Gandhi after 9/11

Gandhi after 9/11

Creative Nonviolence and Sustainability

Douglas Allen

OXFORD
UNIVERSITY PRESS

Oxford University Press is a department of the University of Oxford.
It furthers the University's objective of excellence in research, scholarship,
and education by publishing worldwide. Oxford is a registered trademark of
Oxford University Press in the UK and in certain other countries.

Published in India by
Oxford University Press
2/11 Ground Floor, Ansari Road, Daryaganj, New Delhi 110 002, India

© Oxford University Press 2019

The moral rights of the author have been asserted.

First Edition published in 2019

All rights reserved. No part of this publication may be reproduced, stored in
a retrieval system, or transmitted, in any form or by any means, without the
prior permission in writing of Oxford University Press, or as expressly permitted
by law, by licence, or under terms agreed with the appropriate reprographics
rights organization. Enquiries concerning reproduction outside the scope of the
above should be sent to the Rights Department, Oxford University Press, at the
address above.

You must not circulate this work in any other form
and you must impose this same condition on any acquirer.

ISBN-13 (print edition): 978-0-19-949149-0
ISBN-10 (print edition): 0-19-949149-6

ISBN-13 (eBook): 978-0-19-909709-8
ISBN-10 (eBook): 0-19-909709-7

Typeset in Adobe Garamond Pro 11/13
by Tranistics Data Technologies, Kolkata 700 091
Printed in India by Replika Press Pvt. Ltd.

Contents

Acknowledgements		vii
List of Abbreviations		ix
1	Introduction: The Relevance of Gandhi for India and the Contemporary World	1
2	Gandhian Philosophy: Theoretical Basis with Primacy of Practice	18
3	Is Gandhi a Vedantist?	40
4	How Can Gandhi Interpret His Favorite Bhagavad-Gita as a Gospel of Nonviolence?	60
5	Personal Reflections on Reading *Hind Swaraj* and Indian Reactions	86
6	Is Gandhi's Approach to Technology Irrelevant in the Modern Age of Technology?	99
7	Terrorism and Violence: Gandhi after 9/11 in the USA and 26/11 in India	138
8	Gandhi and Socialism	181

9 Rewriting Marginality: Minority Literature,
Hermeneutical Insights, and Gandhian Challenges 220

Select Bibliography 256
Index 262
About the Author 278

Acknowledgements

In many ways, *Gandhi after 9/11: Creative Nonviolence and Sustainability* is the culmination of 25 years of teaching, lecturing, and writing on the philosophy and practices of Mohandas Karamchand Gandhi. From my youthful experiences in India in 1963–4 and in the Civil Rights Movement, Gandhi was a significant influence on my nonviolent, peace, and justice activism, but I did not approach him as philosophically significant in a scholarly way until the 1990s. In proposing this book project to Oxford University Press (OUP) during my 2015–16 sabbatical in India, my intention was to select my best publications on Gandhi from the previous 20 years, to revise and update them, and to have them published as a collection of essays.

In December 2015, I had a lengthy constructive meeting in New Delhi with the OUP team. They expressed an interest in my preparing two book projects: a volume of essays on Mircea Eliade and the phenomenology of religion and a second volume focusing on Gandhi. With regard to the Gandhi book, they made a valuable suggestion. Knowing that I was giving 20 major lectures throughout India, including many conference keynote addresses and featured plenary presentations, they suggested that I focus on these new papers as the basis for chapters in my Gandhi book.

As a result, most of the chapters in *Gandhi after 9/11* had their origins in lectures I delivered during my last sabbatical, and they have been revised, greatly expanded, and developed in major ways. In many chapters, I provide the background and acknowledge my appreciation for those who invited me to deliver the lectures and sometimes gave me constructive feedback for my revisions. In a few chapters, I have used and greatly revised earlier publications. In each case, I have added endnotes in which I provide the original publication information and acknowledge the permission given to me to use the published material.

It is with gratitude that I acknowledge scholars and other friends who have provided me with invaluable feedback that allowed me to write this book. It is also with some reluctance that I acknowledge such assistance because I know that I am being necessarily selective and omitting many names. Among those who have been dear colleagues and friends and have contributed to my writing this book through our many interactions are the following: Ashok Jhunjhunwala, Usha Thakkar, Bhikhu Parekh, Veena Howard, Fred Dallmayr, Siby George, D. Parthasarathy, Sanjeev Kumar, Hameed Khan, Prafulla Kar, Thomas Pantham, Vinit Haksar, Deepa Mishra, Michael Howard, Sandhya Mehta, K. Ramakrishna Rao, B. Sambasiva Prasad, Rajeev Sangal, Naresh Kumar Sharma, Rajiv Vora, Naresh Dadhich, Sushil Mittal, Nicholas Gier, V.R. Muraleedharan, G. Mishra, and Sandhya Mehta.

Finally, I am most grateful for the support and assistance of Ilze Petersons, who has provided me with constructive feedback throughout the process of writing this book. Ilze is the love of my life, and we have shared a life of 50 years of peace and justice activism and great adventures in India and throughout the world.

Abbreviations

APSC	Ambedkar Periyar Study Circle
BHU	Banaras Hindu University
BJP	Bharatiya Janata Party
CFR	Code of Federal Regulations
CPML	Communist Party of India (Marxist-Leninist)
DOD	Department of Defence
IIT	Indian Institute of Technology
INC	Indian National Congress
IPANA	Indian Peoples Association of North America
IS	Islamic State
ISIL	Islamic State of Iraq and the Levant
ISIS	Islamic State of Iraq and Syria
ISKON	International Society for Krishna Consciousness
LeT	Lashkar-e-Taiba
NDA	National Democratic Alliance
PPST	Patriotic and People Oriented Science and Technology
RSS	Rashtriya Swayamsevak Sangh

1

Introduction

The Relevance of Gandhi for India and the Contemporary World

The title *Gandhi after 9/11: Creative Nonviolence and Sustainability* may be viewed as a shorthand, a short and rather simple way of literally and symbolically expressing major features of the complex world in which we live. It also expresses the major purpose and structure of this book.

On the one hand, the title *Gandhi after 9/11* may be read in a rather literal way. As described in Chapter 7, there was a catastrophic terrorist attack on September 11, 2011. As is often claimed, "9/11 changes everything." Our pre-9/11 ("Gandhi before 9/11") and post-9/11 ("Gandhi after 9/11") worlds are radically different. We now understand and respond to violence and terrorism in very different ways. Even literally, this need not be approached and restricted to some West-centric historical disaster. 9/11 has meaning in India and throughout the contemporary world, revealing a pivotal moment in global history.

On the other hand, the title *Gandhi after 9/11* should be read in a dynamic open-ended way and as symbolically expressing many complex, usually interconnected, structures and levels of meaning.

As will be seen, this is not unlike how we must read and interpret Gandhi's challenging formulations on the central message of the Bhagavad-Gita and his writings in *Hind Swaraj*. In some cases, reading Gandhi only literally presents him as personally idiosyncratic, and often as irrational, unconvincing, and irrelevant for our world of Gandhi after 9/11. More importantly, restricting Gandhi to a literal reading fails to do justice to his broader, deeper, and more relevant philosophy and practice for our contemporary world.

In addition, placing the subtitle, "Creative Nonviolence and Sustainability," directly after the provocative title, *Gandhi after 9/11*, is of greatest significance in expressing my purpose and structure in this book. The provocative title, *Gandhi after 9/11*, is a way of dramatically expressing that we now live in a twenty-first century, which is tragically defined by so much physical, psychological, economic, political, social, cultural, religious, technological, and environmental violence and that is increasingly unsustainable. "Creative Nonviolence and Sustainability" is a response to that title. My central claim in this book is that Gandhi's writings, philosophy, and practices, when selectively appropriated and creatively reformulated and applied, are essential for formulating new positions that are more nonviolent, more sustainable, and provide invaluable resources and hope for dealing with our contemporary personal, social, economic, environmental, and other crises.

There is also an important temporal and historical dimension to the title. Gandhi predates 9/11. As critics and even many sympathizers often submit, the "Gandhi before 9/11," even granting how controversial he was during his lifetime, had great historical and contextual significance for twentieth-century India and the world. But they question and often reject the significance and relevance of "Gandhi after 9/11." This book is intended as a response to that question, attempting, in numerous ways, to show how Gandhi is of greatest temporal and historical significance today.

One of my topics during my 2015–16 sabbatical of lecturing and research in India was whether Gandhi is very significant, or even relevant, for India and the world today. Respondents, raising questions or presenting their alternative views, most often questioned Gandhi's contemporary relevance. As expected, this was not only the case with critics of Gandhi, but it was also the case with many admirers of

Gandhi, who bemoaned the fact that Gandhi was too moral and spiritual for a contemporary India and world that have no place for Gandhi's message.

In this introductory chapter, I maintain that a Gandhi-informed, selectively formulated approach is not only extremely relevant, but it is also desperately needed when addressing various moral, economic, political, cultural, religious, and environmental crises challenging India and the world. Without presenting documentation and detailed analysis, I rather briefly outline seven major topics revealing Gandhi's extreme contemporary relevance. In later chapters, I present more focused and detailed analysis of these topics.

Is Gandhi Irrelevant Today?

This might seem to be a silly question since Gandhi is exalted as Bapu ("the Father of the Nation"), revered as the glorified Mahatma ("the Great Soul"), and memorialized as India's greatest martyr, who was assassinated on January 30, 1948, and gave his life for India's freedom and independence. Nevertheless, large groups of powerful Indians do not really think that Gandhi is relevant for India.

Most prominent are those that Gandhi classifies as "modern Indians," who identify with the worldview and values of Western "modern civilization." As portrayed in Gandhi's *Hind Swaraj* and other writings, most of these Indians adopt modern Western values and approaches, including their promotion of the modern "machine (technology) craze" and the proliferation of endless ego-defined needs and consumption. They now own and/or control the big corporations, the land and natural resources, the financial capital, the modern technology, the media, the military, and the politics. They share the neoliberal, capitalist, globalized, and other anti-Gandhi values of their US counterparts. In terms of these shared economic and other values, priorities, and policies, they usually strike me as more American than I, as they embrace the models of development and other positions rejected by those of us in the USA: peace, justice, and environmental movements.

Next in importance are those now in political power, who adopt an ideology of Hindutva (Hinduness) in which India is an essentially Hindu civilization and nation. This aggressive approach often includes the idealized, ideologically driven rewriting of Indian history and culture that results in a chauvinistic, often violent, Hindu nationalism. In such current formulations of Hindu India's exceptionalism—with a selectively distorted Hindu ideology that fails to address a history of casteism, class exploitation, and patriarchal oppression—India has the best ancient Vedic values, the best culture, the best morality, the best religion, and the blueprint of solutions for all contemporary crises. Gandhi's inclusive, pluralist, tolerant, nonviolent, and democratic approach is antithetical to such a political approach.

Other Indian groups considering Gandhi largely irrelevant for their present and future India include Ambedkerite and other Dalits (formerly best known as the "untouchables" who are below the lowest caste designation), the Adivasis (tribals, original inhabitants), and certain Maoist and other groups engaged in armed struggle. There are also many rigid, conservative, and reactionary Gandhians, at times resembling religious fundamentalists, whose approach to their Gandhi—focused on such issues as chastity and opposition to birth control, prohibition of alcohol, veneration of cows, and embrace of simple living without modern conveniences—is also largely irrelevant to solving India's crises today.

In what follows, the book identifies seven topics for which Gandhi is very relevant today. They are delineated rather briefly and without much of Gandhi's analysis. These topics are just as significant for the USA and the world today as they are for India.

Morality

Gandhi is primarily a moralist with his focus on moral practice. When asked about his philosophy, he typically responds that his life is his message. His major concern is that human beings should live virtuous lives with character, with a major focus on ethical intentions and actions in order to meet the needs and suffering of other beings.

For example, if asked for his views about education today, Gandhi questions whether students, even at the Indian Institute of Technology (IIT) and other elite science and managerial centers and universities in India and throughout the world, graduate as more moral and virtuous human beings. Have they been educated to use their privileged education, with their acquired knowledge and technological and other skills for selfless service? Have they been educated to control and limit their ego, desires, and attachments for maximizing their acquisition of money, power, and status in order to serve the welfare of all? Without the development of ethical values and moral character, such modern education is miseducation, and its graduates have been trained to contribute to and be rewarded by forces upholding modern, immoral, violent, and unsustainable values, relations, and structures.

In contrast to modern distinctions that sharply distinguish ethics from economics, politics, science, technology, media, and other areas of study and life, Gandhi rejects these sharp distinctions. He maintains that moral force (love force, truth force, soul force) establishes integral harmonious relations with all areas of human existence. For example, moral living is necessarily political, since it is concerned with real human suffering, exploitation, oppression, poverty, violence, war, inequality, and injustice. The political is necessarily moral, since it is not value free or an end in itself, but is concerned with establishing relations that are nonviolent, peaceful, compassionate, egalitarian, democratic, and promote welfare for all.

When one examines the contemporary amoral and immoral world of dominant economic, political, military, media, educational, and environmental values and relations, with so much greed, oppression, exploitation, and destruction, the desperate need for Gandhi's emphasis on ethical thinking and living is obvious.

Nonviolence

Gandhi is the most significant proponent of nonviolence of the twentieth century. Even while living in our contemporary world of so much violence, most of us easily affirm that nonviolence is better than violence, peace is better than war, love is better than hatred, generosity is better than greed, compassion is better than meanness and heartlessness, and justice is better than injustice. Usually, we qualify this by stating that we unfortunately live in a world where it is sometimes necessary to use war to achieve peace, to use violence to achieve nonviolence, to be selfish and ignore the suffering of others in order to survive and get ahead.

Gandhi challenges us by submitting that most of us who claim to believe in nonviolence are actually very violent, and most of us who claim to believe in peace actually benefit from or are complicit in the perpetuation of states of war. How does he justify such claims by analyzing our ignorance, hypocrisy, and complicity in perpetuating a world of so much violence? As will be seen in Chapters 2, 7, and sections of other chapters, Gandhi offers these challenges and justifications by introducing such key concepts as the multidimensionality of violence, the structural violence of the status quo, and his means–ends formulations.

In this regard, Gandhi can make such challenging assertions because he broadens and deepens our understanding of violence and nonviolence. Most of us limit our meaning of violence to easily recognizable acts of overt physical violence, such as killing, torture, rape, and bullying. Gandhi is certainly concerned with overt physical violence as he experiences the brutality of war, racism, and violence directed at religious and ethnic minorities, untouchables (Dalits), lower castes, women, and other sentient beings. He, of course, was assassinated through an act of overt physical violence. But in Gandhi's approach, our limited sense of such overt physical violence constitutes only a small part of the overall violence in our lives and in the world.

In his approach to violence (and nonviolence), Gandhi challenges us to become aware of and address the multidimensionality of violence. He emphasizes hatred and other forms of inner violence, linguistic violence, economic violence (equated with exploitation, poverty, and economic relations of inequality), state and other forms of political violence, social and cultural violence, religious violence, educational violence, and environmental violence.

For example, Gandhi lays stress on our recognition of how language can be extremely violent, used as a means for humiliating, intimidating, controlling, and dominating others. That is why he emphasizes the importance of early childhood nonviolent language acquisition in structuring and expressing one's learned experience of one's self and the world. He devotes his greatest attention to economic violence in which some have the economic power, owning or controlling the land and natural resources, financial and industrial capital, technology, media, politics, and are able to establish asymmetrical relations of extreme inequality and domination over those without economic power. As will be seen in Gandhi's radical egalitarianism, such inequality between the haves and the have-nots is always violent.

Gandhi also broadens and deepens our approach to violence (and nonviolence) by focusing on the structural violence (and transformative nonviolence) of the status quo. This is business as usual. For Gandhi, our dominant economic system, political system, cultural and consumerist values, environmental approaches, technological and militaristic values, and hierarchical religious systems, when they seem to be functioning efficiently and "peacefully" without overt protests and disruptions, are extremely violent. The fact that people suffer passively—with self-blame, illusory escapism, or hopeless resignation—and do not resist their humanly caused suffering, expresses and perpetuates the economic, political, cultural, and religious structural violence of the status quo.

In a contemporary world of so much violence, war, injustice, exploitation, racism, sexism, environmental destruction, hatred, and greed, Gandhi's analysis of violence and of the transformative practices to replace it with nonviolent causal conditions, relations, and practices is extremely relevant.

Truth

Gandhi prefers the term "Truth" (*satya*, sometimes used interchangeably with God, Self, Soul, Love, what is Real) as referring to Reality. Ahimsa, as nonviolence and moral nonviolent living, is usually presented as the means for realizing the end or goal of satya, but Gandhi uses the terms interchangeably. Truth and truthful living are also the means for realizing the end of Nonviolence (Love, Compassion, Peace, and so on). I shall mention only two major uses of Truth for Gandhi that are extremely relevant for our contemporary world.

First, Gandhi has an organic, holistic view of the basic interconnectedness of reality. As humans, what unites us is more fundamental than what divides us. This is an experiential realization of a unity with a respect for differences. Truth force (equated with nonviolent force, love force, soul force) is what unifies us and brings us into creative, harmonious, interconnected relations with other humans, other sentient beings, nature, and the cosmos. In the USA, India, and world today, there is so much force that is hateful, violent, oppressive, exploitative, racist, sexist, casteist, religiously divisive, militaristic, and chauvinistically nationalistic. For Gandhi, such force that focuses on what divides us is immoral, violent, and untruthful. More of a focus on the truth of our basic unity and interconnectedness is desperately needed today.

Second, while upholding Absolute regulative ideals of Truth, Nonviolence, Love, Compassion, Pure Ethics, and Pure Religion or Spirituality, Gandhi insists on the primary importance of relative truth. This is developed in Chapters 2 and 3. No one fully knows the Absolute, and in this world, we are always attempting to move from one relative truth to greater relative truth. This distinguishes Gandhi's approach to truth from contemporary religious fundamentalisms, religious terrorisms, and other religious positions claiming to possess the one Absolute Truth. It distinguishes his approach from our contemporary militaristic and imperialistic nationalisms and other political positions that claim that they possess the exclusive Truth. It distinguishes his approach from our huge transnational corporations, with their globalization and ruthless policies to exploit and dominant everything on the planet earth, and which claim to possess the only Truth, the true view of the Reality of human nature and the real world.

For Gandhi, taking what is relative and imperfect and claiming it as the exclusive Absolute Truth is arrogant, egotistical, violent, and false. Such a Gandhi-informed approach, emphasizing some humility in truth claims, pluralism, tolerance, respect for others who may have truths that we do not have and from whom we may learn, is very significant for our contemporary crises.

We may now highlight a most significant feature of Gandhi's philosophy and practice that is expressed throughout this book. This will be seen in the Gandhi-informed analysis of nonviolence and violence, absolute and relative truth and untruth, peace and war, terror and terrorists, courage and cowardice, honor and duty, modern technology and globalization, capitalism and socialism, trusteeship, sustainability, voluntary suffering, class, caste, race, gender, and the marginality of the other. This value-based structure of Gandhi's approach expresses much of what makes him so appealing and relevant for our world of Gandhi after 9/11, but it also reveals possible weaknesses and apparent inconsistencies.

On the one hand, in his dynamic, dialogic, open-ended, contextual approach, with his absolute ideals, relative truths, and embrace of multiple perspectives, Gandhi consistently expresses his personal views and practices with regard to truth, nonviolence, morality, and other values and principles. For example, he consistently affirms his preference for ahimsa, even if his experimental views of nonviolence change significantly over the decades. In this regard, some, but not all, of his apparent inconsistencies are removed when we realize that he rejects some of his earlier positions on violence, war, patriarchy, caste, British "modern civilization," and other topics. My interpretation in this book is that Gandhi develops his philosophy and practice in a more nonviolent, more revolutionary, and more consistent way, late in his life, and this renders his approach more relevant and significant for our Gandhi after 9/11 world.

On the other hand, in his appealing and relevant perspectival approach, Gandhi expresses open-minded inclusive tolerance, insists on mutual respect for multiple relative perspectives of others, and repeatedly advises others to follow their own paths toward truth wherever that takes them. Gandhi is sometimes inconsistent in not following this many-sided perspectival philosophy and practice, as in some of his relations with his wife, Kasturba, his eldest son, Harilal, various ashramites, satyagrahis, and diverse others, with whom he sometimes uses nonviolent coercive measures to resist and change their relative paths to truth. Nevertheless, even when Gandhi is consistent in upholding the valuable perspectival relative truth of the legitimate path of the other, his position often reveals unanswered questions, dialectical tensions, weaknesses, and inconsistencies.

As will be seen repeatedly in the following chapters, these strengths and weaknesses, unresolved issues and tensions often arise from the difficulties that Gandhi had and that we have today in consistently and coherently relating the two perspectives to truth and reality: a Gandhi-informed perspective and path and non-Gandhian and anti-Gandhian perspectives and paths of diverse others. How, for example, does a contemporary Gandhi-informed philosophy and practice relate to others, even sometimes acknowledging that they act with courage and a sense of duty, when they reject Gandhi's absolute ideals of nonviolence, truth, unity with a respect for differences, morality, sustainability, and spirituality? How does a Gandhi-informed philosophy and practice relate to others when they uphold their relative perspectival truths and paths that glorify violence, war, terrorism, egotism, greed, profit, modern technology, environmental destruction, and the control or elimination of the perspectival communal or religious other?

Difficulties in applying Gandhi's many-sided perspectival theory and practice to truth and nonviolence need not prove fatal. As will be seen, at its best, such an approach, when selectively and creatively reformulated and contextualized, offers valuable insights and resources for relating to the world of Gandhi after 9/11. However, it also cautions us not to essentialize, decontextualize, or even deify the Mahatma and claim that he gives us his preferred perspectival blueprint with all of the answers.

Egalitarian

Gandhi is a radical egalitarian, consistently critical of unequal hierarchical structures of domination, and struggling for more equal human relations and alternatives. That is why Gandhi, even when affirming that he is a Hindu (among many other affirmations), is not a traditional Hindu. He repeatedly critiques traditional hierarchical Hinduism for its structural inequalities with immoral, violent, false, cultural, political, religious, caste, gendered, and other relations of domination.

Gandhi would be alarmed by what has been happening in India in recent decades, which is similar to what has been happening in the USA and other parts of the globalized world: the incredible increase in the number of billionaires and multi-millionaires at the top, with insatiable greed, ruthlessness, and concentration of economic and political power, and with the widening gap between the haves and the have-nots. He would focus on the rapidly growing and often unprecedented inequality in which hundreds of millions of Indians and others live in abject poverty, and increasingly large parts of the population are completely marginalized as having little role or future in modern, capitalist, technological, developed India or the world.

For egalitarian Gandhi, with his economic philosophy of *sarvodaya*, or, "the well-being of all," and his focus on addressing the needs of those with the least freedom and greatest need, such inequality today is extremely immoral, unjust, violent, and untruthful. Gandhi goes so far as to assert that if I accumulate great wealth while others live under desperate economic and social conditions of poverty and great suffering, I am living an unjust life of theft. If I benefit from or remain silent in a community, India, and world of such inequality, I am responsible for this economic structural violence. Without a commitment to egalitarian values and relations, moral, nonviolent, truthful living is impossible.

Democracy

Gandhi has a remarkable commitment to democracy, which is much broader, deeper, and qualitatively different from our dominant, modern versions of democracy found in the USA, India, and other nations. Indians typically and proudly state that they live in the world's largest democracy, just as citizens of the USA proclaim that they live in the greatest democracy in the history of the world. Certainly, modern Western versions of democracy, with Constitutions and legal systems upholding various formal individual rights, are in various ways notable achievements over various premodern political and social societies of class, caste, gender, and other hierarchical inequality with no appeal to individual rights. That is why the modernist Ambedkar's vision and achievement of a modern Constitution, legal system, and protection of democratic political rights for Dalits and other oppressed peoples is remarkable. But Gandhi hesitates to extol such modern limited versions of democracy, and questions whether India or the USA is really democratic in true, substantial, meaningful ways.

As Gandhi states, the goal of India's freedom, independence, and democracy is not to replace British exploiters of Indians with Indian exploiters of Indians. This is how he would regard the dominant Indian and US political parties today. Real democracy is not restricted to modern, limited formulations that are hegemonic, hierarchical, and use corrupt, immoral, untruthful means to prevent even minimal Gandhian democratic transformations.

It is often stated that "modern Indians" are descendants of Pandit Jawaharlal Nehru, with his anti-Gandhian vision of a modern India of West-styled, scientific, technological, urbanized, industrial development. Although there is considerable truth to this claim, Nehru, in my view, would be appalled by the dominant amoral and immoral, violent, exploitative, and oppressive values and approaches of modern Indians, with the growing gap between the haves and have-nots and with little concern for the well-being of all.

As this relates to democracy, the modernist Nehru and many others in the freedom movement certainly support a modern Constitution, legal system, and version of formal political democracy for India. However, what is often forgotten is that Nehru and these other leaders are not satisfied with restricting democracy to British-style formal political democracy. They also promote a more robust, more substantive social democracy and socio-economic democracy, so that all Indians will be empowered to overcome poverty, oppression, and exploitation and have a real voice in the democratic process shaping their lives and India. Modern India, which is increasingly under threat to even minimal formal political democracy, has ignored and often undone hard-won gains on any commitment to social democracy. In this regard, Gandhi has a radical view of democracy that goes far beyond the modernist versions.

In ways that are extremely relevant and desperately needed today, Gandhi embraces a view of democracy as consisting in real human development, real human empowerment, real human flourishing. Every citizen should have a meaningful voice in the democratic process that can make meaningful decisions that affect one's life. In his democratic egalitarian formulations of such key concepts as *swaraj* (self-rule), *swadeshi* (aiming as much as possible for decentralized self-sufficient economies with concerns for one's community), and sarvodaya, Gandhi maintains that there is no political democracy without economic democracy. There is no political democracy without a non-egoistic commitment to our interconnected relations of concern for the welfare of all beings. In short, real democracy is impossible without a shared commitment to moral, nonviolent, truthful, egalitarian values and relations.

The Need for Transformative Action

My experience is that most students and citizens in India today, just as most of my students at the University of Maine and most citizens in the US today are rather passive, often alienated and cynical, and feel powerless when it comes to the huge economic, political, military, and environmental problems of the world. They have the accurate sense that those at the top, who run the huge corporations, media, military, and politics, have little true concern for their alternative views and for their democratic participatory input.

In this regard, Gandhi's focus on transformative action, in which we are highly motivated, critically thinking, actively empowered subjects, is extremely relevant. This includes his identification with the path of *karma-yoga*, an action-oriented approach not of renunciation of action but of renunciation in action. In such a Gandhi-informed approach, you act morally and truthfully as informed by your contextualized karmic situatedness, by controlling your ego-desires and ego-attachments to the results of your actions. This includes Gandhi's identification with *satyagraha* (truth-force, love-force, soul-force) in which we come together with others in expressing the active nonviolent and truthful force of resistance to violence, war, injustice, exploitation, oppression, and other forms of humanly caused suffering, in which we actively construct more ethical and truthful alternatives.

Without the activation of moral, nonviolent, compassionate, truth force, and our mobilization directed at transformative action, Gandhi submits that none of the above is realizable in contemporary India and the world: the development of greater moral human relations; the self-transformative and world-transformative process of moving from relative violence to greater relative nonviolence; the moral truthful experiential realizations of our unity, interconnectedness, and movement to greater relative truths; the resistance to the violent and unjust growing inequality and the struggle for a world of greater egalitarian values and relations; and the struggles and action-oriented transformation needed to create a more adequate realization of real substantial democracy.

The Need for a Radical Paradigm Shift

A concern found throughout this book is the need for a Gandhi-informed radical paradigm shift with transformative values and new orientations and models that emphasize creative nonviolence and sustainability. This may be related to Martin Luther King, Jr.'s transformation late in his life. As noted in Chapter 3, in his first book, *Stride Toward Freedom*, King shares how Gandhi is the major formative influence in this "pilgrimage toward nonviolence." In his much more radical formulations in "Beyond Vietnam: A Time to Break the Silence," delivered at the Riverside Church in New York on April 4, 1967, exactly one year before he was assassinated, King calls for a "true revolution of values." King proclaims that "we must rapidly begin the shift from a 'thing-oriented' society to a 'person-oriented society. When machines and computers, profit motives and property rights are considered more important than people, the giant triplets of racism, materialism, and militarism are incapable of being conquered." A true revolution of values makes the connections between the expressions of oppression, exploitation, and injustice. It rejects injustice, poverty and glaring wealth, hatred, and endless war, and recognizes that a "nation that continues year after year to spend more money on military defense than on programs of social uplift is approaching spiritual death." I have cited this remarkable speech by King because I shall submit that a creatively reformulated, Gandhi-informed approach today accepts every word of this King imperative, emphasizing the need for a true revolution of values and radical paradigm shift.[1]

Increasingly, not only peace, justice, and environmental activists, but also many mainstream scientists, engineers, economists, and others with power now recognize that our dominant values, priorities, policies, and models are unsustainable. They are economically and technologically unsustainable, militarily unsustainable, politically unsustainable, culturally and religiously unsustainable, and environmentally sustainable. This is addressed in the following chapters, especially Chapter 6. In several concerns, such as the consequences of climate change or of extreme inequality, we are at the tipping point and face human and global disaster unless we embrace and act on a radical paradigm shift.

A Gandhi-informed approach offers new ways for rethinking our dominant assumptions, priorities, and policies and for a value paradigm shift that allows for new, creative, contextually relevant formulations and practices. For example, rigid Gandhians often dogmatically assert that Gandhi would be against modern technology and globalization. This is certainly true, but we live in an age of technology and in a globalized world, and such Gandhian dogmatism renders Gandhi largely irrelevant to India today and our contemporary world.

A more selective, creatively reformulated, Gandhi-informed approach would instead ask what technology, as integral to a radical paradigm shift, might look like in our future world: appropriate technology to meet real human needs; controlled, limited, not with technology determining us, but with human well-being and moral concerns as central; decentralized swaraj technology, sustainable, and integral to harmonious relations between humans, other life, and nature.

A more selective, creatively reformulated, Gandhi-informed approach in our paradigm shift would not dogmatically reject globalization, but would instead ask what globalization might look like in our future globalized world: globalization recognizing that we are integrally interconnected global beings and that concern for the well-being of the other is a necessary part of our process of self-development; a view of globalized living that critiques and resists the top-down modern globalized power relations of exploitation and domination, and reformulates and transforms them in terms of democratic, egalitarian, moral, nonviolent, bottom-up globalized relations.

Gandhi Does Not Have All of the Answers

My introductory Gandhi-informed formulations in this chapter may have conveyed the impression that not only selectively and creatively reformulated Gandhian responses are extremely relevant and significant today, but also that Gandhi has the exclusive blueprint sufficient for solving our contemporary crises. That would be a false impression. Gandhi is a complex, sometimes contradictory, remarkable human being, but he is human. He describes his life as "my experiments with truth," and he writes hundreds of pages describing his failed experiments with truth. Some of what he proposes is backward, uninformed, reactionary, and irrelevant today. Other proposals are insightful but need to be radically reinterpreted, re-evaluated, reformulated, and reapplied in ways that are contextually relevant today.

In my own approach, Gandhi is a major inspiration and provides me with many, but not all, of the answers when addressing personal, existential, psychological, economic, political, environmental, and other contemporary issues. For me, the Prophetic Hebraic tradition often has more forceful formulations of the need to resist injustice and struggle for justice in this world. Gandhi has profound economic and historical insights, but Marx is a more rigorous economic and historical thinker. In my interpretation, Gandhi is a radical critic of caste, but Ambedkar often has more adequate responses to the oppression of Dalits. When it comes to sexism, Gandhi made remarkable progress in overcoming his patriarchal responses and affirming gender equality, but there are feminists with more developed positions regarding gender relations today.[2] When it comes to our environmental crises, Gandhi offers creative possibilities for a more holistic, harmonious, sustainable approach, but there are contemporary environmentalists with greater contextual insights and knowledge.

A selectively and creatively reformulated Gandhi-informed approach can serve as an invaluable catalyst, challenging us to rethink our dominant presuppositions, values, priorities, policies, and explanatory models. A Gandhi-informed approach, when integrated with complementary non-Gandhian economic, political, social, cultural, and scientific approaches, offers us the best relevant possibilities for an urgently needed paradigm shift of values. This is necessary for actively transforming our lives, India, and the contemporary world of so much violence, war, injustice, hatred, greed, humanly caused suffering, alienation, anxiety, and meaningless existence.

Notes

1. See Martin Luther King, Jr, *Stride Toward Freedom: The Montgomery Story* (New York: Harper and Row, 1968); Martin Luther King, Jr, "Beyond Vietnam: A Time to Break Silence," sometimes referred as the "Riverside Church Speech," accessible through many links online and in several collections of King's speeches. See http://www.mlkonline.net/vietnam.html (accessed on June 1, 2018).
2. There is vast literature of Gandhi's insightful and controversial writings on women and gender relations and hundreds of writings by feminists, anti-feminists, and others on the strengths and weaknesses of Gandhi's approach. Although Gandhi's approach to patriarchy and women as the "other" is cited throughout this book, I do not formulate a detailed analysis or critique of Gandhi's approach to topics such as his personality and relations with specific women and women in general, his essentialized gender formulations, his asceticism and renunciation, his views of purity, *yajna* (sacrifice), *tapas* (austerities), and *brahmacharya* (self-restraint), his controversial practices and experiments testing his self-discipline and purity, and his views of gender in his activist satyagrahas, constructive work, and engaged transformative practices toward greater equality, dialogic mutuality, nonviolence, justice, and sustainability. Consistent with different sections in this book, I submit that Gandhi, late in his life, reformulated many of his positions and developed his most enlightened positions with regard to his wife, Kasturba, the status of women, and gendered relations. At the same time, this does not negate the fact that some of Gandhi's views on women and gender remain idiosyncratic, provincial, and reactionary. These need to be dismissed or reformulated in a Gandhi-informed approach in "Gandhi after 9/11."

2

Gandhian Philosophy
Theoretical Basis with Primacy of Practice

Any philosophical study of Gandhian philosophy must not limit itself to the kinds of abstract theoretical formulations typical of so many dominant approaches in Western philosophy. Gandhi is not interested in abstract theoretical or academic philosophical formulations, but rather in philosophy as practice.[1]

Philosophy as Practice

Gandhi's focus is on living philosophy, on how we can live a life of satya and ahimsa, with the focus on practice. As is often quoted or paraphrased, when Gandhi is asked for his philosophy, he frequently responds that his life is his message. His philosophy is best expressed through how he lives his life in practice.

This is not to endorse a common misconception that Gandhi is simply a practical person with no philosophical interest and no philosophical significance for our contemporary world. Although Gandhi often seems very simple in his practical self-transformative and world-transformative formulations and actions, his practice is actually grounded in a surprisingly complex, dynamic, open-ended, contextually relevant, moral, and ontological theoretical framework.

The common view that Gandhi is a practical person of no theoretical philosophical significance—a view often shared by both Gandhi admirers and Gandhi critics—is clearly illustrated by the formative experiences of my youth with professors in the Department of Philosophy at Banaras Hindu University (BHU), Varanasi, Uttar Pradesh, when BHU was arguably the outstanding philosophy department in India.

Gandhi himself confesses that, say, unlike S. Radhakrishnan or my major teacher at BHU, T.R.V. Murti, and other twentieth-century Indian philosophers, he is not a philosopher in the usual technical, academic, or scholarly sense. Revealing is the inclusion of Gandhi's piece as the very first contribution to the volume *Contemporary Indian Philosophy* edited by Radhakrishnan and Muirhead, published in 1936. The volume is a collection of 25 essays by leading Indian academic and scholarly philosophers. We know from correspondence that Gandhi pleaded incompetence in philosophy. Finally, reluctantly, in response to three questions from Radhakrishnan, Gandhi wrote his untitled one-page "essay."[2]

It is not that Gandhi rejects the importance of philosophy. In various writings, Gandhi, while believing that he has ethical, religious, and philosophical principles, indicates that he will leave it to scholars more competent in philosophy than him to formulate, interpret, and systematize the philosophy underlying his approach, theory, and practice.[3]

Gandhi's own writings, both those lacking systematic philosophical analysis and also those pleading philosophical incompetence, lend credence to the view that he is not philosophically significant. This has led to the common misconception that one may or may not admire Gandhi, the way he lives his life, and his influence on India and the world, but he is not a philosopher or relevant for philosophy.

Illustrating this misconception, during my postgraduate studies at BHU in 1963–4, I do not recall Gandhi ever being mentioned in any philosophy course. In a department that was dominated by proponents of Advaita Vedanta and that included several other influential philosophers, we focused on the theoretical basis of Shankara's philosophy and considered other Vedantic and classical Hindu, Buddhist, and Jain philosophical analysis. The theoretical basis for approaches of Indian philosophical materialism and scepticism were barely considered worthy of our attention. In such a renowned department of philosophy, Gandhi's practical philosophy, with its theoretical basis, was not simply devalued or marginalized. It was completely nonexistent.

To provide a more recent illustration, I participated in the four-day International Vedanta Congress at Jawaharlal Nehru University in December 2015. It is true that most of the presenters were Sanskritists and scholars of Vedanta from disciplines other than philosophy, but most of their focus was on Vedic and Vedantic "philosophy." In the entire conference program, my plenary presentation "Is Mahatma Gandhi a Vedantist?" was the only offering that mentioned Gandhi in its title.[4]

This is not to ignore the fact that "the Philosophy of Mahatma Gandhi" has been incorporated in the course curriculum of many departments of philosophy and other university programs in recent decades, and students write PhD dissertations on Gandhi's philosophy, but the widespread misconception still persists that Gandhi's thought and practice are not philosophical. In my own view, Gandhi may not be a philosopher in some technical academic sense, but his theory and practice are of the greatest philosophical significance. They challenge us to rethink our dominant philosophical approaches and how they are integrally related to a contemporary India and world of so much violence, war, exploitation, oppression, and unsustainable economic and environmental relations.

In his emphasis on the primacy of practice, and not abstract, essentialized, contextually detached theoretical formulations, Gandhi submits that our philosophical analysis must arise from actual practice, and then be applied and tested in terms of new practice. Philosophical theorizing is not devalued or dismissed per se. Grounded in the practice of our human mode of being in the world, our fragmentation and alienation, our lack of meaningful experiences of human situatedness as mind–body–heart beings, theoretical understanding is necessary for any knowledge, and for any moral, philosophical, and spiritual transformative development. Philosophical theory is necessary to inform and guide our philosophical practice. In fact, theorizing is a form of practice, and we can only verify or falsify our theory through ongoing experiments with truth in which we assess the extent to which our new theorizing contributes to new, more adequate, moral, and philosophical practice.

This emphasis on the primacy of practice and on how philosophical theory must be grounded in practice can be seen in the view that Gandhi is primarily a moralist. His primary concern is with moral practice, with developing virtuous human beings of moral character and practice. In Gandhi's emphasis, ethics is first philosophy and morality is first practice. This is different not only from the dominant ways of doing philosophy in the history of Western philosophy, but also from traditional Indian philosophy with its emphasis on the primacy of epistemology and metaphysics.

This is not to deny that the Vedic texts, including sections of the Upanishads, outlining the stages in the course of study, emphasize the moral prerequisites for qualifying as suitable and for being accepted as a worthy student.[5] Without basic moral qualities, without moral character, one is not capable of understanding the sacred teachings. As evidenced in both Upanishadic and other Vedic texts and also in later philosophical and religious traditions, without moral character and development, one is not capable of developing the proper use of the intellect, logic, and rational thinking.

Nevertheless, as has been emphasized by various twentieth-century philosophers, including influential Indians, India and Hinduism have tended not to develop the kind of emphasis on systematic ethics found in Western philosophy, as seen in Aristotle and ancient Greek philosophy and Mill, Kant and modern philosophy, and later philosophical developments. Traditional Indian philosophy has tended not only to lack this emphasis on developing systematic ethics, but it has also tended to embrace the view that the enlightened, highly developed philosophical and spiritual being renounces and transcends the ethical. By way of contrast, in his focus on the primacy of ethical living, Gandhi challenges us to broaden and deepen our philosophical understanding of moral practice and its theoretical basis.

Gandhi's Theory and Practice of Ahimsa

Gandhi's greatest contribution toward the theme of "Gandhi and the Contemporary World" is his moral and philosophical focus on ahimsa and how he greatly broadens and deepens our understanding of nonviolence and its integral relations with truth.[6] The integral relations of satya and ahimsa provide the theoretical basis for Gandhi's philosophy and practice.[7] They reveal the presuppositions, values, and principles informing his approach to swaraj, satyagraha, swadeshi, his constructive program, and other key concepts.[8]

In Gandhi's philosophical approach integrating theory and practice, our contemporary world is characterized by so much violence. But is this true? There are dominant modern approaches, as found in the foundational works of Thomas Hobbes and often justified as "political realism," that view human nature and human relations as motivated by fear, insecurity, greed, glory, and competition. Violent force is necessary to achieve peace and security at home and abroad, to establish law and order, and to allow for realizing rights, freedoms, culture, civilization, and progress. In later chapters, especially Chapter 6, we will analyze how Gandhi critiques this dominant approach as expressing the features of the violent "Modern Civilization." Nevertheless, there are several recent popular approaches to violence and nonviolence, war and peace, that largely reject this dominant modern approach, often on non-Gandhian grounds.

The best illustration of this dissenting approach can be found in the works of Steven Pinker, the Harvard psychologist, best-selling author, and popular public intellectual. In his influential book *The Better Angels of Our Nature: Why Violence Has Declined*, Pinker makes the dramatic claim that the recent decline in violence is "the most significant and least appreciated development in the history of our species." Citing data from peace and conflict research centers, Pinker claims that we live in a world of an all-time low in violence, wars are less frequent and less deadly, terrorism is rare, and we are realizing greater altruism and cooperation. We should have an objectively based confidence in a nonviolent future of progress and human flourishing.[9] In his recent book, *Enlightenment Now: The Case for Reason, Science, Humanism, and Progress*, Pinker goes even further in his optimistic faith in our future. By all rational, scientific, modern, humanistic, quantifiable standards, we are living at an all-time-high level of human flourishing, with unprecedented progress, nonviolence, wealth, health, and happiness.[10]

As is usually stated, if Hobbes and other political, economic, social, cultural, and "modern" thinkers are correct, then Gandhi is out of touch with reality, is at best naïve, and is an obstacle to confronting realistically the issues of violence, war, terrorism, and insecurity in the contemporary world of "Gandhi after 9/11." However, if Pinker and various other upbeat "modern" authors are correct, then Gandhi is also out of touch with unprecedented changes in our contemporary world of nonviolence, security, progress, and human flourishing. Whatever value "Gandhi before 9/11" may have had on violence and modern civilization, his approach is misinformed and misguided when it comes to the contemporary world of "Gandhi after 9/11."

It is easy to agree with much of Gandhi's concern with contemporary violence when focusing on the usual approaches that view violence as overt physical violence. Our world is characterized by so much war and killing—Islamic State (IS), Islamic State of Iraq and Syria (ISIS), Islamic State of Iraq and the Levant (ISIL)—and other forms of terrorism, torture, sexual trafficking, and other blatant human rights violations, acts of religious and communal violence, killing of students in schools, caste and class and gender violence, rape, and bullying.

However, in his philosophical and transformative insights and contributions to our contemporary world, Gandhi submits that such incredible violence is a small part of overall violence. In such a broadened and deepened moral and philosophical approach, most of us who say that we are for nonviolence (peace, love, compassion, justice, and so on), are in reality very violent, either directly or indirectly, in our passivity and complicity in perpetuating a world lacking in ahimsa.

In my own work, I have tried to show at length how a Gandhi-informed philosophical approach bursts opens the limiting constructions of violence and nonviolence by challenging us to become aware of and act on two key concepts: the multidimensionality of violence (and nonviolence) and the structural violence (and nonviolence) of the status quo. In addition to overt physical experience, we experience hatred and other inner or psychological violence, linguistic violence that shapes our experiences and expressions of communication, political and economic and social violence, cultural, religious, educational, and environmental violence. All of these dimensions of violence interact, mutually condition, and reinforce each other, so that we become entrapped in endless causal and conditioning cycles of violence, expressing how we view our self, our relations to others, and our relations to nature and the world.

In addition, we are socialized to accept the social, economic, political, religious, educational, structural violence of the status quo as "normal," as defining the "real world." Especially when there is no extreme disruption, and the dominant economic, political, religious, educational, and other structures and relations seem to be working efficiently, we, unlike Gandhi, normally do not recognize the extreme structural violence that perpetuates so much suffering, poverty, inequality, alienation, and lack of ahimsa.

An excellent contemporary illustration of Gandhi's ahimsa approach to multidimensional and structural violence can be seen in our world of so much economic violence. Gandhi's philosophy and practice, unlike most other Western and Indian philosophical and religious approaches, emphasizing moral and spiritual development, place a primary focus on economic violence. In upholding his philosophical view of the interrelatedness of all of life, Gandhi submits that the economic must be based on the moral, so that economic violence is immoral, but the moral must also value and privilege the economic as we work to overcome economic violence.[11]

In Gandhi's extensive writings on violence, economic violence is equated with exploitation in which those with the finances, land, resources, and technology are able to establish hierarchical relations of domination in which they exploit the labor and limited resources of those lacking such economic power. That is why Gandhi repeatedly maintains that poverty, which is humanly caused and maintained, is extreme economic violence, and he sometimes asserts that it is the worst form of violence. Upholding one of his key concepts of *aparigraha* (nonpossession), Gandhi claims that if I take something I do not need for my immediate use and I keep it, then I am a thief committing economic violence. Gandhi formulates many, interrelated levels and kinds of swaraj, including economic swaraj, and he submits that swaraj is impossible without swadeshi. In dramatic terms, especially significant for contemporary India and the world, Gandhi maintains that hierarchical economic inequality is violence, and "economic equality is the master key to nonviolent independence."[12]

Think of what has been happening in recent decades in the USA, India, and the world, in terms of the unprecedented concentration of so much economic wealth and power in the hands of the relatively few, and with the rapidly growing inequality between the elite economic haves and the overwhelming majority of have-nots. The West and India, of course, have had thousands of years of concentration of wealth and power with the rulers, and the economically powerful establishing various hierarchical relations of domination and control over others. However, even during Gandhi's lifetime, life for the majority of 300,000,000 Indians, living in 600,000 or 700,000 rather isolated and self-contained villages, was still characterized for the most part by economic relations outside the top-down concentration of financial and industrial economic power of the British and Indian elite. This is not to deny that centralized priorities and policies from outside sometimes had devastating consequences for the decentralized peasants, as in catastrophic times of flooding, famine, and starvation.

Such traditional, decentralized, unequal but relatively more egalitarian, socio-economic life has become increasingly unliveable and unsustainable. The whole of India is increasingly brought under the domination of concentrated, centralized, top-down values, relations, and structures of financial capital and big corporate economic structures and relations. These establish interlocking relations with politics and the state, the military and forces of coercion, advertising and endless consumption, the media, and the other interests of what Gandhi critiques as the model of "Modern Civilization." For Gandhi, this contemporary unprecedented concentration of economic wealth and power necessarily leads to growing inequality, and this necessarily leads to growing multidimensional and structural violence.[13]

Gandhi's theory and practice of ahimsa are directed at how we can educate ourselves and others to gain greater awareness of such dominant violence in the world. This necessarily involves becoming aware of how we can nonviolently resist such violence and how we can engage in the dynamic, contextually relevant, action-oriented project of deconditioning such violent assumptions, values, principles, and relations and replacing them with the values and relations of a nonviolent way of being in the world. Gandhi's dialectical theory-practice relational approach involves the integral deconstruction of violence that necessarily involves the construction of nonviolent alternatives.

In this theory-practice moral-philosophical approach, I have focused elsewhere on the following five Gandhi-informed insights and contributions. First, Gandhi offers a very nuanced and complex analysis of the relations of means and ends, often sharing features of the law of karma and the Buddha's Doctrine of Dependent Origination, and presenting a radical critique of the dominant, modern, Western, instrumental approach of the ends justify the means as extremely violent.

Second, we can reflect on the potential for developing Gandhi's philosophy and practice of ahimsa and its significance for the contemporary world by focusing on preventative nonviolence. Especially in Gandhi's major contribution for the need for long-term preventive ahimsa, we need to become more aware of the root causes and basic determinants of the vicious cycles of violence so that we can decondition and replace them with contextually relevant nonviolent causes and conditioning factors. Otherwise, we will remain entrapped within, and keep reproducing the contemporary cycles of violence that are morally, politically, economically, and environmentally unsustainable and threaten our future existence and other life on earth.

Third, informed by his understanding of the Upanishads, various other Indian and Western philosophical and spiritual sources, and especially his favorite text, the Bhagavad Gita, Gandhi's ahimsa approach focuses on how we construct and fuel the separate, I–me ego, with its ego-desires, needs, attachments, possessiveness, defense mechanisms, and aggressiveness. As seen in *Hind Swaraj* and in hundreds of other writings, Gandhi maintains that such ego desires and attachments, which are central to modern civilization and our contemporary socio-economic and political world, express the untruthful, violent, illusory, immoral, and unspiritual Self and violent self-other relations. The only way for us to experience and live lives of ahimsa today is to decondition, control, and eliminate, as much as possible, the functioning of the modern ego at the heart of so much violence in the world.[14]

Fourth, in providing the integral relations of truth and nonviolence, Gandhi's philosophical theory and practice not only challenge us with an insightful ethical approach, but also reveal a valuable ontological orientation and framework. As is easily recognized, Gandhi, in his means-ends moral philosophy and practice, challenges dominant modern approaches. He repeatedly formulates why untruthful, immoral, violent means cannot lead to truthful, moral, nonviolent ends. For example, we cannot use terrorism to overcome terrorism and expect to realize the goal of a world free from terror.

What usually is not recognized is how Gandhi's moral philosophy of ahimsa is grounded in an underlying organic, holistic, interconnected, ontological worldview, and a framework of moral and spiritual reality. Stated briefly, violence is based on the worldview and approach that what is the target of and separates me/us from the other—whether individual, social, or based on ethnic, caste, class, gender, religious, national or other groups—is fundamentally different from me, my social or religious group, nation, and so on. Ahimsa, by way of contrast, is based on the worldview and approach that what unifies us is more fundamental than what divides, expressing our moral and spiritual interconnectedness, a primary realization of unity with a respect for differences. Ahimsa, as the active nonviolent force (love force, truth force, soul force), is not only the basis of Gandhi's moral philosophy and practice, but it is at the same time the unifying moral and spiritual force that brings us together in meaningful, interconnected relations, allowing us to experience greater truth and reality.

Gandhi's Philosophy of Relative Truth

Fifth, essential to Gandhi's philosophy and practice of ahimsa, satya, and other challenges for our contemporary world is his underappreciated analysis of the epistemological, moral, and ontological status of relative truth, and its dynamic, contextually relevant, open-ended relations with Absolute Truth, Nonviolence, Morality, Religion, God, and Self. Many supporters and critics focus on various passages in Gandhi's writings and turn him into some rigid absolutist, uncompromisingly insisting on Absolute Truth and Absolute Nonviolence, but this is not consistent with the overwhelming majority of Gandhi's writings. His primary focus is on relative truth, which, unlike much of traditional Indian philosophy, is not simply devalued or even dismissed in terms of Absolute Reality.

While affirming his belief in the ultimate reality of Absolute Truth and Nonviolence, Pure Ethics and Religion, Gandhi repeatedly confesses that he, at most, has very limited, temporary, imperfect "glimpses" of such Absolutes. Gandhi's ongoing formulations and experimental reformulations of his philosophy and practice consist of his moral, philosophical, action-oriented, transformative project of attempting to move from one relative truth to a greater relative truth, closer to, but never fully realizing the Absolute Truth as Absolute Reality. Much of human egoistic arrogance, violence, and untruth consists in claiming that our relative truths are Absolute, they are the exclusive Truth, and the only true view of Reality.

This challenges frequent philosophical alternatives of essentialism and absolute foundationalism or modern unlimited relativism. In our Gandhi-informed philosophical approach, we embrace absolute regulative ideals of Truth and Nonviolence, but our philosophy and practice always involve the recognition of our human, situated, contextualized world of relative truth with the dynamic, imperfect, open-ended philosophical project of moving closer to the absolute ideal.

In our creative reformulations of such a Gandhian approach that has contextual value for the contemporary world, we must recognize that Gandhi's focus on relative truth and its relation to his Absolutes does not immediately resolve all serious philosophical questions and issues. What is the source for his claims about the ultimate reality of his absolutes? Occasionally, he appeals to his religious faith, but what is most philosophically interesting is his experiential claim that he actually has such imperfect, partial, temporary glimpses of what is the permanent, eternal, ultimate reality. Can Gandhi provide an adequate analysis of how he can distinguish and justify or verify his claim from so many other experiential claims to the Truth, God, and Reality that Gandhi assesses as false expressions of untruth, violence, war, and injustice?

How do Gandhi's philosophical theory and practice relate to his claims about the status of relative truth, relative nonviolence, relative institutionalized religion, and relative situated morality? What are the complex, dynamic, open-ended, contextualized relations in his philosophy between the diverse relative truths and their integral relations with the imperfectly realized regulative absolute ideals?

To provide an illustration of such serious philosophical questions and issues, Gandhi repeatedly advises each of us to follow our own paths to truth wherever they take us. What is experienced as true for him may not be the relative perspectival truth for you. Consistent with much of contemporary philosophy, anthropology, sociology, multiculturalism, postcolonial and racial and gender studies, and other disciplinary approaches, why does Gandhi's position on the significant status of relative truth and nonviolence not lead to an unlimited facile relativism?

Gandhi offers many formulations and reformulations during his life in responding to such a challenging question. He never accepts the modern relativist view that he may uphold a philosophy and practice of ahimsa as what is truthful and real for him, but you may justifiably accept a philosophy of war and violence as truthful and real for you, your social group, your religion, or your nation. This is why the usual liberal interpretation of Gandhi's justification for his remarkable "tolerance," based on a kind of modesty and humility and recognition of uncertainty, with the focus on relative perspectival truth, is not completely accurate. Such a liberal interpretation seems plausible since Gandhi repeatedly asserts that what is true for him may not be true for the other, and that you should follow your own relative path to truth. In addition, he confesses that he has often miscalculated even when he seemed certain about his relative experiments with truth, even if his nonviolent errors and blunders do not have the devastating harmful consequences as do failed violent experiments with truth. Nevertheless, this modern liberal justification for tolerance does not adequately describe Gandhi's approach because, as seen above, Gandhi has no doubt, even in his approach to relative truth, that love is better than hate, that peace is better than war, that compassion is better than ego-driven selfishness, that violence cannot lead to nonviolence, that terror and terrorism cannot lead to a word free from terror, that ahimsa and satya are the only paths to Truth and Reality.

Gandhi's most creative philosophical responses to this challenge involve his claims about the status of his absolutes as regulative ideals, how they relate to relative truths, and how they are essential for a moral and ontological framework that is unifying and brings the diverse fragmented relative perspectives into integral, coherent, interconnected, meaningful, and relational wholes. Such a moral and spiritual framework allows Gandhi to claim that what unites us is more fundamental than what divides us, that our relative truths must affirm this fundamental unity with a respect for diversity, and that our truthful, relative, moral, and spiritual approaches are all aiming at the same Absolutes of Truth, Peace, and Nonviolence.

Obviously, a creatively reformulated Gandhian philosophy and practice must consider the challenges to its responses not only by the many expressions of contemporary relativism. It must also consider the challenges by those absolutist and exclusivist religious and other positions that deny Gandhi's unifying moral and spiritual framework, deny that their relative truth claims are relative, or deny that all of the relative truths are aiming at the same Absolute Truth and Reality.

My attempt at a creatively reformulated proposal of Gandhi's philosophy that has value for the contemporary world includes the following. Our philosophical focus is on our existential mode of being in the world and how we are actually situated as mind-body-heart human beings, pre-reflectively and reflectively, emotionally and conceptually and imaginatively, to experience diverse relative truths and untruths. Our philosophical focus is also on our existential mode of being in the world in which we have imperfect, limited insights and realizations of Absolute Truth that transcend or go beyond our relative truth claims as spatial, temporal, conditioned beings. Such imaginative constituted ideals add to the relative truths that we know as spatial, temporal, conditioned beings.

As relative, imperfect, conditioned, situated human beings, we have limited perspectival experiences of violence and nonviolence, war and peace, ego-driven hatred and greed and selfless action, untruth and truth. In our philosophy and practice, we are engaged in the self-transformative and world-transformative process of attempting to move from our realization of limited relative truth to greater relative truth. In this philosophical project, we reflect on our diverse and complex experiences of relative truth and nonviolence and imaginatively constitute moral, philosophical, political, economic, religious, and other ideals that we express as Absolutes of Perfect or Pure Truth, God, Nonviolence, Peace, Love, Morality, Religion, and Swaraj.

This process of imaginative constitution of absolute ideals is analyzed in Chapter 4 on Gandhi's controversial interpretation of his favorite text, the Bhagavad-Gita, as a gospel of nonviolence. As will be shown, Gandhi interprets the Gita's Krishna as a symbolic creation of our imagination. We are inspired by moral and spiritual beings in this world to construct imaginatively the ideals of perfection, and that includes the Krishna ideal of moral and spiritual perfection. We then attempt imperfectly to realize this Krishna ideal in our own self and in our lives. As will be shown, Gandhi grants that earlier authors, commentators, and devotees of the Gita did not regard it as a gospel of ahimsa. However, we, today, embracing the profound teachings of the Gita as part of an open-ended process of constituting meaning, can use our imaginations to reread, purify, develop, reinterpret, and reapply the teachings of the Gita as expressing the highest ideals of moral and spiritual perfection as a gospel of nonviolence.

It is important to note, as would be granted by Gandhi, that this process of imaginative creation of the Absolute with ideals of perfection has throughout history involved repression, withdrawal, and illusory escapes from the actual world of relative truths. It has often been used to justify so much suffering, violence, war, and injustice. Relevant in this regard are the powerful, modern critiques of such imaginary escapism offered by Karl Marx, Sigmund Freud, and Friedrich Nietzsche. In several of their influential formulations, their critiques focus on a critique of dominant religion, but the form of the critique is extended to most aspects of modern civilization.

Using only the example of Marx, in his early *Contribution to the Critique of Hegel's Philosophy of Right: Introduction*, he analyzes religion as a symptom of the human condition of powerlessness and alienation in this world. Religion is an imaginary projection, an "inverted world consciousness," reflecting a real world of alienation, suffering, and oppression. Rather than dealing with the real causes of alienation, religious people create escapist illusions by an imaginary projection of what is lacking in their world, onto some imaginary supernatural world (God is perfect, omnipotent, omniscient, omnibenevolent, while we are imperfect, weak, ignorant, and evil). Rational, unalienated human beings must demystify and free themselves from these imaginary escapist illusions and address the real causes of exploitation, dehumanization, and injustice that afflict humanity. Then, in his *Economic and Philosophy Manuscripts of 1844*, *The German Ideology*, and *Capital*, volume I, Marx, who is not very interested in religion, extends this form of radical critique to secular forms of alienation, especially to modern political economy, capitalist economic alienation, the fetishism, reification, and imaginary construction and illusory imposition of value on money, commodities, and so on.[15]

Returning to Gandhi, he is certainly aware of the dangers of this imaginative escapism, as clearly seen in his critiques of much of traditional escapist religion and his radical critique of immoral and illusory cultural construction of much of modern civilization. Nevertheless, such imaginary escapism is not necessarily the case. Imaginative creativity and idealization are also essential to what makes us human. They are essential to how we experience what is real. They gave Gandhi and continue to give us hope in times of despair when we are overwhelmed by so much violence, war, and untruth.

In order to avoid illusory escapism, ideological justifications for war and violence and oppression, or renunciation of action with withdrawal from the relative world of untruths, our Gandhi-informed imaginative ideals must be brought into integral dynamic relations with our relative truths. Our imperfectly experienced and constructed absolute ideals do not have the status of abstracted, decontextualized claims to ultimate reality. They serve as our regulative ideals in our philosophy and practice, and are experienced, developed, and expressed through our engaged selfless actions, real struggles, resistance to violence and war and injustice, and projects of nonviolent and truthful constructive alternatives.

Such an approach can be formulated and contextually reformulated in addressing the most difficult counter-examples, usually intended to refute Gandhi's philosophy of ahimsa as naïve, utopian, unrealistic, or even complicit with forces of extreme violence, killing, and injustice in not resisting with violent force. One thinks of the most common large-scale challenges and dismissals: How would Gandhi's approach to truth and nonviolence deal with a Hitler? How would it deal with the 9/11 terrorists in New York or with the 26/11 terrorists in Mumbai? How would it deal with the IS, ISIS, ISIL, and other forms of overt ruthless terrorism today or the dominating structural forms of multinational corporate terrorism? One also thinks of small-scale challenges and dismissals, such as how to deal with the rapist engaged in the violent act of rape or the violent individual with a gun engaged in the act shooting people. In all such cases, it seems obvious that there is no opportunity or willingness to engage in Gandhian dialogue, and any Gandhian attempt to absorb the suffering, violence, or killing without inflicting violence on the other would be completely ineffective.

In my own creative reformulations and applications, arising from many of Gandhi's writings, I have proposed more complex, contextually relevant, open-ended responses that incorporate insights into the relations of relative and absolute truth. In almost all of our challenging situations of violence, war, class exploitation, caste and gender oppression, and other forms of hierarchical domination, we must educate ourselves and recognize how we humans have created the relative, relational, interconnected causes, and conditions of untruth and violence. Therefore, we must focus our philosophy and practice on how we can decondition these causes and conditions, and begin to replace them with truthful, nonviolent, causal and conditioning factors. Nevertheless, we must recognize that there are some relatively contextualized situations in India and the world today in which there are no short-term nonviolent options that can stop or deter the violence or have any possibility for nonviolent transformation.

In the most challenging situations, such as those mentioned above, we must recognize that a violent response, perhaps even involving killing, may be our most nonviolent, relative, contextually relevant option. If we do not use violent force to stop, say, the rapist or the Mumbai terrorist, we perpetuate, and are complicit in the ongoing violence and killings. Gandhi himself has many writings in which he submits that responding to menacing monkeys or to the madman with a weapon may involve violence and sometimes killing that may even count as ahimsa. What distinguishes our reformulations of Gandhi's philosophy and practice today from the normal justifications for violence, war, and nationalistic, ethnic, class, caste, gendered, and other violent actions is that we always uphold the Absolute Truth of Nonviolence as our regulative ideal and its integral relations with relative truths. This means that our imperfect open-ended philosophy and practice attempt to be as nonviolent as possible, but this occasionally involves the need to resort to violence.

Therefore, in our philosophy, with its theoretical basis and primacy of practice, we should never glorify our individual, social group, national, or other appeals to violence. When we act violently, it is never glorious, moral, or spiritual, but is always tragic, revealing our human failure in creating the causes, conditions, values, structures, and constructive alternatives for nonviolent, moral, and truthful living. Always upholding our regulative ideals of Nonviolence, Truth, Morality, and Swaraj, we should do everything in our power to limit the intensity and duration of our necessary relative violence and to change the basic economic, social, cultural, psychological, educational, and other root causes and basic determinants that created the violent situations that necessitated our violent responses.

A Radical Paradigm Shift

A contemporary, creative, and selective re-appropriation, reformulation, and re-application of a Gandhi-informed philosophy, with its theoretical basis and primacy of practice, requires a radical paradigm shift from the dominant, modern, philosophical, economic, political, cultural, and environmental values and orientations. It involves a qualitatively different way of being in the world, a focus on moral philosophy and development, the need to control modern egoistic desires and attachments, the inversion of modern self-other relations, and a hopeful and meaningful way of living philosophy through action-oriented nonviolent resistance and constructive engagement.

Gandhi's theoretical and practical philosophy challenges us with a qualitatively different philosophical view of freedom and human development and flourishing. He critiques dominant modern models as based on egoistic desires and attachments to possessions, as reductionistically materialist and consumerist, amoral and immoral, violent and untruthful, and as resulting in our modern lack of human development that is economically, morally, politically, culturally, and environmentally unsustainable.

Gandhi offers a radically different paradigm, a view of our higher human nature and capacity and a holistic, interconnected view of self and self-other relations. He focuses on non-egoistic selfless service, especially to meet the needs of the most disadvantaged, and on our integral sustainable relations with other beings and nature. He challenges modernity with a qualitatively different view of what it means to live a morally and spiritually developed life. Only a qualitatively different, radical paradigm shift, providing the philosophical framework for our creatively reformulated philosophy and practices, will allow for the nonviolent, truthful, moral, and spiritual future of India and the world.

In evaluating Gandhi's philosophy and practices as contextually significant for the contemporary world, Gandhi does not have all of the answers or simple solutions in his critique of dominant "Modern Civilization," as seen in his influential formulations in *Hind Swaraj*. Some of what Gandhi wrote was inadequate during his lifetime, sometimes lacking truth and at times even blatantly immoral. Some of his formulations were contextually of value at the time, but are no longer valuable for analyzing some of the changing contextual situations now confronting India and the world. These formulations by Gandhi must be reformulated as we develop our contextually relevant philosophy and practice today.[16]

Nevertheless, Gandhi serves as a catalyst, not unlike the role of Socrates as philosopher in many of the Platonic Dialogues, constantly challenging us to examine and rethink our dominant philosophy and practices. In that regard, the key assumptions, values, principles of multidimensional and structural violence, exploitation, oppression, alienation, unsustainability, and false standards of development, success, and freedom that Gandhi critiqued, seem much more widespread and dominant in our contemporary world. We will not be able to develop a reformulated philosophy today, with its theoretical basis and primacy of practice, unless we address his invaluable insights and alternatives.

Notes

1. At the International Conference on Gandhi and the Contemporary World, organized by the Gandhi Study Circle of Zakir Husain Delhi College and held at the University of Delhi in February 2016, the title of a major plenary session was "Gandhian Philosophy: Theoretical Basis and Practical Dimensions." I changed the emphasis in the wording of my submission to "Gandhian Philosophy: Theoretical Basis with Primacy of Practice." Gandhi is not interested in abstract theoretical or academic philosophical formulations, but rather in philosophy as practice.
2. See S. Radhakrishnan and J.H. Muirhead, eds, *Contemporary Indian Philosophy* (London: George Allen and Unwin, 1936), p. 21. Gandhi's

letter on January 23, 1935, to Radhakrishnan, which is his contribution in *Contemporary Indian Philosophy*, is published in M.K. Gandhi, *The Collected Works of Mahatma Gandhi* (CWMG) (New Delhi: Publications Division, Ministry of Information and Broadcasting, Government of India, 1974), vol. 60, pp. 106–7. The following are the three questions Radhakrishnan sent to Gandhi: What is your religion? How are you led to it? What is its bearing on your social life?

3. See Gandhi's letter on September 16, 1934, to Radhakrishnan, cited in S. Gopal, *Radhakrishnan: A Biography* (Delhi: Oxford University Press, 1989), p. 138. Anthony J. Parel, *Gandhi's Philosophy and the Quest for Harmony* (Cambridge: Cambridge University Press, 2006), pp. 3–5 and 104, correctly submits that Gandhi has an underlying philosophy. For Parel, the key to Gandhi's underlying philosophy is the Indian theory of the *purushastras* (the four aims of life). I discuss Gandhi's contribution to the volume *Contemporary Indian Philosophy* in Douglas Allen, "Mahatma Gandhi's Philosophy of Violence, Nonviolence, and Education," in *The Philosophy of Mahatma Gandhi for the Twenty-First Century*, ed. Douglas Allen (Lanham, MD: Lexington Books, 2009), pp. 33–62, and Douglas Allen, *The Philosophy of Mahatma Gandhi for the Twenty-First Century* (New Delhi: Oxford University Press, 2009), pp. 33–62.

4. See Chapter 3, "Is Gandhi a Vedantist?," in this volume. While Gandhi was not featured at the Vedanta Congress, it is revealing how the situation has changed from my experiences with the philosophers of Advaita Vedanta at BHU in 1963–4. In response to my presentation on "Is Gandhi a Vedantist?" at the Vedanta Congress in 2015, the overwhelming response of the Vedantists was that Gandhi's philosophy was clearly grounded in Vedanta, and, more specifically, was an expression of Advaita.

5. There are numerous passages outlining the Upanishadic path of realization, with the appropriate course of discipline and stages of development leading to the realization of truth and reality, in which the student must be morally qualified as a preliminary requisite. As expressed in "The Upanishads," in *Sourcebook in Indian Philosophy*, ed. S. Radhakrishnan and C. Moore (Princeton: Princeton University Press, 1957), and other versions of the Upanishads, goodness, character, and virtue are necessary for Vedic study, moral detachment from egoistic desires and attachments is necessary, the student must resist temptations of wealth and power (Katha Upanishad), honesty is extolled, as when the student admits that he does not know who his father is (Chandogya Upanishads), and so on. As with everything else, orthodox Hindu

philosophers then debate which of these moral prerequisites is absolutely necessary to be accepted as a student and how to interpret and apply them.
6. Etymologically, *himsa* is derived from the Sanskrit root "to strike" and has the meaning of to injure or to harm. Ahimsa has the opposite meaning: to cause no injury, to cause no harm, in words, thoughts, or deeds. I shall use the usual definition of ahimsa as "nonviolence," while recognizing that it encompasses much more than our usual English-language meanings of nonviolence. Ahimsa is an essential principle and value in Jainism, much of Buddhism and Hinduism, and in Gandhi's philosophy and practice. Noteworthy are my experiences, especially in the contexts of contemporary India, in which Indian scholars, Hindu political figures, and Hindu religious leaders, often claiming to appropriate Gandhi, challenge the meaning of ahimsa as "nonviolence." They reformulate Gandhi ideologically so that ahimsa now encompasses and justifies all kinds of violence that Gandhi would reject.
7. Gandhi, of course, has thousands of pages of writing on his views of Truth (Satya, God, Self, Being, Reality), Nonviolence (Ahimsa, No-Harm, Love), and their integral relations. See, or example, the following key formulations: *CWMG* 37, 348–9; *CWMG* 48, 404; *CWMG* 84, 229; M.K. Gandhi, *From Yeravda Mandir: Ashram Observances*, trans. V.G. Desai (Ahmedabad: Navajivan, 1957 [1933]), pp. 12–13.
8. For an attempt to formulate Gandhi's philosophy and practice of Satya (Truth), Ahimsa (Nonviolence), and the integral relations between Truth and Nonviolence, see Chapter 6 "Gandhi's Philosophy: Truth and Nonviolence," in Douglas Allen, *Mahatma Gandhi* (London: Reaktion, 2011), pp. 105–30, which contains citations from Gandhi's writings. This formulation is based on my previous writings, including Douglas Allen, "Gandhi, Contemporary Political Thinking, and Self-Other Relations," in *Gandhi's Experiments with Truth*, ed. Richard L. Johnson (Lanham, MD: Lexington Books, 2005), pp. 303–29; "Mahatma Gandhi's Philosophy of Violence, Nonviolence, and Education," in *The Philosophy of Mahatma Gandhi for the Twenty-First Century*, 33–62.
9. Steven Pinker, *The Better Angels of Our Nature: Why Violence Has Declined* (New York: Viking, 2011). As will become clear, Pinker and some other recent optimistic writers, who maintain that we have unprecedented nonviolence, peace, security, and human flourishing today, usually restrict their quantifiable criteria for what counts as violence, war, killing, terror, insecurity, and so on, and do not include most of what a Gandhi-informed approach interprets as contemporary violence.

10. Steven Pinker, *Enlightenment Now: The Case for Reason, Science, Humanism, and Progress* (New York: Viking, 2018). Pinker claims that the all-time low levels of violence and unprecedented high levels of progress, education, wealth, health, happiness, and human flourishing are the result of the modern Western Enlightenment. Interestingly, as will be analyzed in Chapter 6 and other sections in this book, Gandhi, while positively influenced by the Enlightenment and other modern developments, primarily offers a radical critique of the Enlightenment tradition. This dominant modern orientation is the cause of so much violence, amoral and immoral living, dehumanization, alienation, exploitation, destruction of nature, lack of spirituality and unsustainability today.

11. For my attempt to formulating Gandhi's philosophy and practice of economics and economic violence and my evaluation of the strengths and weaknesses in his approach, see Douglas Allen, "Gandhi and Socialism," *International Journal of Gandhian Studies*, 1, no. 1 (2012): 109–37.

12. See *CWMG* 30, 33; "Ashram Vows," *CWMG* 13, 225–34, especially "vow of non-thieving," 230–1; "Constructive Programme," *CWMG* 75, 146–66, especially the section "economic equality," 158–9; "Implications of the Constructive Programme," *CWMG* 72, 378–81, with Gandhi's conclusion that the "whole of this programme will, however, be a structure on sand if it is not built on the solid foundation of economic equality"; *CWMG* 25, 475, where Gandhi claims that economics disregarding moral values are untrue and that the introduction of non-violent economics means the introduction of moral value to Indian and international economic relations.

13. This is not to deny that maintaining some features of semi-feudal exploitative and oppressive relations of domination can be integral to the specific nature of capitalist development in India. One must contextualize one's analysis, avoiding the uncritical, universal, theoretical imposition of a model of capitalism, its class relations, development, exploitation, domination, and globalization and being aware of the specific contextual variables necessary to analyze what is happening in India.

14. The need for self-purification, involving understanding the physical, mental, and imaginary construction of the false, immoral, violent ego and the deconstruction, deconditioning, and overcoming of the ego with its ego-driven desires, needs, and attachments, is one of the major themes in Gandhi's philosophy and practice. In his *Autobiography*, pp. 504–5, he describes this difficult path of self-purification, and how "I must reduce myself to zero. So long as a man does not of his own free

will put himself last among his fellow creatures, there is no salvation for him. Ahimsa is the farthest limit of humility." In *CWMG* 33, 452, after affirming that "Truth and Love have jointly been the guiding principle of my life," Gandhi writes the following: "It is impossible to reach Him (God), that is, Truth, except through Love. Love can only be expressed fully when man reduces himself to a cipher. This process of reduction to cipher is the highest effort man or woman is capable of making. It is the only effort worth making, and it is possible only through ever-increasing self-restraint."

15. Relevant sections from all of these works by Marx can be found in *The Marx-Engels Reader*, ed. Robert C. Tucker (New York: W.W. Norton, 1972). The *Contribution to the Critique* begins with the influential critique of religion as imaginary projection; *The 1844 Manuscripts* contain the critique of the imaginary construction of capitalist political economy, the four structures of alienation (alienated labor), and the humanistic alternative of unalienated life; *Capital*, volume I, contains the basic analysis of capitalist production as based on exploitation of alienated labor-power and includes the section on the illusory imaginary construction of the "fetishism" of commodities. Sigmund Freud's critique of religion can be found in Sigmund Freud, *The Future of an Illusion*, trans. W.D. Robson-Scott (New York: Liveright, 1961), Chapter 8, and Freud extends this critique beyond religion in such works as *Civilization and Its Discontents*.

16. Gandhi's radical critique of "Modern Civilization," using the controversial example of Gandhi's approach to technology, as well as his alternative of a radical cultural and civilizational paradigm shift with a swaraj technology, is presented in Chapter 6, "Is Gandhi's Approach to Technology Irrelevant in the Modern Age of Technology?"

3

Is Gandhi a Vedantist?

Mohandas Karamchand Gandhi, while always controversial during his lifetime and the source of continuing extreme controversy in India and the contemporary world, is certainly the best-known Indian of the twentieth century. In India, Siddhartha Gautama, the Buddha, and he are frequently identified as the two greatest moral and spiritual figures in the history of India. Surveys not only in India, but also throughout the world usually list Gandhi at or near the top of the most admired human beings of the modern world.

Vedanta is the best-known Indian philosophy. Many in India have simply presented Vedanta, and especially the non-dualistic Advaita Vedanta, as Indian philosophy. Often it is acknowledged that there are indeed other Indian philosophies, but Advaita and sometimes other Vedantic approaches are then presented as the essence of Indian philosophy, the philosophy expressing the highest and deepest level of Truth, Being, and Reality.

This has also been a common, albeit inaccurate and oversimplified, misconception in the West of the pluralistic, dynamic, diverse nature of India's philosophical tradition. Western philosophers, other scholars, and others interested in Indian thinking and spirituality frequently identify Indian philosophy and spirituality with Vedanta and especially Advaita. There is a historical context for this. As most evident in the life, lectures, academic and political positions, and writings of S. Radhakrishnan, many modern influential Indian scholars studied and taught at Oxford, Cambridge, and other leading institutions. Many of these philosophers and other influential Indians were fluent in English and sometimes established Vedanta centers in Europe and the USA. They often promoted the view that Vedanta, especially Advaita, is the essence of or highest realization of Indian philosophy.

With the influence of M.K. Gandhi and the influence of Vedanta, it is of great significance to ask: Is Gandhi a Vedantin? This topic is also central to significant research today.[1]

Personal Introduction

Sharing some of my background may provide a personal context for my interest in this topic.[2] During my youthful Fulbright year of 1963–4 at BHU, I taught in the department of English and did postgraduate studies in the distinguished department of philosophy. My major mentor was the head of the department, T.R.V. Murti, the president of the Indian Philosophical Congress and a proponent of Advaita Vedanta. Other Advaitins, including my other major mentor, R.K. Tripathi, dominated the department. There were a few non-Vedantins in the department, most notably J.L. Mehta, who had a strong background in continental philosophy and especially the philosophy of Martin Heidegger. Reflecting his feelings at that time of his life, Mehta would privately tell me that I should not be seduced by the Vedanta rubbish, but his was a rare dissenting voice. As with almost all postgraduate students at that time, reflecting the dominant orientation not only at BHU but also at the other advanced philosophy centers in India, I left my BHU studies convinced that Shankara was the greatest Indian philosopher and Advaita Vedanta was the best Indian philosophy.

What was the presence of Gandhi and his philosophy in the department of philosophy and at BHU at that time? Put briefly, Gandhi's presence in the department of philosophy was nonexistent. Unlike Nagarjuna, Shankara, Ramanuja, or twentieth-century Indian philosophers, Gandhi was not considered a philosopher, and we never studied him in our postgraduate courses. Gandhi's name and presence, of course, were everywhere at BHU and in India at the time, but one could soon realize the pervasive atmosphere of hypocrisy. As an illustration, the vice-chancellor of BHU, consistent with Indian politicians and other leaders, would wear his Gandhi cap, wear his khadi, and give the same Gandhi ritualized speeches, invoking the name of the Mahatma and repeating the same Gandhi slogans. He, along with so many others, would then return to their non-Gandhian and anti-Gandhian values, priorities, and policies. Such Gandhi invocations and slogans did not express Gandhi's philosophy or practice.

Returning to the US in 1964 to pursue my PhD in philosophy at Vanderbilt University in Nashville, Tennessee, and to become deeply engaged in the Civil Rights Movement, my Advaita influence led to an ambivalence and self-critical attitude. I certainly admired my teachers at BHU and in Varanasi. However, as I was confronted by and engaged in the struggle to overcome segregation and racism, poverty, oppression, and injustice, I began to feel that my Indian journey, with the focus on my ego-needs, desires, and attachments and the pursuit of my moral and spiritual development, was, ironically, a kind of selfless selfishness, with so much of my focus on my own self.

I was not unaware of this in Banaras. Repeatedly, I experienced remarkable pandits and yogis, with untouchables/Dalits and other impoverished, exploited, and oppressed Indians living nearby, and the presence, philosophies, and practices of the spiritual masters seemed to make no difference in improving the lives of the downtrodden. I recall being shaken by an experience in which one of India's most renowned philosophers, a high Brahman Vedantist, publically screamed at and humiliated an untouchable rickshaw wallah. Traditional Vedanta, at least how I had been taught it, now seemed largely irrelevant, and even a self-indulgent obstacle, to expressing civil rights solidarity with and struggling with the victims of racism, class exploitation, and injustice.[3]

One other relevant formative Vedanta development occurred when I submitted my PhD dissertation topic to work on Nagarjuna's Madhyamika Buddhism and Shankara's Advaita Vedanta. My dissertation committee turned this down because they did not feel competent to supervise such a dissertation, acknowledging that I knew more than they did on the topic. Instead, they proposed that I work in the area of philosophical phenomenology, and I could incorporate some of the Indian material. What this meant was that although I continued to teach and write on Vedanta, I never became a Sanskrit or Vedanta specialist.

The formative influence of M.K. Gandhi was very different. Martin Luther King, Jr, was the most influential leader in the civil rights movement, and I soon realized that one could not understand King's nonviolent activism, resistance, boycotts, and civil disobedience without understanding Gandhi's major influence on his philosophy and practices.[4] For the next 30 years, while I did not focus on a scholarly approach to Gandhi, he was a major influence in my personal life, civil rights, human rights, anti-war, anti-apartheid, and other peace and justice struggles.

This changed in the mid-1990s, when I engaged in scholarly research and began to lecture and write on Gandhi's philosophy. I developed the position that Gandhi is not a philosopher in a technical academic or disciplinary way, but he makes moral and philosophical assumptions, has moral and philosophical principles, and is more morally and philosophically insightful and significant than most work done in academic philosophy.

Although it may not reflect the dominant philosophical approach of traditional Vedanta, the question remains whether it is possible to be a Gandhian Vedantin. More specifically, is M.K. Gandhi a Vedantin? Leaving aside various Indians who claim that everyone, whether they realize it or not, is really a Hindu or even a Vedantin, there are serious Indian scholars who claim that Gandhi is a Vedantist. Rather than citing the writings of several well-known Indian scholars on Gandhi and Vedanta, we shall examine the scholarship of two young Indian scholars, who have been exposed to a wide range of philosophical positions and claim that it is obvious that Gandhi is not only a Vedantist, but, more specifically, a proponent of Advaita philosophy.

Ved Mitra Shukla: Gandhi Is an Advaitin

According to Ved Mitra Shukla, "Mahatma Gandhi is one of the recent well-known followers of Advaita philosophy. The influence of this philosophy can be easily traced out in his writings as well as in his life."[5]

After classifying Advaita Vedanta philosophy in two parts—classical Advaita Vedanta, with the focus on Shankaracharya, and neo-Advaita Vedanta, with the focus on Vivekananda—and with a later quotation from Glyn Richards asserting that Gandhi is closer to the neo-Advaita Vedanta, Shukla focuses on classical Advaita Vedanta in his section on Gandhi's Position as Advaitin (216–19).[6] After a brief delineation of key principals in Shankara's Advaita Vedanta, Shukla claims that Gandhi is an Advaitin, and he cites the following six passages from Gandhi's writings as evidence that Gandhi's proclaims himself an Advaitin.

Gandhi writes: (*a*) "I believe in absolute oneness of God and therefore of humanity.... We have but one soul"; (*b*) "I believe in Advaita. I believe in the essential unity of man and for that matter of all that live"; (*c*) "The forms are many, but the informing spirit is one. How can there be room for distinctions of high and low where there is this all-embracing fundamental unity underlying the outward diversity"; (*d*) "What I want to achieve ... is self-realization, to see God face to face, to attain *moksha*" (salvation); (*e*) "I am endeavoring to see God through the service of humanity, for I know that God is neither in heaven nor down, but in everyone"; (*f*) "I am a part and parcel of the whole, and I cannot find Him apart from the rest of humanity.... And I worship the God that is Truth or Truth which is God through the service of these millions."[7, 8]

Shukla asserts: "Without a doubt, his (Gandhi's) belief in the essential quality of oneness of Advaita tradition is loud and clear. The attainment of the *moksha* is the goal of his life." However, Gandhi's means, his *marga* (path) of karma, with involvement in the political field, is very different from Shankara's Advaita focus on *jnana* (spiritual knowledge path). Rejecting Shankara's "extreme aversion (*vairagya*) to all perishable things," Gandhi's endorses full participation in social and political activities in service to humanity. "The reason behind the full participation is the identification of non-duality between the all-pervading *Brahman* and the human beings" (218).

Then, under Gandhi's socio-political practices, Shukla briefly considers satyagraha, prayer meetings, mass singing of the devotional *ramadhuna* (rhythmical chanting of the name of Rama), his favorite *bhajana* (devotional song), elimination of untouchability, his version of *varnashrama* (divisional structure of the Indian society into four major castes), and religious harmony. Shukla maintains that all of these are based on Gandhi's Advaita philosophy.[9]

Kumar Rahul: Gandhi Is a Cosmopolitan Advaitin

Before delineating major features of Kumar Rahul's ambitious, creative, and thought-provoking essay, I shall offer a summary and overview. With a commitment to cosmopolitanism and knowledge of recent scholarship, Rahul correctly notes that this has assumed a Western-centric, liberal, Enlightenment, theoretical, universalizing framework. Rather than completely rejecting such cosmopolitanism, as so many post-modernists, subaltern scholars, cultural relativists, and others have done, Rahul offers Gandhi's self-other inversion and framework as an alternative for a more adequate cosmopolitanism.[10]

Rahul focuses on how Gandhi's analysis and practice on self and self-other relations is grounded in Advaita Vedanta theoretical/metaphysical foundation and framework, with the other main complementary influence of the Bhagavad-Gita. His main claim is that Gandhi's approach and framework are cosmological, not the limited, Western teleological or deontological alternative frameworks. The self, self-other, and the other (as part of self) are grounded in the nondual cosmic view of Brahman, *Atman* (the true spiritual Self or Soul), Truth, God, providing the source, the origin, the rootedness, and the energy. Prayer, self-purification, and the ideal of the perfected being are important for such self-realization. This Gandhian grounding and framework can also provide the political theory and practice for more adequate cosmopolitanism, with the other as valued other, and not marginalized or erased through othering.

Under "Metaphysics of the Advaita-Vedanta," Rahul begins with an oft-cited and controversial quotation from Gandhi: "I am an Advaitist and yet I can support 'Dvaitism' (dualism)." Gandhi continues that the world is ever-changing, impermanent, and therefore unreal, but it has something about it that persists and is to that extent real.[11] He can accept that the world is real and unreal, and can be called an "Ankantavadi" (upholding Jain theory of "many-sidedness") and a "Syadvadi" (upholding Jain theory of "conditional predication"), but his "Syadvadi" is not of the scholar, but peculiarly his own.[12]

Then, in "Metaphysics of the Advaita Vedanta," "the Absolute," "the Self," and "Nondualism," Rahul focuses on the philosophical approach of Adi Shankaracharya, briefly including the appeal to Vedic Upanishadic revelation, the distinction and dialectical relation between *para* (higher) and *apara* (lower) *vidya* (knowledge), the distinction and relation between *Nirguna Brahman* (*Brahman* without qualities) and *Saguna Brahman* (with qualities), the nature of the Absolute as *Brahman*, the nature of the Self as Atman, and their identity in the Advaita philosophy of nondualism. At various points, Rahul both identifies Gandhi with this Advaita philosophy and contrasts him with Shankara's approach.[13]

Under "Gandhi and the Advaita Vedanta" and using some of the same Gandhi writings and Richards and other citations found in Shukla's article, Rahul develops the case for Gandhi as Advaitin. This includes consideration of Truth alone as eternal Being, Truth as God, and Gandhi's acceptance of God as personal and impersonal, with his preference for the Advaita. In reaffirming his Advaitin position, Rahul submits that the following writing "illustrates it more unambiguously than any other:" "I believe in the absolute oneness of God and therefore of humanity. What though we have many bodies? We have one soul. The rays of the sun are many through refraction. But they have the same source."[14]

Rahul's other argument supporting Gandhi's Advaitin position focuses on his conceptualization of swaraj, with the emphasis on dharma, the para–apara relation, and the guide to more egalitarian and democratic moral action. "Thus, having acquired Swaraj, one is motivated not to differentiate oneself from others as one would treat oneself" (p. 341).

For the second half of his article, for which I shall not provide detailed exposition, Rahul develops his argument for Gandhi's philosophy of Advaita Vedanta with the thought-provoking emphasis on how Gandhi's Advaita necessarily leads to a strong commitment to a creative and insightful cosmopolitanism. He cites Gandhi's emphasis on following dharma, daily prayer, and the process of self-purification, and maintains that this is grounded in and supported by an Advaitin metaphysical system and cosmological orientation.

This is developed through a detailed consideration of Gandhi's many controversial writings about the "inner voice" and how this leads to the ethical primacy of "the other" as integral to Gandhian cosmopolitanism.[15] Rahul's most interesting move is to distinguish the inner voice as a spiritual device, a temporary invocation, prompting our conscience as part of the process of self-purification drawing us to the truth, and as both personal and relational. The inner voice is distinguished from but also metaphysically grounded in the Gita's ideal of the state of *sthitha-prajna* (the perfected person of stable wisdom). The temporary inner voice, which calls on us to recognize and address the suffering of the relational other, cannot replace its ideal of the self-perfected state of sthitha-prajna (344–7).

As summarized in my above overview, the remaining sections of Rahul's article address the need for an alternative cosmopolitan framework, and how Gandhi's cosmopolitan dharma, grounded in his cosmological framework from Advaita Vedanta and from the Gita, provides for such a dharma approach. Gandhi's morally informed cosmopolitan approach, rejecting traditional self-negation and world-renunciation, purifies politics and worldly engagement, with the "supreme primacy of the other." Our cosmopolitan dharma is to invert the self-other relationship and serve the needs of the other. The Gandhian other, as integral part of our selves, can provide the cosmological basis for an alternative cosmopolitan framework in India and throughout the world.

Is Gandhi an Advaitin? Two General Responses

We shall begin with two general responses to the excellent detailed expositions and Vedantic and Advaitin interpretations by Shukla and Rahul. This will be followed by detailed responses to the key issue of whether Gandhi is a Vedantin.

In both articles, as well as in writings by some other Vedantists, the assumptions and arguments are that Gandhi is clearly an Advaitin. Gandhi, of course, has writings in which he affirms his preference for Advaita, just as he has many more writings in which he affirms bhakti and other ethical, religious, nonreligious, philosophical, nondualistic, and pluralistic perspectives. Most of the writings cited in the two articles for Advaita evidence refer to unity, permanence, oneness, with the Absolute, the Self, God, what is Truth and Reality.

The first general response is to question why such Gandhi formulations specifically and necessarily lead to his identification with Advaita Vedanta philosophy. Hindu philosophy in general—with all of its pluralism, dynamic tradition of vigorous argumentation and debate, and with some notable exceptions—tends to emphasize unity over diversity, permanence over impermanence, and structure over disorder and chaos. This can be contrasted with the orientation of Buddhist philosophy, especially in its foundational doctrines of *anicca* (impermanence), *anatta* (no-self), *dukkha* (suffering), and dependent origination. In other words, an emphasis on permanence, unity, oneness, Soul or Self, God, and so on, may commit one to a more Hindu philosophical and religious orientation, but not necessarily to a strict or exclusive Advaitin philosophy.

Second, as formulated in previous writings and as expressed in the chapter in this book on Gandhi's unusual approach to the Bhagavad-Gita, it is necessary to adopt a contextualized anti-essentialized approach in which one recognizes the dynamic integral relations between text, contexts, and interpretations of meaning. This attempt at new, open-ended, creative readings and interpretations is in contrast to how more traditional Vedantic and other Indian scholars have studied and commented on the Vedas, Upanishads, Gita, Ramayana, and Gandhi's writings. They have focused on essentialized questions and truth claims, such as what is the most adequate philosophy of what is real, what is the true interpretation of the text, or why Gandhi is an Advaitin.

By way of contrast and trying to avoid a kind of anti-essentialized, unlimited, fashionable, often facile, completely subjective, contemporary relativism, we may ask the following questions: Which Vedas? Which Upanishads? Which Mahabharata? Which Gita? Which Gandhi writings? Even, which Gandhi?

We may briefly illustrate this approach to Gandhi's key and controversial reading and interpretation of his favorite Bhagavad-Gita, as developed in the Gita chapter in this book. As relevant to the previously formulated articles by Rahul and Shukla, Shankara and later proponents of Advaita Vedanta philosophy privilege the *jnana-yoga* Advaita passages. Unlike Gandhi, these Vedantists submit that the

Advaita passages in the Gita focusing on the knowledge path express the highest, deepest, most philosophically and spiritually perfected claims about Truth and Reality. Gandhi, while affirming and sometimes expressing his personal preference for the Advaitin passages, also affirms the truth of the Krishna teachings in which bhakti-motivated devotees follow their Lord's will and desire union or unity with God without a complete nondualistic meaning. What is especially distinctive about the Gita is its philosophical, religious, foundational focus of karma-yoga, and what is special in Gandhi's reading and commentary on the meaning of the text is his specific interpretation of privileging karma-yoga as renunciation in action and especially his claim that the Gita is gospel of nonviolence.

Our hermeneutical encounter involves the process of understanding how Gandhi—in terms of his reading of Hindu, other Indian, and Western texts, his reading of other commentaries on the Gita, his own contextual situations that shaped him and that he influenced, and so on—arrives at his own, insightful, and often controversial readings and interpretations of meaning. We are always involved in the dynamic open-ended process of how we mediate and connect our contextualized readings and interpretations of Gandhi's writings with our own insights, disclosures, silences, reformulations, selectively appropriating what is most significant in Gandhi's approach for our lives and for the contemporary and future world.

Is Gandhi an Advaitin? Specific Responses

Is Gandhi a Vedantin, and, more specifically, a proponent of Advaita Vedanta philosophy? In many ways, the answer is a qualified "yes" and a "no." A key to this response is how one uses the terms "Vedanta" and "Vedantist": whether in a narrower sense referring to Advaita and other formulations of Vedanta philosophy or in a much wider sense encompassing the Vedas, Upanishads, Gita, epics, the *Manusmriti* and other Dharmashastras, the *Arthashastra*, the Sutras, and later philosophical and religious texts, commentaries, and developments. In any case, Gandhi is not a traditional Indian or Vedantic philosophical thinker, and while identifying with much of the wider Hindu Vedanta tradition, he critiques and rejects much of it.

The following focus will not be on Gandhi's action-oriented karma-yoga with his unusual ahimsa interpretation, but instead on his strong nontraditional emphasis on the world of relative truth. This is not only the case in Gandhi's approach to the Gita, but it defines one of the most significant features of most of his writings and how he lives his life and engages in the world.

In contrast to most traditional Vedanta philosophy and most clearly in traditional Advaita philosophy, Gandhi engages in and grants a much higher moral, epistemological, social, political, economic, and metaphysical status to the world of relative truth. While recognizing that Vedanta can be more engaged with the world, as seen in some formulations of neo-Vedanta, most Vedantins, including Advaitins, have not been action-oriented and have not had a Gandhi focus on renunciation in action. Instead they focus on the goal of renouncing and transcending the action-oriented illusory karmic world of relative truth, so that the process of ego-transcendence and self-realization involves world transcendence. With limited exceptions in some of his writings, this is not Gandhi's position. He resists such a renunciatory move of world transcendence, and primarily focuses on the status and significance of relative truth.

As previously indicated, Gandhi does emphasize permanence, oneness, and unity, but this is a unity with a deep respect for differences. The relational other, as integral to the self, is not devalued or transcended. Acting to serve the needs of the bodily and mentally and spiritually unfree other, who is impoverished, oppressed, exploited, unjustly treated, and suffering, necessarily means active, selfless engagement in the world of relative truth.

Sometimes ignored and usually underappreciated is Gandhi's key methodological, moral, epistemological, and ontological distinction between Absolute Truth and relative truth.[16] For Gandhi, satya is Truth, and he equates this with Being, God, Self, Soul, that which is Real. Therefore, any claim to Absolute Truth is identical with any claim to Absolute Reality. Various Gandhi writings express his affirmation of Absolute Truth as Reality with his rigid uncompromising judgments. This has led to the frequent interpretation, really a misinterpretation, that Gandhi is concerned exclusively or primarily with Absolute Truth. For many Gandhi devotees, this shows the admirable Mahatma upholding his extraordinary moral and spiritual absolutes, while for many critics, this shows the Gandhi who is inflexible, coercive, and abusive in relating to his family, striking workers, satyagrahis, and others.

Throughout his writings, Gandhi tells us that he only has "glimpses" of the truth. He writes: "As long as I have not realized this Absolute Truth, so long must I hold by the relative truth as I have conceived it."[17] Even more, going beyond any claim to his own imperfection, Gandhi writes: "Nobody in this world possesses absolute truth. This is God's absolute alone. Relative truth is all we know. Therefore, we can only follow the truth as we see it."[18] In his philosophy and practice, we are always engaged in the process of attempting to move from relative truth to greater relative truth, closer to the ideal of Absolute Truth. This does not mean that the unrealized perfect Absolute Truth is irrelevant. Through our limited experiential glimpses of the pure absolute and our imaginative idealizations, we are provided with the regulative ideals, the motivation and hope in times of darkness, and the moral, spiritual, nonviolent, truthful force that allows us to become aware, struggle and resist, and work for constructive alternatives in our world of relative truth.

As Gandhi repeatedly warns us, everything he says about Absolute Truth, Nonviolence, God, and Self remains on the level of relative truth. For example, in upholding the pure perfect ideal of ahimsa, he asserts that no one knows absolute ahimsa and that we can at best act to realize the greatest relative truth of the least violence and most nonviolence in our values, intentions, and actions. This absolute-relative distinction, with the focus on relative truth, shapes Gandhi's approach to economic, political, social, cultural, and religious concerns, his formulations on violence and nonviolence, his writings and actions on swaraj, swadeshi, satyagraha, and his constructive program. This key distinction, with his focus on relative truth, shapes his views on anti-colonial independence, untouchability and caste, gender oppression, decentralized economic and political institutions and technology, socialism, and education.

There is a persistent tension in Gandhi's philosophy, practice, and approach that arises from the essential, contextualized, complex, at time contradictory, absolute-relative relations. On the one hand, Gandhi repeatedly emphasizes limited relative truths, the inner voice, individual consciousness, a tolerance and respect for the plurality and diversity of others, recognizing the legitimacy of their perspectives and advising others to follow their own paths to their truths. On the other hand, Gandhi grounds his commitment to an essential unity, oneness, and permanence, with the absolutes of Truth, Reality, Self, and Nonviolence, by assuming a metaphysical, spiritual, ethical framework. Such an ideal framework, constituted by Absolute Truths, allows us to unify the diverse perspectives and allows Gandhi to resist a position of endless, individual, fragmented, and disconnected relative truths. There are many relative truths, many legitimate contextualized paths to climbing the mountain. But as imperfect human beings, moving from one relative truth to greater relative truth, we are interrelated and unified in our experiments with diverse imperfect ways to climb the same mountain; in our attempts to realize the Absolute Truth and experience Reality.

The tension in Gandhi's approach arises from the fact that he has assumed a metaphysical foundation, a spiritual essentialism, which holds together and unifies the plurality of individual selves and cultural and religious groups with their diverse relative perspectives and relative truths and relations. What if the philosophical, cultural, or religious others claim that their relative approach is the true path and the other relative paths are false or evil? That we are climbing different mountains, and their path is the only way to ascend the one mountain of truth and reality? That they realize the exclusive Absolute Truth and Reality? How does Gandhi justify adopting his spiritual, philosophical, ethical, metaphysical, unifying framework? Through reason and critical reflection? Through Vedic and other scriptural revelation? Through faith? Through the imposition of a metaphysical spiritual framework, even when the other claims that this involves a unifying Hinduization or Vedanta philosophical imposition and does violence to the absolute and relative perspective of the other?

One way that Advaitins, other Indian scholars, and even some Gandhians attempt to resolve this tension, even claiming that there is no tension, is to present a traditional Indian philosophical distinction between relative truth and Absolute Truth as seen in the theory of two truths, of two levels of reality and truth. This theory is most often associated with Buddhism, with the best-known and most influential philosophical approach in Nagarjuna's Madhyamika philosophy and with numerous diverse Buddhist formulations found in different philosophical expressions throughout the world. Influenced by Nagarjuna's formulation, Shankara's Advaita Vedanta formulates its own influential version of the theory of two truths and levels of reality.

It is not my intention to present and analyze the complexities of the Buddhist and Advaitin formulations and the ensuing philosophical debates. In a somewhat oversimplified manner, the focus will be on the differentiation of two levels of experiential reality, with the distinction between Absolute Truth and relative truth, in order to determine whether this resolves the tension in Gandhi and renders him a Vedantin or more specifically an Advaitin.[19]

Consistent with the theory of two truths, we should not confuse or conflate the two levels of analysis expressing two radically different levels of truth and reality. When Gandhi is discussing individual selves, individual consciousness, social selves, inner voices, separate diverse perspectives, and limited relative contextualized economic and political and cultural variables, his approach functions on the limited conditioned level of empirical, worldly, and relative truth. When Gandhi is discussing Truth, Brahman (Nirguna Brahman), Atman, Self, (absolute) God, and Nonviolence, his approach functions on the deepest, ultimate, spiritual level of unconditioned, noncausal, nonempirical, transcendent Absolute Truth. Tension only results when we confuse these two levels of analysis by not distinguishing relative truth and reality from the Absolute Truth and Reality.

Regardless of how one formulates and assesses Shankara's Advaita Vedanta theory of two levels of truth and reality, such a Vedanta approach does not easily remove all tensions and questions regarding Gandhi's approach. What follows presents two of many possible complicating relevant considerations.

First, relative truth is not simple, empirical, worldly, apparent illusory truth. Even Gandhi's relative truths have a nonempirical, ahistorical, spiritual dimension. This is why many of Gandhi's claims about relative truth, seemingly arising from his empirical worldly experiments with truth, often prove so frustrating to scientists, philosophers, and other scholars attempting to subject them to a process of strict empirical, rational, social, political, historical verification.[20]

Second, unlike many traditional Vedantins, Gandhi maintains that there is an integral necessary relation between relative truths and Absolute Truth. A traditional Advaita Vedanta philosopher may claim that on the level of Absolute Truth, when we experience the true or real Self as the pure spiritual Atman and we experience the complete nondual identity of Atman–Brahman, we reject and transcend the illusory world of relative truths. The world of relative truth is sublated and negated as constituted by false, karmic, *mayic* (illusory), human constructions devoid of Truth and Reality. Such empirical, social, political, cultural, historical, contextualized, relative truths may have limited epistemic status, but they have no ultimate ontological Truth and reality.

This is not Gandhi's approach. For Gandhi, relative truth is our only limited access to Absolute Truth. We can only gain access to the ideals of pure Self, Truth, the Absolute, through the imperfect, limited, relative perspectives of relative self, truth, and reality. At no point can we speak of transcending moral, social, economic, political, religious, educational, environmental, and other relative dichotomies, including self-other relations, and transcending the world of relative truth.

* * *

Is Gandhi a Vedantin? As previously indicated, it is possible to respond with a qualified "yes" and a "no." It is also possible to respond that Gandhi is a Vedantin, even an Advaitin, but he is also more than a Vedantin. Is this a coherent approach that makes sense and is significant today?

Similar to what some Advaita Vedanta philosophers do, one can examine Gandhi's diverse writings and actions and then selectively privilege Gandhi as an exclusive Advaitin; as embracing an approach in which the nondual, monistic, Advaita Vedanta philosophy expresses the realization of what is true and real. However, this is not a comprehensive adequate interpretation of Gandhi's approach. Gandhi values and wants to do justice to many non-Advaitin and non-Vedantic Indian approaches, other Eastern approaches, and Western approaches, some of which deeply influence his own philosophy, spirituality, and practices.

Is Gandhi's inclusivist, pluralist approach to truth and reality confused, irrational, and incoherent or is it brilliantly insightful and especially contextually significant for us today in our world of so much intolerance, conflict, exploitation, oppression, and violence? My own view is that Gandhi is philosophically significant and serves as a needed catalyst in continually challenging us to rethink our own philosophical assumptions, principles, theories, and practices.

Notes

1. I would like to thank the organizers of the Vedanta Congress held at Jawaharlal Nehru University, New Delhi, India, December 2015, especially Bal Ram Singh and Girish Nath Jha, for inviting me to present a Gandhi-informed plenary lecture. The topic of "Is Gandhi a Vedantist?" is my response to that invitation. I would also like to thank Prof. Sukalyan Sengupta, organizer of the Vedanta Congress held at the University of Massachusetts Dartmouth, August 2017, for inviting me to present my revised work on this topic.

    Humorously, after I accepted the invitation, I began to question whether I had been foolish in selecting the topic of whether Gandhi is a Vedantist. After reading other authors on the topic, including recent publications, and considering the views of most participants at a Vedanta Congress, it seemed to me that there would be a shared affirmation that Gandhi is obviously a Vedantist, and, more specifically, an Advaitin. Again somewhat humorously, but also informed by the scholarship, I began to wonder if I had selected a non-topic, a pseudo-topic; whether participants would think that I was mentally impaired or at the minimum unscholarly. After all, would this be similar in its ridiculousness to my proposing a topic such as "Is Shankaracarya an Advaitin"? As will be seen, my response is that the topic of whether Gandhi is a Vedantist raises serious controversial questions and issues of great scholarly and practical significance.
2. In Chapter 2, "Gandhian Philosophy: Theoretical Basis with Primacy of Practice," in this book, I describe some of my experiences in the department of philosophy at BHU and the complete omission of Gandhi in the philosophy course curriculum.
3. This is not to deny that one can be a Vedantist who is deeply engaged in struggles that address the plight of Dalits, Adivasis, lower castes, women, victims of religious and communal violence, and so on. There are Vedantic approaches, some classified as Neo-Vedanta, that are activist, do not devalue worldly engagement as *maya* (illusion), and struggle to overcome violence and oppression and to create nonviolent,

egalitarian, nonhierarchical relations in this world. My personal experiences were that this was not the approach of traditional, dominant Vedanta.

4. See Martin Luther King Jr, *Stride Toward Freedom: The Montgomery Story* (New York, Harper & Row, 1968), especially King's Chapter 6, "Pilgrimage to Nonviolence," for King's formulation of the major characteristics of nonviolence and how Gandhi was the most important formative influence on King in developing his theory and engaged practices of nonviolent resistance, including civil disobedience.

5. Ved Mitra Shukla, "Significance of Advaita Philosophy in Mahatma's Gandhi's Life," *GITAM: Journal of Gandhian Studies* 4, no. 1 (January–June 2015): 214–24.

6. The quotation cited by Shukla is from Glyn Richards, "Gandhi's Concept of Truth and the Advaita Tradition," *Religious Studies* 22, no. 1 (1986): 14.

7. *Young India* VI, 39: 313; *Young India* VI, 49: 398; *Harijan* I, 45: 3; *Autobiography*, p. xii; *Young India* IX, 30: 244; *Harijan* VII, 5: 44.

8. In various writings, Gandhi does identify specifically with Advaita, although in far more writings, he is more inclusive, pluralistic, and identifies with many other positions. In terms of six quotations cited by Shukla as evidence that Gandhi is clearly an Advaitin, I shall submit that most of these statements about underlying unity, experience of God, moksha, and so on, can also be accepted by Hindu and other Indian philosophers who are not Vedantists and not Advaitins.

9. Several of Shukla's socio-political illustrations are open to discussion, such as Gandhi's controversial and changing views of varnashrama, and the Rama and other bhakti emphasis that usually do not have a clear non-dualistic focus.

10. Kumar Rahul, "On the Self-other Relationship: Lessons from Gandhi for an Alternative Cosmopolitan Framework," *Gandhi Marg* 37, no. 2 (July–September 2015): 333–54.

11. This formulation that the karmic world of maya is both real and unreal might suggest the move to Shankara's Advaitin theory of illusion as *anirvachanyakhyati* in the *Vedanta Sutra*, in which the illusory object is indeterminable or indescribable as fully real (*sat*, existence, being) or unreal (*asat*, nonbeing, nonexistence). However, Gandhi does not develop such a scholarly analysis and is also willing to affirm other approaches to illusion and worldly existence.

12. M.K. Gandhi, *Truth Is God* (Ahmedabad: Navajivan Publishing House, 1955), p. 10. This quotation has led some Gandhi scholars to conclude that he is remarkably insightful with an admirable commitment to inclusivism, pluralism, diversity, tolerance, and mutual respect and

other scholars, such as Nicholas Gier, to conclude that he is muddle-headed, inconsistent, incoherent, and lacking in critical reflective thought. Gandhi's acceptance of *ankantavadi* (many-sidedness) and *syadvadi* (conditioned viewpoints) are two foundational concepts in Jainism, and this approach is usually presented as a Jaina philosophical, epistemological, logical, and ontological alternative to Shankara and Advaita Vedanta. Kumar continues that Gandhi never abandons his nondualist premise of understanding "the Real" and "the Truth," and he provides the following evidence from Gandhi, *Truth Is God*, p. 12: "He (God) allows us freedom, and yet His compassion commands obedience to His will." It is not clear to me why this provides evidence for a specific commitment to Advaita Vedanta philosophy.
13. Although it is not important for my essay, some of Rahul's historical, chronological, and philosophical background assertions are a source of considerable debate by Indian and other scholars. Significantly, Rahul claims: "Vedanta is the only philosophy which directly plays a part in modern Indian civilization" (Kumar Rahul, "On the Self-Other Relationship," p. 336).
14. N.K. Bose, *Selections from Gandhi* (Ahmedabad: Navajivan Publishing House, 1948), p. 92.
15. In my own writings, I analyze Gandhi's numerous writings on the key concept of the "inner voice," which is contextually invoked with a wide variety of possible meanings and truth claims and with complex dialectical relations, considerable tensions, and contradictions between them. In most cases, Gandhi's use of "inner voice" refers to his inner individual self, his purified inner moral voice, his conscience, and sometimes as the voice of the God within him.

This is usually the inner voice of the interrelated social individual, the moral and spiritual relational self that embraces the voice of the other. One's inner voice is revealed by transcending one's ego and realizing that the relational other is an essential structure of being a moral and spiritual self. However, what complicates this are many other passages in which Gandhi appeals to his inner voice as that of the nonsocial individual, even the autonomous self that is opposed to the social. In addition, there are many passages in which Gandhi identifies his "inner voice" with the Atman or Absolute Spiritual Self. What complicates even further is that even when the inner voice is not identified with the Atman or highest spiritual Self, but instead with that of the worldly conditioned and limited individual self, this is not the karmic ego-self. It is a spiritual self and is often not capable of inter-subjective historical, empirical, rational, or philosophical verification.

Are these diverse formulations of Gandhi's inner voice complementary or contradictory and can they be united in a coherent philosophical framework? Rahul's creative attempt to resolve these controversial issues by distinguishing between the spiritual aid and temporary nature of the "inner voice" from the "*sthitha-prajna*" does not, in my view, resolve all of these issues. See, for example, my "Gandhi, Contemporary Political Thinking and Self-Other Relations," in *Contemporary Political Thinking*, ed. by B.N. Roy (New Delhi: Kanishka Publishers, 2000), pp. 129–70, and revised in Richard L. Johnson, ed., *Gandhi's Experiments with Truth: Essential Writings by and about Mahatma Gandhi* (Lanham, MD: Lexington Books, 2006), pp. 305–33.

16. Most of the following presentation on relative truth, including the formulation on the Indian philosophical theory of two truths, is based on parts of my "Gandhi, Contemporary Political Theory, and Self-Other Relations," in *Gandhi's Experiments with Truth*.

17. M.K. Gandhi, *An Autobiography or the Story of My Experiments with Truth*, trans. Mahadev Desai (Ahmedabad: Navajivan Publishing House, first published in 2 vols. in 1927 and 1929; 14th reprint), pp. xi–xii.

18. M.K. Gandhi, *The Collected Works of Mahatma Gandhi*, vol. 84 (New Delhi: Publications Division, Ministry of Information and Broadcasting, Government of India, 1958–91), p. 199.

19. A more complex presentation of Shankara Advaita Vedanta's two theories of truth includes the distinction between the level of reality of the Absolute, Nirguna Brahman, Atman, and the level of the experiential world of apparent reality of the illusory object that is sublated by right knowledge. A more adequate consideration involves Advaita's theory of illusion, *anirvachanyakhyati*, with an understanding of superimposition and sublation, as integral to analyzing the dynamic of *avidya* (ignorance) and maya. In addition, a more comprehensive presentation would include a differentiation and analysis of a third level of reality and truth in terms of Saguna Brahman, personal God, and *jiva* (individual self) with a different dynamic of superimposition and sublation.

20. As indicated in note 9, even when it comes to Gandhi's writings about the level of seemingly worldly truths with regard to diverse formulations of the inner voice, often equated with the divinity within and other expressions, Gandhi's position is complex and often inconsistent. Consistent with Rahul's resolution, it is tempting to conclude that Gandhi is referring to the temporary, transitional, imperfect level of relative truth and reality. Certainly, Gandhi writes that many others

claim to listen to inner voices, often claiming that God is speaking to them, when these are false voices of violence, immorality, and untruth. Gandhi himself acknowledges that his own experiences of his inner voice have led him to errors, miscalculations, even Himalayan blunders. What complicates matters and creates complexity is that Gandhi, in other writings, seems to assert that the nonempirical, ahistoric, moral, spiritual inner voice, the voice of divinity and of truth, is not tentative and transitory, but is an expression of Truth and Reality. Our miscalculations are based on our contextualized mind-body situatedness, on the fact that we are not sufficiently pure and are not able to listen to the inner voice. Only through the ongoing process of self-purification and moral and spiritual self-development are we capable of experiencing the moral, spiritual inner voice of truth/Truth.

4

How Can Gandhi Interpret His Favorite Bhagavad-Gita as a Gospel of Nonviolence?

Gandhi repeatedly avows that the Bhagavad-Gita is his favorite text, his moral and spiritual guide to daily living. He expresses the following personal sentiments:

> When doubt haunts me, when disappointments stare me in the face, and when I see not one ray of light on the horizon, I turn to the Bhagavad-Gita, and find a verse to comfort me; and I immediately begin to smile in the midst of overwhelming sorrow. My life has been full of external tragedies, and if they have not left any visible and indelible effect on me, I owe it to the teachings of the Bhagavad-Gita.

He later writes:

> As for myself, I run to my Mother *Gita* whenever I find myself in difficulties, and up to now she has never failed to comfort me. It is possible that those who are getting comfort from the *Gita* may get greater help, and see something altogether new, if they come to know the way in which I understand it from day to day.[1]

The Bhagavad-Gita is Gandhi's greatest resource for formulating and living his primary moral, philosophical, and practical approach of karma-yoga. In his commentaries, theoretical analyzes and practices, embracing his understanding of the Gita, what is most distinctive is Gandhi's identification with and primary emphasis on the path of karma-yoga.[2]

In his "Introduction," written in 1929 for his Gujarati translation of the Bhagavad-Gita, Gandhi writes the following about the Gita's central message of renunciation.

> He [or she] is the devotee who is jealous of none, who is a fount of mercy, who is without egotism, who is selfless, who is ever forgiving, who is always contented, whose resolutions are firm, who has dedicated mind and soul to God, who causes no dread, who is not afraid of others, who is free from exultation, sorrow, and fear, who is pure, who is versed in action, and yet remains unaffected by it, who renounces all fruit, good or bad, who treats friend and foe alike, who is untouched by respect or disrespect, who is not puffed up by praise, who does not go under when people speak ill of him [or her], who loves silence and solitude, who has a disciplined reason. Such devotion is inconsistent with the existence at the same time of strong attachments.[3]

In his formulations, Gandhi is consistent with most previous interpretations of renunciation and its approach in karma-yoga, an action-oriented approach of renunciation in which the karma-yogi fulfills one's dharma, consistent with one's karma, with an attitude or spirit of complete non-egoistic attachment to the results of one's action.

In his interpretation of the Bhagavad-Gita as a whole, its central message of renunciation, and its specific treatment of karma-yoga, Gandhi is influenced by traditional Indian, and more specifically, Hindu sacred texts and philosophical and religious traditions in their approaches to the karmic world and liberation or moksha. These include the dualistic Samkhya philosophy with its key distinction between *purusha* (pure spirit) and *prakriti* (nature, matter), and its analysis of karmic prakriti in terms of the three *guna*s (the three primary qualities); the Vaishnava bhakti tradition of Gandhi's youth and later life with the devotional focus on incarnational Rama and Krishna; key Upanishadic passages and later Vedantic jnana traditions with the focus on knowledge of the absolute Brahman and its unity or identity with the higher self or Atman as distinguished from the karmic world of maya or illusion; and the different yoga approaches, including the yoga-sutra and the traditional distinction between jnana-yoga, karma-yoga, and bhakti-yoga. In his approach to the Gita's renunciation and karma-yoga, Gandhi is certainly influenced by Jain, Buddhist, and other Indian-sources, and by Christian and other Western sources; but one must appreciate how the radically nontraditional Gandhi is deeply influenced by traditional philosophical and religious Hindu sources.

The Gita, consistent with other classical Hindu texts, emphasizes the goal of self-realization, which is impossible without self-control, which is impossible without the control of the senses, the mind, desires, and attachments. Our normal karmic world of maya, with the functioning of the three gunas within the physical and mental prakriti, is characterized by the uncontrollability of our senses, the instability of our minds, our undisciplined and endless desires and attachments that result in evil, immorality, untruthful living, and make wisdom impossible. Krishna instructs Arjuna that although the mind is fickle and difficult to curb, it can be controlled through self-restraint and constant practice. Although it is difficult to perfect, yoga allows one to stabilize the mind, control the senses with their sense-object attractions, desires, and attachments, to allow the higher Soul or Self (Atman, Purusha, untouched by change) to control the lower karmic unstable self (Chapter 6, verses 34–6).[4]

For Gandhi, this ideal of the perfected yogi, the ideal moral and spiritual human being, is best expressed in the last part of Gita's Chapter 2, verses 55–72, upon which Gandhi meditates every day. These 18 verses present the ideal, which provides Gandhi with daily practical guidance, of the sthita-prajna, the person of steadfast wisdom, of self-controlled and self-disciplined mind, with no ego-attachment to results, with control of senses, of desires, of thoughts, and living a life full of equanimity, peace, truth, reality, and joy.[5]

What is it that makes Gandhi's approach to karma-yoga so distinctive, self and world transformative, and potentially revolutionary for our contemporary world? Gandhi's approach is distinctive in at least two major ways,

First, what differentiates Gandhi's Gita-informed karma-yoga from many past philosophical and religious interpretations is his greater emphasis on the significance of the karmic world of relative truth. More specifically, this involves Gandhi's major focus on selfless service, self-discipline, self-renunciation and self-sacrifice (yajna), in which one sacrifices the ego-self with its desires and attachments, so that one realizes the moral and spiritual Self that necessarily includes the karmic world of unfree and suffering others. One limits, resists, and sacrifices the traditional desire to achieve moksha or nirvana by transcending and liberating one's self from the karmic world. This involves Gandhi's emphasis on developing a moral and spiritual action-oriented practice of self-realization, with no ego attachment to results, by focusing on acting to meet the needs of the other, especially the others who are least free, most disadvantaged, and experience the greatest suffering.

Second, what most renders Gandhi's approach to the Gita so idiosyncratic, controversial, and seemingly bizarre is his claim that it is also a gospel of nonviolence. As Gandhi writes:

> Let it be granted that, according to the letter of the Gita, it is possible to say that warfare is consistent with renunciation of fruit. But after 40 years' unremitting endeavor fully to enforce the teaching of the Gita in my own life, I have, in all humility, felt that perfect renunciation is impossible without perfect observance of ahimsa [nonviolence] in every shape and form.[6]

As Gandhi also acknowledges at the beginning of his "Introduction" to his translation of the Bhagavad-Gita, his co-worker and devoted follower Swami Anand remarked on Gandhi's nonviolent message of the Gita: "I do not think it is just on your part to deduce *ahimsa* [nonviolence] from stray verses."[7]

It should be acknowledged that there are many references to ahimsa and nonviolence in the classical texts of Hinduism, including the earlier Vedas, the Upanishads, the Yoga-Sutras, and later philosophical and religious formulations.[8] These passages can be found within

Vedic *shruti* scriptures, the great epics, and the social and political texts that are full of violent deities, violent rituals, and violent, patriarchal, class and caste relations. These are not Hindu writings that are often read as ahimsa texts.

An excellent illustration of passages focusing on nonviolence can be found in the *yamas* (moral disciplines) and *niyamas* (moral observances), the ethical rules for moral restraint, ethical duty, and right living that appear in numerous classical texts of Hinduism and yoga. Best known is the formulation in Patanjali's Yoga-Sutra 2.30 in which ahimsa is listed as the first of the five yamas.[9] To provide only one other example, in Shandilya Upanishad, ahimsa is listed as the first of the 10 yamas. Although Gandhi goes far beyond these classical formulations, he clearly is influenced by the earlier Hindu and yoga analysis that himsa always involves injury, harm, and only ahimsa and nonviolence, involving renunciation, nonattachment, and equanimity, allow for moral and truthful living.

Turning to the Gita, how is it possible for Gandhi to provide his dramatic, seemingly bizarre, nonviolent interpretation of the true meaning of the Gita? After all, the dramatic setting for the Gita is the battlefield, and Krishna instructs the morally challenged, conflicted, and indecisive Arjuna to engage in battle, fulfilling his dharma as a warrior, based on his karmic self-knowledge, but renouncing any attachment to the fruit of his action. In order to convince Arjuna to fulfill his dharma, Krishna provides him with a variety of responses as to why he should not be attached to such inevitable results as winning or losing the battle and killing other human beings.

For example, in Chapter 2, verses 31–7, Krishna presents a variety of reasons, some of which many readers have found morally objectionable. Arjuna, as a caste Kshatriya warrior, should fulfill his dharma, engage in the righteous war, stand up and fight the battle. If he does not fulfill his duty by fighting, he will lose his honor and be disgraced, which is worse than death. Others will believe that he did not fight because of fear, will deride his prowess, and will speak ill of him.

In Chapter 3, verse 30, Krishna instructs Arjuna to cast his acts on Krishna, fix his mind on the indwelling Self (Atman), with no attachment to results and no sense of mine, "shake off thy fever (of ignorance and illusion) and fight!" Gandhi comments that when

Krishna here says "fight," he means that Arjuna should do his duty, and to do one's duty means to fight and struggle.

In the powerful and terrifying Chapter 11 of divine revelation, verses 33–4, Krishna instructs Arjuna to arise and win glory, defeat the foes and enjoy a thriving kingdom. The enemies have already been destroyed by Krishna, and Arjuna as an archer, skillful with either hand, will be no more than Krishna's instrument. The warrior chiefs have already been killed by Krishna, and Arjuna should now slay them. Do not hesitate. Fight! Victory is yours over your foes on the battlefield.[10]

It seems not to have occurred either to Shankara or Ramanuja and other classical philosophers, the nineteenth-century Hindu revivalists, the twentieth-century Indian nationalists who wrote influential commentaries on the Gita, or to the hundreds of millions who have identified with the Gita, that this could possibly be a text with Gandhi's essential message of ahimsa.

Just as we noted that there are references to nonviolence in classical Hindu texts, it should be acknowledged that there are references to nonviolence in the Bhagavad-Gita, although, as we will see, Gandhi goes far beyond these in his interpretation of the Gita's essential message of ahimsa. For example, in Chapter 10, verses 4–5, Krishna lists 20 attributes, including nonviolence, of the person of wisdom, who has no attachment or trace of egotism and is unaffected by the pairs of opposites. As Gandhi then writes:

> All the qualities then mentioned in these two verses—intellect, knowledge, the absence of ignorant attachment, forgiveness, truthfulness, control of the senses, serenity, happiness and suffering, birth and death, fear and absence of fear, ahimsa [nonviolence], inward poise and contentment, *tapas* [austerities], making gifts, good name or evil reputation among men—these conditions exist in all creatures and I [Krishna] am the cause of each one of them.[11]

Gandhi concludes: "The Creator of all beings is also the cause of all the good and evil in which we see in these beings."[12]

To provide a second example from the Bhagavad-Gita, at the beginning of Chapter 16, Krishna distinguishes the divine from the devilish or demoniacal individual. He describes one born of divine nature by listing about 30 traits that include: "'Nonviolence, truth, slowness to wrath, the spirit of dedication, serenity, aversion to slander, tenderness to all that lives, freedom from greed, gentleness, modesty, freedom from levity" (verse 2).[13]

In Chapter 6, Gandhi relates his key focus on nonviolence to Krishna's presentation of *sannyasa* (stage of renunciation) and yoga in which the sannyasi and yogi experience the identity of the Self (Atman, the spirit within, Krishna, the Absolute) in all beings. "Nonviolence will have become direct experience for us in this sense when our whole life comes to be permeated with the spirit of compassion, when nonviolence manifests itself in its true essence. That boy who comes to feel compassion as his own experience will, to that extent, have purified himself, or attained knowledge of the Self." Gandhi continues that the yogi, whose Self is filled with perfect equanimity and contentment, having attained wisdom and understanding through reason (jnana) and the higher consciousness of knowledge of the Atman in direct experience (*vijnana*), having become inwardly purified and controlling the senses completely, has attained freedom.[14]

Critics, examining how Gandhi uses such occasional passages in the Gita to justify his interpretation that it is a scripture with its essential meaning of ahimsa, assert that Gandhi's nonviolent interpretation is a hermeneutical disaster. It has nothing to do with a rigorous objective interpretation of the meaning of the actual text. Gandhi's readings and commentaries may reveal a lot that is of autobiographical and biographical interest, his own personal idiosyncrasies, his contextual history, and his own moral and spiritual values. However, his imposed nonviolent interpretation does violence to the actual nature of the real text. As is well known, others, usually Gandhi defenders, who see value in Gandhi's commentaries, often use Gandhi's own writings on the Gita to assert that Gandhi is offering an allegorical, highly symbolic reading that cannot be taken literally.

Symbolic, Mythic, and Allegorical Interpretation of the Bhagavad-Gita

Gandhi's commentaries on the Gita often present an allegorical, highly symbolic reading and interpretation of the essential meaning of the sacred text. Others most frequently uphold Gandhi's claim that the battle is not some actual, historical, or literal warfare.[15]

Instead, the Gita directs us to the battle within each of us when we are confronted with moral conflicts and when we are full of doubt as to how to deal with our internal forces of good and evil. Gandhi, in his translation and interpretation, repeatedly upholds such a symbolic approach to the dramatic setting and message of the Gita.[16]

For example, Gandhi submits that he does not regard Krishna as some historical human being who literally appears at some specific time in history as the charioteer, as the battle is about to commence, in order to advise the warrior Arjuna. Instead, in his symbolic approach, Gandhi submits that the Gita's Krishna is a creation of our imagination. When we encounter exceptional moral and spiritual beings in our actual experiential world, they inspire us to use our imaginations to create an ideal of perfection, just as we may imaginatively construct and then imperfectly live ideals of perfect Nonviolence, perfect Truth, perfect Ethics, and perfect Religion. Through the imaginative creation of this Krishna, the ideal of the perfect being, we are then able to realize the Krishna (God, Self, Atman, Brahman, Truth, and so on), within each of us.[17]

Gandhi certainly intends to offer a symbolic, mythic, and allegorical interpretation of the Gita, but making this claim does not resolve the serious hermeneutical issues and debates. After all, we have a long tradition, going back at least to Aristotle, in which myths and mythologies are analyzed as works of fiction. They may be highly imaginative, fascinating, and have great aesthetic value, but they have nothing to do with critical, rational, objective, scientific, philosophical accounts of truth and reality. This is reflected in the history of philosophical and other scholarly approaches in which the scholar must demythicize and critique the mythic or simply ignore it if the scholarly focus and goal is to formulate and justify claims to truth and reality. This approach is reflected in the most common meaning of myth in everyday discourse, as in "five myths about effective dieting" or "myths about Bollywood stars." People believe and act on such myths, but to describe something as a myth is to expose it as false.

There are many, very diverse, more recent approaches that often focus on myth and allegory, but they also deny that such symbolic expressions reveal and justify objective, universal claims to truth and reality. Variations of such approaches to myth, allegory, and other subjective narrative formulations have become very fashionable in the late twentieth century, as evidenced in much of cultural studies, cultural and other forms of relativism, postmodernism, postcolonial and ethnic studies, gender and race studies, and other scholarly approaches. To claim that Gandhi's highly symbolic, mythic, and allegorical interpretation of the Gita, or any other interpretation, has some objective, universal status with regard to the truth and reality revealed by the text would be another illustration of hegemonic, objectifying, universalizing violence.

Consistent with such twentieth century and more recent approaches, Gandhi may offer us his own mythic and allegorical account of the Gita's narrative. In terms of our own personalities and contextual situatedness, we may find Gandhi's interpretations emotionally and imaginatively pleasing or displeasing, rational or irrational, liberatory or repressed, insightful or hopelessly ignorant. In any case, Gandhi's symbolic formulations of the Gita's narrative have nothing to do with some universal objective claims to truth and reality.

There is a radically different sense of truth and reality of the mythic and the allegorical for those who believe in and live the mythic and allegorical and for phenomenological, hermeneutical, and other scholarly approaches that examine such phenomena. It seems noncontroversial to assert that for the mythic person, the mythic is much more than some subjective fictional story. On the contrary, the mythic reveals an existential orientation, an experiential way of being in the world, in which the narrative is experienced as an exemplary true story, allowing one to live the myth and realize its truths and realities.[18] Certainly, this is what Gandhi intends when he describes and interprets the meaning of the devotional and other dramatic stories that so impressed him in his childhood or his identification with the Gita's powerful narrative. He is doing more than simply sharing his own personal story.

However, Gandhi intends much more than the descriptive phenomenological and hermeneutical claim that the Gita has such meaning for the believer, who accepts the moral and spiritual truths of the narrative. For Gandhi, his symbolic, mythic, and allegorical approach to the Gita reveals profound truths and realities about our human existential mode of being in the world. Such an approach reveals profound insights about our false and limited, materialistic and consumerist, egoistic and ego-attached relations today, and about our inauthentic and alienating, violent and destructive, modern mode of being in the world. His symbolic reading and interpretation of the Gita provides not only a radical critique of dominant values, but also opens up a new approach for constructive nonviolent resistance and for self and world transformation. Such a process of transformation is necessary for more meaningful, authentic, sustainable, moral relations of peace, harmony, and true human development.

Nonviolent Interpretation of Bhagavad-Gita as Open-Ended Dynamic Text

While such allegorical, mythic, and symbolic interpretations are invaluable for understanding Gandhi's approach to the Gita's narrative, they do not, by themselves, leave us with Gandhi's most important moral, spiritual, and hermeneutical claim in his nonviolent interpretation. After all, one could grant almost everything said above about an allegorical and mythical approach to the Gita while rejecting an interpretation of the Gita as a gospel of nonviolence. One can back this up with the obvious observation that myths, allegories, and other symbolic narratives throughout history are often extremely violent.

What has generally been overlooked is Gandhi's surprisingly complex, nuanced, and insightful methodological claims about texts, contexts, the interpretation of meaning, and a dynamic, open-ended approach to formulating and applying the values and principles of the Bhagavad-Gita and other texts. Gandhi grants that earlier formulators and interpreters of the Gita did not view it as a gospel of nonviolence. The Gita, the Mahabharata and the Ramayana, and the traditional religious and philosophical texts reveal profound moral and spiritual values and meanings, but they are often full of violent narratives or simply marginalize or are completely silent on questions of ahimsa.

In Gandhi's approach, earlier formulators, interpreters, and devotees of the Gita were often situated in contextual worlds defined by psychological, linguistic, economic, political, and cultural violence. They were socialized through language acquisition, not expressing ahimsa, that then shaped their experiences, and through which they communicated their understanding of the message of the Gita.

Therefore, Gandhi grants that in earlier readings and interpretations of the moral and spiritual truths of the Gita, including the path of karma-yoga, the Gita is not regarded as a scripture of nonviolence.

Gandhi, for all of his admirable simplicity, has a surprisingly complex, nuanced, and insightful methodological approach, with a symbolically expressed, but often hidden, epistemological and ontological framework for uncovering and interpreting meaning. The three components that I have identified—the Gita as narrative text, the contexts within which the Gita is read and understood, and the diverse interpretations of meaning of the Gita—are always integrally related in Gandhi's dynamic open-ended approach. In an actual, experiential world of how we are presented, relate to, understand, and apply or practice the Gita, none of the three components can be abstracted, objectified, and reified, as if it had any separate, self-defined and self-sufficient, independent existence in reality. Each is integrally related to the others as part of our actual dynamic process of experiential realization.

To provide a revealing, contrasting, personal anecdote, during one of my research sabbaticals in India, I engaged in work in comparative philosophy with different philosophical approaches to self and self-other relations. I gave a lecture at the department of philosophy in BHU, focusing on four approaches: the karma-yoga analysis of the Bhagavad-Gita, the *anatta* analysis of the Buddha in the Pali canon, the dialectical analysis of self-alienation and self-realization by Karl Marx, and the existential feminist analysis of the patriarchal self by Simone de Beauvoir. After delineating each approach, I attempted to analyze their similarities and differences, their relative strengths and weaknesses, and to bring them into dialogue in order to explore what new formulations and meanings might develop.[19]

My commentator was a senior, influential philosopher of Advaita Vedanta at BHU. He was clearly exasperated by my approach and analysis. He began his response with a very emotional outburst: "When it comes to the *Bhagavad-Gita*, Professor Allen knows absolutely nothing!" He did not say that I had misinterpreted the text, that my analysis was inadequate, but rather made a startling assertion that I knew absolutely nothing. He then went on: "The *Bhagavad-Gita* has nothing to do with women," by which he meant that the overt or actual text did not address the status of women, male–female relations and patriarchal structures. He had other comments on how I did not understand the real or true Gita. As an aside, the next day he told me that his wife had chastised him for being so rude and told him to apologize to me. Since I had not personalized this, I was able to maintain the collegial relationship I had with him.

My response to this attack was to acknowledge that when I first studied the Bhagavad-Gita in my youth, as taught to me by T.R.V. Murti and other distinguished Advaita Vedantins at BHU, I would have taken the same position toward the text that my commentator did. I would have agreed that there was one, essential, decontextualized, actual Gita, the real Gita, and that Shankara and his followers had formulated the most profound and most accurate interpretation of the true meaning of the text.

I then responded that I now rejected my earlier position as inadequate and that is why I now approached the Gita as a complex open-ended text. It is a text with hidden meanings in need of disclosure and new meanings that need to be constituted and formulated. Even the apparent silence of questions of, say, the status of women, gendered relations, and hierarchical, patriarchal structures is poignant with significant meaning. Textual omissions, silences, and marginalizations are most relevant in understanding how texts are constructed and what they reveal of the contextual worlds in which they have been formulated, read, interpreted, and applied.

Therefore, the Gita, including Gandhi's Gita, should not be approached as one, decontextualized, nonhistorical, permanent text, as if our philosophical or religious objective is to uncover and argue for the one true Gita. Instead, we should be asking: Which Gita? The Gita of the jnana-privileged Advaitins or the Gita of the bhakti-devotional masses? Shankara's Gita? Rammohun Roy's Gita? Vivekananda's Gita? Tilak's Gita? Aurobindo's Gita? Gandhi's Gita? Indeed, one should not necessarily rule out the possibility that there may be several Gandhi philosophies and several Gandhi Gitas expressing different stages in his personal, moral, political, and spiritual development.

This is not to confuse Gandhi's approach with many modern, fashionable approaches that would reduce such an acknowledgment of the wide diversity of Gita to some position of complete subjectivism and unlimited relativism. Just as Gandhi—unlike some of traditional Indian philosophy and spirituality—is a philosophical realist to the extent that he takes very seriously the existence of a real world of violence and suffering, he accepts that there is a Gita text that actually exists. There is a real Gita, with actual independent existence, that exists independently of Gandhi's readings and surprising nonviolent interpretations.

However, even while affirming the Gita as a text with some significant independent status in real existence, we need to make sense of the wide diversity in how Gandhi and others have approached the Gita as text. We cannot understand this without appreciating how this textual diversity is necessarily related to the diverse, changing, contextual situations within which Gandhi and others read and relate to the Bhagavad-Gita. There can be no absolute decontextualized approach. For over 2,000 years, Indians and others have lived under complex, diverse, changing linguistic, economic, cultural, political, religious, hierarchical, caste-based, class-based, gender-based, and other violent and nonviolent contextual variables and structures. They have mediated and filtered their readings, receptiveness, expressions, and understandings of the Gita through such contextual situatedness. Just as we must ask which Gita, we must always relate this to the question of asking which contextual situatedness.

Therefore, in trying to understand how Gandhi could read the Gita and interpret its message of selfless action as a gospel of nonviolence, we must analyze how Gandhi was one of the most fascinating human beings, being shaped negatively and positively by numerous changing contextual variables, experimenting with truth in ways that appreciated much of his traditional world and its Gita, and introducing radically new contextual breakthroughs and new contextual worlds of meaning with his new formulations of the Gita.

Gandhi would not have read the Gita narrative as symbolically expressing an essential message of ahimsa if he had not been exposed to Jainism and other influences in his childhood, and to Tolstoy and other influences after he was first exposed to the Gita while a student in England. He would not have read the Gita narrative as nonviolent if he not developed an appreciation for the incredible violence of "modern civilization," much of which he has earlier embraced, the violence of British colonial rule, and the violence in traditional Indian contexts toward Dalits or untouchables, lower classes and castes, women, and other suffering beings.

In short, without understanding these multiple contexts with their variables and influences, both within the contextual worlds in which Gandhi was raised and socialized, and also the new contextual worlds in which he played a major part in creating, we cannot understand how Gandhi gradually developed his philosophy of ahimsa and how he could regard the Gita as a scriptural text of nonviolence.

In developing the dynamic, interrelated, open-ended relations between texts, contexts, and interpretations of meaning, we must recognize that even on the seemingly simple level of what is presented or given to us as the Gita, what is received by Gandhi and by us, is a text that is already constituted and structured in contextually complex ways. In our broader and deeper hermeneutical approach, what is presented to us at the first stage of experience is not some simple, given, actual Gita narrative that then requires our contextually shaped reading, interpretation, evaluation, and application. At the first experiential stage, what is recognized as the given Gita text as violent or nonviolent, what captures our attention or is marginalized or completely silenced and omitted, what is given priority and strikes us as meaningful or what is devalued, must be analyzed as integral to a dynamic process of experiential realization.

A second personal anecdote will illustrate this hermeneutical claim. 20 years ago, a young man, wearing a conservative suit and with a very conservative appearance visited our campus, he told me that he was deeply involved in studying and lecturing on the message of the Bhagavad-Gita, and asked if he could give his presentation to my Philosophy of Hinduism class, which was then reading the Gita. There was no indication in his appearance or in anything he said that he was a very intelligent devotee of the International Society for Krishna Consciousness (ISKCON) movement, with A.C. Bhaktivedanta Swami Prabhupada as its founder and *acharya* (one who teaches by their example and conduct). For this movement, Bhaktivedanta's version of the Gita serves as a foundational text. The young man gave his articulate lecture for about 40 minutes, with his complete focus on the bhakti-yoga path as "the" message of the Gita. When it came to questions, one of my students, influenced by what we had been studying, asked: "What about *karma-yoga* which you never mentioned?" His revealing response was the following: "Oh, yes, *karma-yoga* is mentioned in the *Bhagavad-Gita*, but it is a minor and insignificant approach!"

It would be hermeneutically inaccurate to charge that this Krishna Consciousness devotee was dishonest or even that he misinterpreted the true message of the Gita that had been given to him.[20] In his received Gita, a specific approach to bhakti-yoga is the essence and true reading and message. Diverse karma-yoga readings and interpretations, including Gandhi's preferred nonviolent reading and interpretation are omitted or are devalued as nonessential in this given Gita text.

This is not to deny that when reading the entire Gita, the bhakti-yoga devotional approach with devotees focusing on Krishna is certainly the most emphasized yoga in the scripture. This has led to numerous Krishna bhakti approaches that present this devotional emphasis in their translations and specific commentaries. However, the Gita is not one unified coherent text. Its tremendous appeal for 2,000 years has been that diverse approaches, different philosophies, and religions can read the Gita in diverse ways. This is reflected in the diverse translations and commentaries about the true meaning of the Gita. Diverse philosophical and religious approaches always recognize all of the other yogic approaches, but they then usually privilege one of them.

For example, many influential philosophers privilege their jnana-yoga focus of the knowledge-based experiential realization of Brahman-Atman as expressing the highest attainment of truth and reality. They cannot avoid acknowledging the numerous bhakti-yoga chapters, but they typically analyze them as expressing easier approaches, more accessible to ordinary people, and at a lower level of self-knowledge and self-realization.

In a similar way, Gandhi certainly recognizes and is deeply influenced by bhakti-yoga in the Gita, as well as the need for jnana-yoga. However, what is so unusual in his translation and commentaries is how he privileges his specific action-oriented, renunciatory approach of karma-yoga, and especially his interpretation of this as revealing its deepest message of ahimsa at the highest experiential level of truth and reality.

The Key Hermeneutical Move in Gandhi's Interpretation of the Bhagavad-Gita as a Gospel of Nonviolence

This brings us to the key hermeneutical move in Gandhi's approach in which the Gita is not some gospel of nonviolence in some fixed, essentialized, nonhistorical, and decontextualized reading of the true meaning of Bhagavad-Gita. As we have seen, Gandhi acknowledges that the original author, earlier formulators, and earlier interpreters of the Gita did not view it as a gospel of nonviolence. In his translation and commentary on the Gita, there are many similar acknowledgements.

For example, Gandhi expands and develops his understanding of yajna as sacrifice. Since this is one of the key concepts in Gandhi's view of philosophy, religion, and practice, and his treatment dramatically illustrates his hermeneutical moves, I shall document his commentary in considerable detail.

In many passages in the Gita, he critiques earlier Hindu formulations, including definitions and understandings by Vyasa. One cannot become a yogi or an enlightened being practicing true yajna by simply performing thousands of sacrifices, by rejecting body yajna, or by renouncing and sacrificing the world.

In Chapter 3, verses 9–16, Gandhi begins by telling us to accept a broad definition of yajna, meaning any activity for the good of others, spending our body in their service. "The word *yajna* comes from the root *yaj*, which means 'to worship,' and we please God by worshipping Him through physical labor." Gandhi then grants that Hindus practiced human sacrifice and continue to practice animal sacrifice, but "it is not a true sacrifice in which we kill other creatures. We serve the good of the world by refraining from causing suffering to them," because we cherish the lives of others as we do our own. As we become more enlightened, the meanings people attach to "sacrifice" and other words become more morally and spiritually enlightened.

Gandhi submits "there is no harm in our enlarging the meaning of the word yajna, even if the new meaning we attach to the term was never in Vyasa's mind. We shall do no injustice to Vyasa by expanding the meaning of his words." Gandhi then expands the meaning by focusing on two of his interrelated themes.

First, as influenced by John Ruskin's *Unto This Last* in his commentary on these passages from the Gita,[21] Gandhi proposes that the special meaning in these passages in the Gita is on engaging in bodily yajna, in bodily labor, in the spirit of service and dedicated to Krishna. As he develops in other writings, such bodily *yajna* allows one to identify with the lives of other suffering and unfree beings, and to serve their needs through selfless action. Second, in expanding this focus on bodily labor and nonegoistic service, Gandhi submits that as we develop our spirit of *yajna*, "our service will enlarge itself to embrace the whole world. We ... should serve the humblest human beings, even those whom we never see, with respect and honor and looking upon them as gods and not our servants. We should, in other words, serve the whole world."[22]

In Chapter 4, Gandhi comments on how Krishna created and ordered the four varnas, each with its special dharma. The lowest of the four varnas by tradition, the Sudras, who were not allowed by traditional upper-caste Hindus to study the Vedas or Gita, have, according to Gandhi, a special dharma of service. If they combine their service with the spirit of yajna, motivated by public good, they will realize the reward of their lives. "There is here no question of higher and lower. If we regard the person who cleans lavatories as lower and another who reads the Gita as higher, that will be the end of us."[23]

Later in Chapter 4, verses 23–34, Gandhi formulates his most developed analysis in the Gita of the wide variety of yajna. "Every *karma* done in the spirit of *yajna* (sacrifice) leaves no effects behind it." Those who offer the sacrifice to Brahman, relate all their karmas to Brahman, will merge into Brahman. Krishna then lists many types of sacrifice, ranging from those that are more accessible to the masses and easier to perform, to those that require a high level of yogic, moral, and spiritual development.

Gandhi then comments on how the "Gita teaches us to look upon all activities for the supreme good as forms of yajna. The idea that we work for others is only an illusion. We always work for ourselves. We shall attain deliverance only if we work exclusively for our highest Self. All activities for the supreme good, therefore, aim at one's own good." In reinforcing his earlier assertion that the goal of all philosophy and religion is true self-realization, Gandhi does, in fact, affirm that we must sacrifice the lower, karmic, illusory self, but this is necessary for directing our yajna to and realizing the Atman, the highest Self, which is Brahman. Nevertheless, Gandhi submits that as long as we are embodied souls or selves in this world, we necessarily have relations with others. "To become disinterested in the body, therefore, means that one should devote oneself exclusively to the service of others, so that one may attain the Brahman beyond time."[24]

In his radical hermeneutical move, Gandhi claims that the Gita is a gospel of nonviolence for him (and for us today) because along with him, we can also purify and develop the text in more moral and spiritual ways. We can, and must, do a re-reading of the Gita, reformulating it, re-applying it, in dynamic, open-ended experiments with truth. This involves embracing the traditional insights of renunciation, karma-yoga, and other yoga paths, but that addresses our contextual situatedness, living in a contemporary world of so many violent relations in how we relate to our self, other beings, and nature.

In such a hermeneutical approach, we recognize that Gandhi exists in a complex dynamic world of texts, contexts, and interpretations of meaning. Born on October 2, 1869, Gandhi first reads the Gita through Sir Edwin Arnold's English translation, *The Song Celestial or Bhagavad-Gita*, during 1888–9. How Gandhi receives, reads, and relates to the Gita is shaped by his lived world, consisting of his personality and cultural upbringing and socialization, shaped by a long history of cultural, linguistic, political, social, religious, and other determinants. These include diverse past expressions, readings, and interpretations of the Gita and other formative texts in his life.

Gandhi offers his first focused series of talks on the Gita at his ashram from February 24 until November 26, 1926. In explaining why his translation and understanding of the Gita, including his claim that it is a gospel of ahimsa, seems so different, Gandhi submits that unlike other translators, he has been actively engaged for 40 years in transformative practice in living the Gita. Through his experiments with truth and action-oriented transformative engagements, Gandhi then transforms his life world, including his radical interpretations and applications of karma-yoga and other paths in the Gita as expressing a more moral and spiritual message of ahimsa.

At the same time, in such a hermeneutical approach, we recognize that we today exist in a very different, complex, dynamic world of meaning with new relations of texts, contexts, and interpretations of meaning. Although Gandhi's moral approach and profound insights into truth and nonviolence speak in the most significant ways to our contemporary values and crises, we cannot decontextualize, worship, or uncritically appeal to the Mahatma, his philosophy of truth and nonviolence, and his interpretation of the message of the Bhagavad-Gita. We must reject a kind of Gandhi fundamentalism or decontextualized essentialism in which Gandhi has already given us the infallible blueprint with all of the clear solutions to our problems. In fact, such an uncritical authoritarian approach would violate the experimental spirit and lessons of Gandhi's own life and his moral and philosophical formulations.

In analyzing how we receive, read, and relate to the Bhagavad-Gita, we exist in our own, developing world of texts, contexts, variables, structures, and meanings. Our new, actually lived world has been shaped by Gandhi's remarkable readings and interpretations of how we can develop nonviolent interpretations and applications of karma-yoga and the Gita. We can now appreciate how Gandhi's innovative approach provides us with invaluable resources for addressing our contemporary violent, moral, philosophical, social, economic, cultural, educational, and environmental crises.

Thus, we have multiple interconnected, but also different perspectives, horizons, or worlds of meaning—Gandhi's and our own—that are highly complex, sometimes with values and meanings that are transparent and coherent, and at other times hidden and contradictory, opened-ended, and resisting any final closure. Our hermeneutical challenge is to connect, mediate, or fuse Gandhi's contextually structured understanding and interpretation of the meaning of the Gita's text, including his radical claim that it is a scripture of nonviolence, with our contemporary contextually structured approaches to the text.

First, in connecting our perspective with Gandhi's, we may decide that Gandhi is insightful in claiming that the ego is *necessarily* violent. Our construction and functioning of the false, untruthful, violent ego necessarily limits our realization of nonattachment and nonviolence with its separation of the I–me ego self, its ego-desires and possessive attachments, and its generation of conflict, war, hatred, greed, and relations of disharmony toward other beings and toward nature. Therefore, a morally and spiritually developed karma-yoga approach today necessarily involves a commitment to nonattachment that involves a commitment to ahimsa. It may be granted that Indian philosophers for thousands of years have made connections between the ego and violence, but Gandhi develops his karma-yoga, nonviolent approach in new action-oriented transformative ways that can be reconstructed to address our violent contemporary world.

Second, in his reading and interpretation of the Gita and karma-yoga as nonviolent, Gandhi adopts a cause-effect, means-ends moral approach in his formulation of a kind of law of karma. Stated briefly, violent, immoral causes, structures, and conditioning factors lead to immoral violent and untruthful effects, which then become new immoral causes and conditioning factors. We thus become entrapped in relative, immoral, untruthful, violent cycles. Karma-yoga, as a morally developed approach, allows us to control and decondition those violent interconnected causes and conditions and to introduce more moral nonviolent causes and conditioning factors. Only by addressing the basic violent causes and conditions and engaging in nonviolent transformation, through the developed karma-yoga understanding of ahimsa, will we be able to break the causal links in the cycles of violence. Only then will we develop as self-realized nonviolent beings, relating with love, compassion, and justice, as moral beings integrated with a morally unified, interconnected, sustainable world.

Third, Gandhi's moral approach, illustrating and justifying his nonviolent reading of karma-yoga and the Gita, is grounded in his ontological view of truth and reality.[25] This also provides an ontological framework of our previously analyzed approach to the dynamic, interconnected, open-ended relations of texts, contexts, and the interpretation of meaning. We can develop an understanding today in which we realize that violence, including violent interpretations of karma-yoga, not only leads to violent immoral unsustainable consequences, but it also separates us from truth and reality.

Put briefly, Gandhi repeatedly upholds an organic, holistic view of the interconnected unified nature of truth and reality. Violence separates us from truth and reality. It is based on a primary ontological distinction that the other—whether individual, social, ethnic, caste-based, class-based, gendered, racial, or national other—is othered as fundamentally different from me, my caste, my religion, my gender, or my nation. Ahimsa, by way of contrast, is the active, transformative love-force, truth-force, soul-force, and nonviolent force that brings us together in non-egoistic, compassionate, loving, meaningful, unified, interconnected, and sustainable relations. This involves the purification and development of the self-realization of our basic unity, with a respect for legitimate perspectival differences. In other words, a developed Gandhian approach today would be grounded in the underlying ontological philosophy and practice that maintains that only a nonviolent interpretation of ahimsa is commensurate with truth and reality.

Finally, these claims and issues lead to key unresolved challenges for Gandhi's reconstituted nonviolent readings, interpretations, and applications of the Bhagavad-Gita. These challenges can be related to Gandhi's insightful, often nontraditional, and often controversial claims about his inclusivistic, pluralistic, perspectival approach; the status of relative truth in which we are always attempting to move from one relative truth to greater truth, closer to the Absolute ideal; and his moral, epistemological, and ontological view of the organic, interconnected, unifying nature of truth and reality.

In his tolerant approach involving real respect for the views of the other, Gandhi repeatedly affirms a contextualized pluralism and diversity, often using such images as the many branches on the tree or the many paths ascending the mountain. He repeatedly asserts that what may be true and real for him may not be true and real for the other. Gandhi upholds the necessity for numerous, legitimate approaches expressing diverse relative truths and different paths to developing greater relative truths. We must respect that the other must develop her or his legitimate approach to truth, that is, commensurate with one's karmic personality and contextualized situatedness, and we can even learn from the diverse other in developing our own moral and spiritual self-transformation and realization.

This sounds very admirable, especially when dealing with so much intolerance, hatred, conflict, and multidimensional and structural violence in our contemporary world, but such an approach faces serious questions and challenges. In the above images and claims,

Gandhi submits that there are diverse legitimate paths climbing to the same mountaintop; that there are diverse relative truths that express our incomplete realizations of the same, unifying, nonviolent, truthful Absolute ideal. In his moral, epistemological, and ontological view of truth (Truth), Gandhi submits that we only have partial, incomplete, perspectival, temporary "glimpses" of the unified, meaningful, interconnected, harmonious, moral, and spiritual nature of reality.

In his approach to the Gita in general and karma-yoga in particular as a gospel of nonviolence, how does such a Gandhi-informed interpretation meet the challenges of many Muslims and Christians, dominant post-Enlightenment approaches, secular, political, and scientific thinkers, those focusing on contemporary violence and terrorism, and others who may recognize, but reject the legitimacy of many or all diverse paths and claims to relative truth? Who may reject Gandhi's view that they are climbing the same mountain with the shared goal of reaching the same mountaintop or that they share the same Absolute ideal? Who may reject Gandhi's moral and ontological view of reality? Who may be devout Hindus embracing the Gita, but who reject his interpretation of it as a gospel of nonviolence, as inadequate and even immoral? These, of course, are challenges that Gandhi faced during his lifetime and that continue to challenge his claims about the Gita as a nonviolent text today.

My own view is that Gandhi's approach to the Gita and karma-yoga, as an evolutionary developmental reformulation expressing the key message of ahimsa, is of the greatest significance for us today. In such a Gandhi-inspired approach, we are challenged to rethink our basic assumptions, theories, paradigms, and practices in developing deeper and broader nonviolent approaches. This means selectively appropriating and reconstituting what is insightful from Gandhi's interpretation of the Gita and integrating this with complementary non-Gandhian approaches and insights. Gandhi has valuable answers to the key questions and challenges that confront us, but he does not have all of the answers.

In his nonviolent reading, interpretation, and application of the Bhagavad-Gita, Gandhi invites us to engage in developing more nonviolent theories and practices. In this complex, dynamic, openended process of nonviolently transforming ourselves and our world, we are able to develop more moral, spiritual, and pragmatically effective ways for addressing our contemporary ethical, social, economic, cultural, religious, educational, and ecological crises that are violently unsustainable, and threaten the future of our planet.

Notes

1. M.K. Gandhi, *Young India* (1925), p. 274 and *Young India* (1930), p. 1.
2. The major treatment of karma-yoga is in Chapter 3, the Yoga of Action, in the Bhagavad-Gita. Gandhi's translations and commentaries on the Bhagavad-Gita can be found in various pamphlets and in M.K. Gandhi, *The Collected Works of Mahatma Gandhi* (New Delhi: Publications Division, Ministry of Information and Broadcasting, Government of India, 1958–91), especially *CWMG* 32 ("Discourses on the Gita"): pp. 94–376 and *CWMG* 41 ("Anasaktiyoga," published in English under the title *The Gita according to Gandhi*): pp. 90–133. In this chapter, I primarily use Mahatma Gandhi, *The Bhagavad Gita according to Gandhi*, ed. John Strohmeier (Berkeley, CA: North Atlantic Books, 2009), which is taken almost entirely from "Discourses on the Gita" in the *Collected Works*.
3. "Introduction," M.K. Gandhi, *Bhagavad Gita according to Gandhi*, p. xx. Gandhi translated this 1929 "Introduction" into English and published it in 1931 in *Young India* under the title "*Anasaktiyoga*: The Gospel of Selfless Action."
4. Gandhi, *Bhagavad Gita according to Gandhi*, p. 98.
5. Gandhi, *Bhagavad Gita according to Gandhi*, pp. 26–32. In his interpretation and application of the lessons of the Gita as central to decades of struggle in India's Independence Movement, Gandhi focuses on the sthita-prajna as necessary for renunciation with no ego-attachment to results, and he uses this to organize his satyagrahas. In the Freedom Movement, Gandhi thus emerges as the exemplary satyagrahi, and the lessons of the Gita are used to organize individual and mass satyagraha.
6. Gandhi, *Bhagavad Gita according to Gandhi*, pp. xxiii–xxiv.
7. Gandhi, *Bhagavad Gita according to Gandhi*, p. xv.
8. It is important to note the widespread recognition of ahimsa in ancient India. There is an Indian civilizational context in which ancient *rishis* (spiritually perfected seers, sages, divinely inspired saints) identify with ahimsa as necessary for dealing with and transcending worldly karmic violence. As Gandhi submits in *Hind Swaraj* and other formulations, there is an ancient Indian civilizational ideal that embraces ahimsa in diverse expressions. Nevertheless, what Gandhi does in translating,

commenting, and applying the Bhagavad-Gita, as essentially a gospel of ahimsa, is something innovative and controversial.
9. Georg Feuerstein, *The Yoga-Sutra of Patanjali: A New Translation and Commentary* (Rochester, Vermont: Inner Traditions International, 1989).
10. Gandhi, *Bhagavad Gita according to Gandhi*, pp. 19–20, 48–9.
11. Gandhi, *Bhagavad Gita according to Gandhi*, p. 132.
12. These passages indicate that Krishna (the Divine, Atman, Brahman, the Absolute) is immanent in the sense of being the foundation and cause of all of the pairs of opposites found in all beings, including good and evil, nonviolence and violence. Other chapters in the Gita indicate that Krishna (the Divine, Atman, Brahman, Purusha) is transcendent in the sense of being the essence, eternal, unchanging, Absolute Reality beyond all pairs of opposites and dichotomies, including cause and effect, good and evil, appearance or illusion and reality. These differing passages in the Gita, as well as in the Upanishads and other Hindu texts, have given rise to differing philosophical and religious interpretations, such as the analyzes of Saguna Brahman and Nirguna Brahman.
13. Gandhi, *Bhagavad Gita according to Gandhi*, p. 177.
14. Gandhi, *Bhagavad Gita according to Gandhi*, pp. 89–90.
15. In Gandhi, *Young India*, CWMG vol. 26, 289, Gandhi writes: "The fact is that a literal interpretation of the Gita lands one in a sea of contradictions." Gandhi is responding to a correspondent and to others who claim that the Gita advocates and teaches violence.
16. See, for example, Gandhi, *Bhagavad Gita according to Gandhi*, p. xvii.
17. Gandhi, *Bhagavad Gita according to Gandhi*, pp. xvii–xviii. Gandhi continues by interpreting this approach to divine incarnation, how we experience perfected beings in this world, as intended to bring out self-realization, the central subject of the Gita. Gandhi grants that the author did not write the scripture to establish that doctrine. Nevertheless, the Gita shows Gandhi the most excellent way of attaining self-realization through renunciation, right knowledge, devotion, and especially desireless action and service renouncing all attachment to the fruits of action.
18. The attempt to formulate such a radically descriptive, hermeneutical, structural, phenomenological approach has been a major focus of my work. In this regard, I have been most influenced by the works of literary writer, historian of religion, and phenomenologist of religion Mircea Eliade, whose major works on the mythic and the symbolic include *Myth and Reality*, trans. Willard R. Trask (New York: Harper and Row, 1963), *The Myth of the Eternal Return*, trans. R. Trask Willard (New York: Pantheon Books, 1954), also published as *Cosmos and History:*

The Myth of the Eternal Return, 1959, and *Patterns in Comparative Religion*, trans. Rosemary Sheed (New York: World Publishing Co., Meridian Books, 1963). In Eliade's theory and approach, the human being is *homo symbolicus, homo religiosus*, and *homo mythicus*, and the scholar attempts to describe the structural experience and interpret the meaning of the mythic and other phenomena for the religious, mythic believer. I have attempted to provide such a phenomenological account in several writings, including *Myth and Religion in Mircea Eliade* (New York: Routledge, 2002) and more recently in Douglas Allen, "Eliade's Phenomenological Approach to Religion and Myth," in *Mircea Eliade: Myth, Religion, and History*, ed. Nicolae Babuts (New Brunswick, NJ: Transaction Publishers, 2014), pp. 85–112.

19. This is formulated in Douglas Allen, "Social Constructions of Self: Some Asian, Marxist, and Feminist Critiques of Dominant Western View of Self," in *Culture and Self: Philosophical and Religious Perspectives, East and West* (Boulder, Colo.: Westview Press/HarperCollins, 1997), pp. 3–26.

20. *Bhagavad-Gita As It Is*, with translations and elaborate purports, by His Divine Grace A.C. Bhaktivedanta Swami Prabhupada (New York: Bhaktivedanta Book Trust, 1972).

21. John Ruskin, *Unto This Last*, ed. P.M. Yarker (London: Collins, 1970). In M.K. Gandhi, *An Autobiography: The Story of My Experiments with Truth* (Boston: Beacon, 1993), in his chapter entitled "The Magic Spell of a Book," Gandhi reports how he read the book on his 24-hour train trip from Johannesburg to Durban, and "I determined to change my life in accordance with the ideals of the book." Starting in May 1908, Gandhi translated into Gujarati and published a series of articles in his Gujarati *Indian Opinion*, paraphrasing Ruskin's book, for which Gandhi used the Gujarati title Sarvodaya ("the Welfare of All"). Gandhi summarized the key teachings of Ruskin's work as follows: the good of the individual is contained in the good of all; a lawyer's work has the same value as a barber's; a life of labor, that is, the life of the tiller and the handicrafts person, is the life worth living. Gandhi's work was published in English as M.K. Gandhi, *Unto This Last: A Paraphrase* (Ahmedabad: Navajivan Publishing House, 1956). Gandhi developed sarvodaya, the well-being and welfare of all, as his key economic concept. In his Gita commentaries, one can observe the strong influence of Gandhi's understanding of Ruskin's *Unto This Last* in the egalitarian inclusivist focus on sarvodaya and in the focus on the value of bodily yajna, bodily labor, as developed in Gandhi's emphasis on everyone engaging in "bread labor," a major concept he learned from reading Tolstoy.

22. Gandhi, *Bhagavad Gita according to Gandhi*, pp. 39–41.
23. Gandhi, *Bhagavad Gita according to Gandhi*, p. 60. Gandhi here, in his more egalitarian and idealized view of the four varnas, with the spirit of yajna and specific dharma, is not only offering a critique of past traditional Hinduism, but also of dominant, oppressive, and violent, caste-based practices in Hinduism today. Such idealized formulations of the four varnas in the Gita and other writings by Gandhi have led to controversies and widely opposed views as to whether Gandhi is in reality a supporter, or at the least, an apologist for the hierarchical Hindu practice of casteism. My own position is that Gandhi in his personal life and practices was always strongly anti-caste, that many of his idealized varna formulations and questionable actions raise serious concerns, and that he evolved in his views so that the Gandhi of the 1940s had no interest in defending any formulation of varna and caste.
24. Gandhi, *Bhagavad Gita according to Gandhi*, pp. 67–71.
25. This key interpretation of Gandhi's ethics, philosophy, practice, nonviolence, sustainability, and spirituality as grounded in his ontological view of truth and reality was mentioned rather briefly in Chapter 2 on Gandhi's philosophy; it will be essential to Chapter 6 with his approach to technology, to Chapter 9 with his approach to minorities and marginality, and to other sections on violence, terrorism, and untruth in this book.

5

Personal Reflections on Reading *Hind Swaraj* and Indian Reactions

As formulated in Chapter 6, Gandhi's *Hind Swaraj*, arguably his most challenging and most significant work for *Gandhi after 9/11*, is structured by Gandhi as a dialogue and illustrates his inclusive dialogic methodology. In *Hind Swaraj*, as well as in his other writings and engaged practices, Gandhi invites "the other" to join him in a nonviolent and truthful dialogue that is essential for mutual transformation, self-development, and self-realization of moral and spiritual reality.

One can read *Hind Swaraj* as Gandhi having a dialogue with himself. He engages his Gandhian other historically, temporally, and imaginatively, challenging himself to pursue his experiments with truth and greater self-realization. As will be seen in the next chapter, *Hind Swaraj* is most clearly a dialogue with the contextualized non-Gandhian and anti-Gandhian Moderate and Extremist others. In his dialogic methodology, in which the other is an integral part of one's self-development, Gandhi is attempting to relate to these diverse others. The non-Gandhian Moderate and Extremist others are part of Gandhi's creative, nonviolent transformative process toward greater truth and reality. In other chapters in this book, Gandhi's inclusive dialogic methodology is illustrated by how he relates to capitalists and upper-caste Hindus, trusteeship, and proponents of "Modern Civilization" with their modern technology. In addition, Gandhi's dialogic approach embraces those upholding violent interpretations of the Bhagavad-Gita, exploited peasants and workers, oppressed women and religious minorities, as well as marginalized others.

Consistent with this dialogic approach and methodology, this introductory essay to Chapter 6 can be seen as how Gandhi's *Hind Swaraj*, in the historical and temporal period of "Gandhi after 9/11," continues to challenge contemporary Indians, me, and others to engage in a dynamic, open-ended dialogue with Gandhi. This dialogic project involves our reading and re-reading, interpreting and selectively re-interpreting, formulating and critically reformulating Gandhi's moral, nonviolent, truthful, and spiritual insights and values in new creative and contextually significant ways.

A review of my reactions to reading and re-reading *Hind Swaraj* is not only personally instructive, but it also reveals changing attitudes of some influential Indians and others in India and in the contemporary world. This personal journey of encounters with the text discloses contradictions and dramatic changes.[1]

In 1963–4, I lived in Varanasi, taught one course, and attended postgraduate courses in the distinguished department of philosophy at BHU. At that time, Vedantists, especially Advaitins, dominated the philosophy department. I studied Shankara, Ramanuja, and other Hindu, Buddhist, and Jain philosophers under Professor T.R.V. Murti and other philosophers, but not Gandhi.[2] I know that I read *Hind Swaraj*, because I still have the small marked copy of the Navajivan edition. However, unlike other Indian philosophy texts, it made no impression on me. This was probably because the text would have struck me at that time as simplistic, exaggerated, one-sided, often irrational, and at odds with reality.

In the 1970s, especially around the time of the Emergency, I was part of a branch of the Indian Peoples Association of North America (IPANA).[3] Very bright and talented Indians, sometimes influenced by Naxalbari and the rise of the Communist Party of India (Marxist-Leninist) (CPML) and the later split into different CPML groups, would come to Maine for long, intense, often contentious discussions and debates about what needed to be done. To say that *Hind Swaraj* was irrelevant to such Indian leftists would be an understatement.

One's attitude toward Gandhi was sometimes the litmus test. If one dismissed and perhaps even indicated a hatred for Gandhi, the young Indian was considered to have potential.[4]

In the 1980s, much to my surprise, some of these dedicated Indians, including some in the Patriotic and People Oriented Science and Technology (PPST), flip-flopped from their absolute anti-Gandhi position of the 1970s. I was now told that Gandhi has the answers for understanding that pre-modern India was not scientifically and technologically backward, and he was in favor of creating an Alternative Science Movement. *Hind Swaraj* had become the key foundational text. As an almost mirror image, an act of absolute negation, with self-purging and eradication of their earlier sins, they now seemed to idealize and romanticize the text.[5]

For the young talented Indians in the PPST and Alternative Science Movement, Dharampal (1922–2006) was most often praised as the inspirational leader and guru of the movement. A dedicated Gandhian, Dharampal's research led to a rethinking of dominant negative views of India's social, cultural, technological, and scientific accomplishments in pre-British Indian society.[6] Young Indians searched for and found the most remarkable accomplishments, including astounding mathematical and scientific achievements, in a pre-modern, pre-industrial, pre-colonial, harmonious, rather idyllic village India.[7]

I re-read *Hind Swaraj*, and I found the text and the current reactions of these very bright Indians, both understandable and bewildering. I could relate to what Gandhi is saying about the evils of modern civilization, the lack of ethics, the alienation and dehumanization, the violence and war, the exploitation and domination, the materialistic reductionism and worship of endless consumption, the misplaced concepts of "development" and "progress," and the destruction of human relations and of nature. I could relate to what Gandhi is criticizing about modern civilization's glorification of its modern Western-centric technology, with its narrow view of reason as instrumental rationality, and the need to open up alternative, more Indian-informed approaches to culture, science, and technology. But parts of *Hind Swaraj* still struck me as rather bizarre and confusing, overly simplistic and irrational, escapist and romantic, irrelevant and unreal. *Hind Swaraj*, while sometimes insightful and suggestive, certainly did not seem adequate for dealing with contemporary crises with regard to technology in India, the US, and the rest of the world. As a somewhat surprising revelation, I was told 25 years later by one of the Indians who had identified with the PPST and similar efforts, that with some exceptions, most of those former "leftists" and "progressives" he knew, later identified with the rightwing Bharatiya Janata Party (BJP). On reflection, this rightwing direction is not completely surprising. In their flip-flopped conversion to the pro-Gandhi and pro-*Hind Swaraj* positions of the 1980s and early 1990s and their extolling of indigenous, ancient, Vedic, and other Indian alternatives to the modern West and its views of technology, there were the seeds for developing rightwing, aggressive, nationalist, often chauvinist positions regarding India, its exceptional civilization and culture, and its technology.

Fast forwarding to my 2009–10 sabbatical in India, I was very fortunate to participate in the remarkable *Hind Swaraj* Centenary International Conference, entitled "Hind Swaraj–Gandhi's Manifesto of Non-violence, Civilisation and Forms of Violence: A Twenty-First Century Agenda for Non-violence," held from 19 to 22 November 2009 in Surajkund, Delhi. This gathering included some of the most influential and significant scholars, writers, cultural figures, and dedicated activists. At one point, we were reminded that that very day, 22 November, marked the precise day when Gandhi finished *Hind Swaraj* 100 years ago. Most of the participants seemed to agree that *Hind Swaraj* was not only Gandhi's most important work, but it was also the most important work for our contemporary world of violence, war, oppression, exploitation, injustice, and environmental devastation.

Nevertheless, key participants at the conference reflected on the non-Gandhian and anti-Gandhian state of India and the world in 2009, and what this reveals about the dominant modern worldview, with its values and policies and the seeming irrelevance of *Hind Swaraj* and its view of modern technology. India is developing a more assertive, self-confident, wealthier, and more powerful economic, political, and technological elite, which embraces the very values of "Modern Civilization" that Gandhi critiques in *Hind Swaraj* as amoral and immoral, violent, untruthful, dehumanizing, and unsustainable. In terms of Gandhi's textual structure of a dialogue in *Hind Swaraj*, dominant modern Indian views seem to express the values and worldview of the "Reader," not Gandhi the "Editor," and are more the legacy of a Nehru and a Savarkar than a Gandhi.[8]

Finally, fast forwarding to my 2015–16 sabbatical in India, there are changing attitudes toward Gandhi and his philosophy and practice and his approach to technology. In many ways, the atmosphere seems more sympathetic to Gandhi with widespread praise of the Father of the Nation, who continues to inspire and teach us. A dramatic illustration of this is the blockbuster Bollywood comedy hit *Lage Raho Munna Bhai* (2006), which exposes and critiques dominant modern values with their ego-driven obsessions with wealth, power, status, and self-other domination and with the amoral, dehumanized, alienated nature of modern relations and ways of living. The underworld don Murli (Munna Bhai), initially motivated by romantic anti-Gandhi fantasies, later experiences the vision and spirit of Gandhi and the film's alternative of *Gandhigiri* (Gandhism, the Gandhi way). This launches a larger cultural and social movement in which relating to Gandhi is now "cool," and in which we can find the Gandhi spirit and the Gandhi way within each of us. This allows us to resolve conflicts through control of our ego selves, to act with kindness and for the good of others, and to transform ourselves and our relations in moral, truthful, and pragmatically effective ways. It is true that Gandhigiri's focus is usually limited to one's inner self and one's personal relations, and does not focus enough on the systemic economic, political, militaristic, and other structural relations of power. Nevertheless, it does offer an alternative to the contemporary orientation and framework within which modern technology plays a central role.

More revealing has been the dramatic changes in the approach of many with political power in how they speak of Gandhi and *Hind Swaraj*. Just as we saw an earlier reversal of positions from anti-Gandhi to pro-Gandhi among some leftists and progressives, there has been an apparent flip-flop among significant rightwing power orientations. With its landslide victory in 2014, the National Democratic Alliance (NDA) took power, with Narendra Modi of the BJP becoming the prime minister. The NDA is a rather ad hoc combination of many diverse regional and other parties and groups. The largest party is the conservative BJP, with some of the most aggressive base members coming from the Rashtriya Swayamsevak Sangh (RSS), Shiv Sena, and other militantly rightwing groups. This expresses itself with the ideology of Hindutva, a term first coined by Vinayak Damodar Savarkar in 1923, and adopted as the official ideology of the BJP. Hindutva usually expresses itself as a proud, aggressive, nationalistic, often chauvinistic view of India with an essentially Hindu essence. In his *Hind Swaraj* and other writings, Gandhi, while embracing the need for national swaraj, is very critical of such a Hindutva approach.[9]

What has struck me as revealing is an apparent, dramatic shift in many Hindutva and other rightwing attitudes toward Gandhi. This is not to deny the fact that there are tensions, contradictions, and diverse tendencies between the NDA parties and groups within the BJP and the other rightwing parties. This is also the case within the Indian National Congress (INC) and its often ad hoc changing alliances within various leftist parties and groups.[10] Having recognized such diversity, my experiences, especially in the 1990s, were that many within the BJP and other Hindutva groups were extremely anti-Gandhi in their rhetoric, ideology, and policies: Gandhi is a traitor, prefers Muslims to Hindus, is responsible for Partition and Kashmir, appeases and rewards Pakistan, makes us weak, and so on. They are often in full agreement with the detailed defense that Nathuram Godse—a former Gandhian who later became an extreme anti-Gandhian influenced by Savarkar, the RSS, and the Hindu Mahasabha—gives at his trial after his assassination of Gandhi. Such anti-Gandhi views continue today.

Nevertheless, in recent years, the rightwing BJP and most of the various other Hindutva groups have seemingly undergone an incredible pro-Gandhi transformation: they honor Gandhi in their rhetoric as one of the greatest Indians and a national treasure, and they appropriate him as part of their Hindutva ideology. Just as it was expedient to run against Gandhi at an earlier time, it now appears that using Gandhi and taking a pro-Gandhi stance can be a means for getting votes and achieving party success.

In making some sense of how those upholding Hindutva ideologies can claim to appropriate Gandhi as a Hindutva Hindu/Indian and then to appropriate his *Hind Swaraj* as their own text, we can observe changes in formulations of this orientation in recent decades. These often depart from the earlier, narrower, militant, "hard Hindutva," BJP, RSS, and other anti-Gandhi formulations. In very vague formulations, sometimes presented as approaches of "soft Hindutva," Hindutva is defined as the "way of life of India." The prime minister and influential political, cultural, and religious leaders can then appropriate leaders who rejected Hinduism or at least major features of Hindutva Hinduism, such as Ambedkar and Gandhi, as exemplary Hindutva figures. An extreme expression of this broadened Hindutva perspective can be seen in recent interviews and speeches by Mohan Bhagwat, RSS chief.[11]

One should not overstate the real substance of such a pro-Gandhi reorientation. When one examines and deconstructs the pro-Gandhi rightwing ideology, it is usually combined with anti-Gandhi neoliberal economic policies favoring globalization, international capital investments and relations, and rapid economic capital growth with the top-down centralized concentration of wealth and political power, and growing inequality between the haves and the have-nots. In such economic and political priorities and policies, there is an emphasis on the rapid growth of modern technology as key to India's rapid development that Gandhi critiques in *Hind Swaraj*.[12]

Finally, there is another even more revealing and significant sign of more receptiveness to Gandhi and his view of technology among some of those who embrace the values of what Gandhi formulates as "Modern Civilization," acknowledging that this receptiveness can also be overstated and misleading. In earlier decades, I found that for such modern, usually Westernized Indians, Gandhi and the values of his *Hind Swaraj* are completely irrelevant. They do not know or care about what they ignore or dismiss as the pre-modern and anti-modern Gandhi, who plays no part in their views of technology, development, progress, and standard of living. The many hundreds of millions of traditional peasants, villagers, slum dwellers, and other impoverished Indians, who are the central focus of Gandhi's philosophy and practices, are at most a backward inconvenience, a drain on India's development, and largely irrelevant to their approach to a new modern India. Similarly, Gandhi, the Mahatma, and his critique of modernity and its modern technology—that would today focus on the rapidly growing inequality in India and the world with the unjust and violent concentration of wealth and power in the hands of the few—are at most an inconvenience, an occasional irritant, irrelevant to the actual real world of modern India. This remains the case.

Nevertheless, there is an increasing recognition by many modern Indians that their dominant modern approaches may be improved through Gandhi-informed innovations, and also, more significantly, that their assumptions, values, priorities, and policies may be economically, technologically, and environmentally unsustainable. Therefore, some of Gandhi's philosophy and practices may have some relevance and may be useful for modern India.

In terms of how Gandhi-informed innovations may improve the priorities and policies of corporate and other modern Indians, one finds the proliferation of popular articles, books, posters, and slogans praising Gandhi as invaluable for improving management, corporate environment and productivity, and technology. This often overlaps with the first two illustrations of more receptiveness to Gandhi, as seen in the usefulness of Gandhigiri for Gandhian management reforms or the appropriation of Gandhi for Hindutva priorities. For example, if corporate executives and others with institutional economic and political power can appeal to Gandhi slogans and introduce some Gandhi practices with more human-centric technologies, employees will feel less alienated, will be more content with their jobs, and will work harder and more efficiently to increase profits. For example, if customers are treated in a friendlier and more respectful manner, consistent with a Gandhi-influenced approach with customer-first technologies, they will have a more positive attitude, will be more loyal, and will buy more of the firm's products. In such illustrations, I would submit that in terms of his analysis in *Hind Swaraj*, Gandhi is being used in very limited and often non-Gandhian ways as a means for achieving non-Gandhian and usually anti-Gandhian ends.

In terms of the more substantial recognition by an increasing number of modern Indians that their modern models and approaches may be economically, technologically, and environmentally unsustainable, there are significant openings for constructive Gandhi-informed changes. This recognition has increasing urgency with the awareness that we are now at the "tipping point" in which the humanly caused destructive consequences of climate change and the economic consequences of modern technological development and levels of consumption threaten future life on this planet. Today we have large numbers of modern Indian scientists, engineers, and others with economic and technological training and power, engaged in developmental alternatives, such as the need for alternative, decentralized, village-focused, less costly, more environmentally friendly, more self-sufficient, and more solar and other technologies.[13]

Nevertheless, if we consider India today, there is an alarming concentration of wealth and power in the hands of a few, with increasing inequality between the haves and have-nots. This is not unlike what is happening in the US and rest of the world, with the development of corporate and financial capitalism, with its neoliberal economics and imposition of structural adjustments and severe austerity measures, and its ever-expanding technological globalization. As presented in his critique of modernity in *Hind Swaraj*, this expresses the priorities and policies of the anti-Gandhi modern power elite to dominate and exploit human labor, resources, and nature. In such a modern worldview, with its dominant modern approaches, technology is an essential means for achieving anti-Gandhi ends.

Therefore, most of the significant minority of modern Indians who now recognize that their present models and approaches are unsustainable, still live within, and function as part of a dominant world of financial and corporate capitalism, and its political, cultural, media, and other relations. This limits what they can learn, or are willing to learn from *Hind Swaraj*, in terms of Gandhi-informed significant changes. What this means is that most of these modern Indians, even with their greater awareness, are still driven by ego-desires, needs, and attachments to their status quo, high levels of consumption, wealth, status, and power, and continue to perpetuate their modern unsustainable relations with those with economic, technological, military, media, and other dominant relations of power. Often, they support alternative, more Gandhi-influenced reforms, such as decentralized appropriate technologies, but these do not threaten the dominant modern power relations or bring about fundamental qualitative structural transformations.

This is not to deny that there are numerous exceptions among dedicated modern Indians and non-modern Indians who take Gandhi's critique and his alternative of swaraj culture and technology seriously. They are attempting, as much as possible, to decouple direct dependency and control by top-down, centralized, hierarchical state power and corporate capitalist power, thus creating alternatives of multiple decentralized, empowered, and empowering, more sustainable sites of power. They are developing and experimenting with all kinds of Gandhi-informed technological innovations and alternatives, and are often engaged in Gandhi-informed grassroots struggles and resistance to the dominant values and relations of India's "Modern Civilization."

What are my present reflections on the contemporary significance of Gandhi and *Hind Swaraj* for India and the world? Undoubtedly, because of my greater knowledge of Gandhi's philosophy and practice, my recent rereading of *Hind Swaraj* and my preparation of Gandhi-informed lectures during my 2015–16 research sabbatical in India as well as recent developments in Gandhi scholarship and developments in India, the US, and the world, I have gained a much greater appreciation for *Hind Swaraj*. This should not be confused with the positions of conservative, rather dogmatic admirers of the Mahatma, who often regard the Gandhi text as a kind of scripture that provides the perfect blueprint that just needs to be applied in the words of its author. If one ignores the changing contextual world of 2018 and the future, and dogmatically asserts that Gandhi is against modern technology, against globalization, against modern medicine, against alcohol consumption, against modern birth control, against sexuality for anything other than biological reproduction and so on, then Gandhi has limited relevance for India and the world. This is certainly far from the positions of extreme critics of Gandhi, who regard him and *Hind Swaraj* in equally rigid, essentialized, noncontextualized, absolute terms, and then reject his philosophy and practice as completely uncritical, inadequate, and hopelessly irrelevant for our contemporary technological world.

Instead, I have come to the present conclusion that *Hind Swaraj* is a brief manifesto, an argumentative work, and an invitation to rethink our dominant modern values and priorities, and to live radically different lives. It is a work with brilliant insights of contemporary relevance. It is indeed a valuable resource for our modern world. We can learn much from Gandhi's critique of post-Enlightenment, industrial, modern civilization and from his formulations of Truth and Nonviolence, swaraj, swadeshi, *swadharma* (one's duty according to one's own nature), satyagraha, and constructive work. But Hind

Swaraj is at the same time, a rather cryptic dialogic text that is difficult, nuanced, complex, and confusing, that must be situated historically and contextually, and has weaknesses and limitations, and needs to be interpreted, re-interpreted, and applied in new, open-ended, creative ways.

Notes

1. My original intention was to include this chapter of "personal reflections" as the introductory section of the next chapter on Gandhi's approach to technology, with my major emphasis on his *Hind Swaraj*. However, because of the length of next chapter, I reformulated this as a rather brief Chapter 5. It is not until the first section of Chapter 6 that I present some of the dialogic structure and historical background of *Hind Swaraj*. In many respects, these reflections on changing Indian responses to *Hind Swaraj* are consistent with my more general reflections on changing attitudes toward and evaluations of Gandhi each time I returned to India since 1963.
2. I share this experience at BHU at greater length in the section "Personal Introduction" in chapter 3 "Is Gandhi a Vedantist?"
3. "The Emergency" was a 21-month period from 25 June 1975 to 21 March 1977 when Prime Minister Indira Gandhi had a state of emergency declared across India. The Emergency gave the prime minister unprecedented authority to suspend elections, restrict civil liberties, imprison political opponents, censor the press, and impose a campaign of forced mass-sterilization.
4. I observed a dramatic, intense, rather brutal illustration of such a litmus test: several visiting Maoist M-L members conducted a kind of aggressive interviewing process of University of Maine students from India. These students from engineering, science, and technology were very intelligent, very familiar with computers and technology, but like most modern Indians, they had little or no knowledge of Gandhi's writings or Gandhi scholarship. The students were asked what they thought of Gandhi. If the students expressed vague admiration for Gandhi, or, more likely, hesitated because of lack of knowledge, they were contemptuously dismissed as hopelessly reactionary.
5. In these dramatic and revealing personal reflections on how these progressive Indians seemed to flip-flop in their evaluations of *Hind Swaraj* and especially in the later reflections on how many of these Indians were transformed from leftist to rightwing BJP and other

anti-Gandhian positions, it is imperative not to overstate the case. For example, my limited knowledge is that most of the active young Indians in IPANA remained in the US and did not reject some of their formative progressive values. More significantly, and open to debate among Indian scholars and activists, it is not the case that almost all former Gandhi scholar-activists in India converted to anti-Gandhian positions, including those that now try to appropriate Gandhi in anti-Gandhian ways that will be analyzed in the next chapter. Nevertheless, it is revealing how many did.

6. Among Dharampal's major works are *The Beautiful Tree, Indian Science and Technology in the Eighteenth Century*, and *Civil Disobedience and Indian Tradition*. These and other writings are contained in *Dharampal: Collected Writings*, 5 vols (Mapusa, Goa: Other India Press, 2000).
7. See, for example, Sunil Sahasrabudhe, *Gandhi's Challenge to Modern Science* (Goa: Other India Press, 2006), and R.R. Gaur, R. Sangal, and G.P. Bagaria, *A Foundation Course in Human Values and Professional Ethics* (New Delhi: Excel Books, 2010).
8. This is analyzed at some length in Chapter 6, "Is Gandhi's Approach to Technology Irrelevant in the Modern Age of Technology?"
9. It may be objected that Savarkar did not coin and promote the term Hindutva in writing under 14 years after Gandhi wrote *Hind Swaraj*, and Gandhi does not mention Hindutva in his *Hind Swaraj* formulations. It may be noted that Gandhi and Savarkar were invited to an Indian celebration, and shared the stage and spoke in London in October 1909, one month before Gandhi wrote *Hind Swaraj*; Gandhi was aware of Savarkar's followers and his approach. Most importantly, without mentioning the term, Gandhi presents a radical critique in *Hind Swaraj* of what emerged and continues to express itself as Hindutva Hinduism. He develops this critique through his engaged practices and writings during the 39 years after writing *Hind Swaraj* until his assassination in 1948.
10. In terms of significant political changes in India in the past decade, it may be noted that Rahul Gandhi and some others in the more "liberal" Congress Party began to appeal in different contexts to what may be described as a "soft *Hindutva*" approach.
11. See, for example, "The Truth That Mahatma Gandhi Was Searching for Was Hindutva, Says Mohan Bhagwat," *news18.com*, March 20, 2018 (accessed on June 12, 2018). The RSS chief claims that Gandhi was a *kattar* (fundamentalist) Hindu, and Hindutva is the set of values, such as satya and ahimsa, that allows different individuals and groups to approach them in different ways. "Gandhiji also talked about the

'consistent search for truth' and that truth is Hindutva." Remarkably, this is offered as the same Hindutva of Vivekananda, Subhas Chandra Bose, Rabindranath Tagore, B.R. Ambedkar, and even Ram and Krishna.

12. For some of the significant differences between the Hindutva Hinduism and Gandhi's approach in *Hind Swaraj*, see Chapter 6, "Is Gandhi's Approach to Technology Irrelevant in the Modern Age of Technology?" This next chapter also analyzes at length Gandhi's approach to modern civilization, instrumental rationality, modern technology and other topics raised in *Hind Swaraj*.

13. These orientations by modern Indian businesspersons, scientists, engineers, and others, advocating greater corporate responsibility and the need for decentralized alternative technologies, should not be confused with various non-modern and anti-modern positions, sometimes assumed by dedicated Gandhians, who embrace Gandhi's views of trusteeship and advocate Gandhi-inspired views of business ethics and corporate responsibility.

6

Is Gandhi's Approach to Technology Irrelevant in the Modern Age of Technology?

When reading Gandhi's major work on technology, *Hind Swaraj*, it is easy to conclude that Gandhi is hopelessly ignorant and extremely anti-modern and anti-technology.[1] He often seems completely irrelevant to what is happening in modern India and in the contemporary world. In my approach to Gandhi, technology, and his relevance today, we need to be creatively selective in appropriating, reformulating, and reapplying what remains insightful in Gandhi's philosophy and practice in ways that are contextually significant today.[2]

I shall analyze how a creatively reformulated, Gandhi-informed approach presents a radical critique of our dominant modern paradigms and views of technology. These are critiqued as dehumanizing, alienating, immoral and amoral, violent, exploitative, unjust, and economically and environmentally unsustainable.

A Gandhi-informed approach to technology allows us to rethink the possibilities for a radical paradigm shift with qualitatively different values and a different framework and way of living. This challenges us to rethink how we view the self and self-other relations, our relations to nature, the nature of technology, our reconceptualization of freedom and development and standard of living. In most general terms, this challenges us to rethink what it is to live a meaningful, moral, truthful, nonviolent, and sustainable human existence. A selectively and creatively reformulated Gandhi-informed approach to technology, when integrated with complementary non-Gandhian approaches to technology, is profoundly insightful and urgently needed today.

Hind Swaraj: The Text and Some Historical Background

In many ways, *Hind Swaraj* is a very peculiar and troubling book. This little book, pamphlet, or manifesto of only 90 pages was written in Gujarati by Gandhi in the 10 days between November 13 and 22, 1909, on the ship Kildonan Castle, while he was returning from England to South Africa. It takes the form of a rather simple dialogue, at times irrationally and embarrassingly simple, between the Reader (largely a collection of expatriates and other "modern" Indians in their approaches to Indian Independence) and the Editor (Gandhi). It is easy to dismiss the work, as Jawaharlal Nehru and so many others have done, as completely unreal and irrelevant when trying to deal with problems of modern India and the contemporary world with the need for modern technology and economic development.

As I recently reread *Hind Swaraj*, I kept noting that the Reader's views, that Gandhi, the Editor, repeatedly refutes, have indeed prevailed through the dominant power of the descendants of Nehru, the followers of Savarkar, and other economic, political, social, and cultural values and positions that define modern India, the USA, and the rest of the contemporary world.

Much of what is happening politically, socially, culturally, religiously, and educationally in India today can be related to the increasing acceptability and even glorification of Savarkar and his legacy. This is most clearly seen in the Hindutva ideology of the ruling NDA, with the dominant BJP, the RSS, and other rightwing groups. This political approach has adopted and developed Savarkar's vision of India as an essentially Hindu nation that is increasingly expressed today in aggressively nationalistic, militaristic, often chauvinistic values, actions, and policies. Although the BJP and some other proponents of Hindutva have in recent years praised Gandhi and attempted to incorporate him within their ideology as a great Hindu Indian, it is evident, in *Hind Swaraj* and his other writings, that Gandhi rejects Savarkar's approach, the recourse to violence, and the intolerance and national chauvinism of much of the legacy of Hindutva.[3]

What is this Hindutva India like for the descendants of Savarkar? How does it compare with Gandhi's vision for swaraj India that will be developed in this chapter, including his views of Hinduism and of technology? First, it is tempting to conflate the Hindutva ideology, with its imagined construction of an ancient Bharat/India, with Gandhi's imagined construction of Ancient Indian civilization. After all, in the Hindutva ideology, usually embracing a view of the greatness and superiority of ancient India, one might think of what will be seen as Gandhi's idealized claims about the moral and spiritual superiority of Ancient Indian civilization. Such a comparison brings out several similarities, but it primarily brings out profound differences. Savarkar regards ancient and later Indian texts and historical developments as often violent and highly militarized—characteristics that can be regained in a strong Hindutva India. This is radically different from Gandhi's essentialized claims of a moral, nonviolent, truthful, ancient village India.

Second, it is inaccurate to regard Hindutva ideology as simply expressing a traditional religious formulation or to equate Hindutva with Hinduism. Savarkar opposes most of traditional Hinduism as not necessary for, or even as antagonistic to, modern Hindutva Hindu identity. I have previously analyzed how Gandhi, in a nontraditional way, religionizes/spiritualizes politics, while simultaneously politicizing religion/spirituality. Savarkar, in his nontraditional Hindutva orientation, provides a religious ideological justification for political followers while politicizing and militarizing Hinduness, but in non-Gandhian and anti-Gandhian ways.[4]

Third, Hindutva ideology emphasizes unity, as does Gandhi, but these are radically different formulations. Gandhi upholds the value of pluralism, diversity, our basic interconnected unity, with a respect for legitimate differences. Savarkar's approach to Hindutva unity, India's Hindu essence, is aggressively hostile to diversity and pluralism, and valued differences.

Fourth, one might think that with its Hindutva ideological focus on ancient Hindu India and its imagined nation of collective Hindu identity, the descendants of Savarkar would share Gandhi's radical critique of modern civilization, with its glorification of modern technology, but one would be mistaken. This was not Savarkar's view, and his descendants have embraced modern, Western assumptions, values, and policies. Unlike Gandhi, the Hindutva proponents favor a developed, neoliberal, capitalist, economic superpower and militarized superpower; a nuclearized, technologically and scientifically advanced, globalized, powerful modern India.

It is even more common for many Gandhians and other critics of modern India to place the blame on Nehru and his descendants. Nehru rejects Gandhi's vision, and this is decisive in what has become modern India. Nehru envisions a modern India that is industrialized, urbanized, and is scientifically and technologically advanced. This is the model for economic development, the way to overcome premodern backwardness and alleviate poverty and suffering, and for realizing modern standards for progress and raising the standard of living. Nehru's vision for rural India is of villages becoming modernized with the benefits of urbanized technological developments. Until the end, Gandhi and Nehru engage in dialogue and debate over their conflicting visions for future India, and Gandhi clearly rejects the path modern India has taken.[5]

Nevertheless, the extreme criticisms of Nehru by many Gandhians and other critics of modern India, while generally true, are not always completely accurate or fair. It is true that Nehru has a vision of a developed, technological, modern India. However, he would be appalled by the concentration of wealth and power in the hands of the financial and corporate capitalist elite, the growing intolerance and undermining of inclusiveness, pluralism, and democracy, and the insensitivity to and disregard of the needs of those in rural India and other impoverished and exploited parts of Indian. True, modern Indians in major respects are descendants of Nehru, but they have also rejected much of Nehru's vision for modern India.

In *Hind Swaraj*, Gandhi the Editor engages in dialogue and rejects many views of the various Readers. Why does he reject the diverse values, views, and practices of these expatriates and other modern Indians, who, he grants, are often dedicated, courageous,

Gandhi's Approach to Technology Irrelevant in the Modern Age 103

and self-sacrificing in their determination to achieve the admirable goal of Indian independence from the exploitation and oppression of British colonialism? A major focus of Gandhi's many refutations of the Reader's views involves his rejection of violence. He focuses on expatriate and other Indians, whom he identifies as anarchists and terrorists, and who believe in using any means necessary to drive out the British and achieve India's freedom.

On July 1, 1909, a few days before Gandhi arrives in London, Madan Lal Dhingra, a revolutionary engineering student at Imperial College, London, assassinates Sir William Curzon-Wyllie, the aide-de-camp to Lord Morley, secretary of state to India. Gandhi writes that what Dhingra did harms India, is indefensible and cowardly, but he is "innocent" in the sense that he is "incited" by reading the extremist literature, such as Shyamji Krishnavarma's Indian nationalist journal, *The Indian Sociologist*, first edited by Krishnavarma from 1905 to 1914. Dhingra is "incited" by others, especially Savarkar, and commits the assassination in a "state of intoxication," intoxicated by a mad idea. It is those who incited Dhingra that deserve to be punished.[6]

For Gandhi, such "Extremists," while they may appear to be much more radical than Gandhi in their anti-British violent approaches, actually share the modern civilization values and worldview of their British oppressors. They "want English rule without the Englishman. You want the tiger's nature, but not the tiger ..." They want to replace the "British tiger" with the "Indian tiger," in which they imitate the British, and, if successful, will simply replace British dominators with Indians, who will control the wealth, economic and political power, and technology and will then dominate and oppress other Indians. For Gandhi, this is not his vision of Indian independence as true swaraj, real self-rule of self-determining citizens, a swaraj that is not realized in India, the UK, the USA, and other modern nation states today. For Gandhi, true swaraj is necessary for real egalitarianism, freedom, and democracy. In this sense, Gandhi's qualitatively different approach is far more revolutionary in his vision for a future India with appropriate technology than the views of the Extremists.[7]

In the dialogue between the Editor and the Reader, Gandhi also makes a basic distinction between the Moderates and the Extremists. This distinction is evident in the divisions within the Congress Party and other Indians emphasizing the need to change British colonial Rule. The Moderates, including Gandhi's initial Congress Party political mentor Gopal Krishna Gokhale, favor gradual, legal, constitutional, reformist moves, including petitioning the British over legitimate grievances. Although Gandhi appears in *Hind Swaraj* to be more sympathetic to the Moderates, probably because they do not appeal to violence, he finds their approach is often ineffective. Usually caste and class-privileged, and highly Westernized and modernized, the approach to swaraj of the Moderates lacks the nonviolent, proactive force of satyagraha, including civil disobedience, and a qualitatively different vision that rejects the British approach to development, progress, and technology.

Gandhi, even more strongly, rejects the approaches of the Reader as Extremist. The Extremists, including Bal Gangadhar Tilak who thundered "Swaraj is our birth right," do not restrict their values, methods, and views of swaraj to legal, constitutional, or nonviolent means. They embrace any means necessary to overcome British rule, even if it involves legitimate violence, killing, and terrorism. In engaging the Extremists in dialogue, Gandhi wants to convince them not only about their approach being immoral, untruthful, and unworthy of what is best in India, but also that it is pragmatically ineffective. As previously indicated, he submits that their oppositional approach is actually very modern and very British, and that it will replicate the violent, untruthful, unjust, unsustainable relations of domination, exploitation, and technological development evident in modern civilization.

Throughout *Hind Swaraj*, Gandhi critiques the varied positions of the Reader as embracing the approaches and shared worldview of a "Modern India" that identifies with Western "modern civilization." A central feature of this modern civilization is its approach to modern technology, illustrated more powerfully today in our "Age of Technology."

Hind Swaraj: Gandhi's Controversial Technology Assertions

Hind Swaraj is certainly a very controversial work, and its most controversial section, that has received the strongest criticism and has been used to substantiate Gandhi's hopeless ignorance and irrelevance, is the short chapter on modern technology. Consider the following citations on machinery (technology) from that chapter. "Machinery [technology] is the chief symbol of Modern Civilisation: It represents a great sin." "I cannot recall a single good point in connection with machinery." In focusing on the major evil, "the machine craze" that now defines so much of contemporary life, Gandhi writes: "Do not, therefore, forget the main thing. It is necessary to realize that machinery is bad. We shall then gradually be able to do away with it."[8] In earlier chapters, Gandhi dogmatically trashes modern hospitals as "institutions for propagating sin" and "modern medicine" for narrowly focusing on the body and not including the moral and spiritual basis of bodily and all health.[9] He dogmatically rejects modern railways as propagating evil, spreading plague, and impoverishing and dividing India. We rush from place to place on railroads, but this is against our human nature that allows us to know our Maker. We need to go only as far as our hands and feet will take us. This is confirmed by how God created us.

This is not to ignore the fact that these seemingly reactionary, anti-modern, irrational, and dogmatic assertions by Gandhi are sometimes remarkably insightful and relevant to contemporary India and the world. For example, in his rejection of how in modern civilization we are always speeding things up, trying to save time, and rushing from place to place, Gandhi correctly notes how we are not mindful of what is happening in our own bodies, minds, and moral and spiritual selves, and have little time to experience and enjoy our relations with our neighbors and with nature. Gandhi's severe criticisms of modern railways are also relevant to how recent worldwide pandemics have been spread by global transportation and how development and control of modern means of transportation are essential to contemporary globalization, imperialism, concentration of wealth, and growing inequality. Finally, as related to Gandhi's criticisms cited from *Hind Swaraj*, his intemperate dogmatic assertions about doctors and hospitals correctly note that "modern medicine" has often not taken the time and placed the well-being of the patient first, as a self with freedom and dignity. Modern medicine has overprescribed pills and other medications that lead to addictive and other dependent behavior without self-awareness, and it has not treated the patient as a whole, integrated, mind–body–spirit being.

Among Gandhi's many controversial claims from later writings, we may simply note his position on the Bihar earthquake of 1934 in which over 15,000 people died and his debate with Rabindranath Tagore over this.[10] Gandhi, who is focused at the time on his campaign against untouchability, claims that the Bihar earthquake is a punishment for the sin of untouchability.

Tagore responds furiously and with powerful attacks. Primarily, Gandhi is "unscientific," as earthquakes and other physical disasters have to be described and explained with physical facts, natural phenomena, and laws of nature. Tagore then gives strong arguments as to why giving divine and moral explanations for natural disasters lead to unacceptable moral and theological conclusions, such as questions as to why a worthy God would use the sin of untouchability to kill untouchables and other innocent people.[11] Tagore concludes that the unscientific Gandhi is adopting and promoting the blind faith and superstition that has so plagued India.

Gandhi, who has great admiration for Tagore, just as Tagore has for Gandhi, primarily defends his position by submitting that Tagore is wrong in completely separating the physical, matter, natural phenomena from the moral and spiritual. In Gandhi's view of truth and reality, all of life is interconnected, so that natural phenomena are influenced by the moral and the spiritual. Gandhi cannot prove that the Bihar earthquake is a result specifically of the sin of untouchability or other sins. In fact, how the moral and spiritual affect the natural remains a mystery to Gandhi and other mortal human beings. Yes, this is a matter of "faith" for Gandhi, just as he claims that Tagore's completely naturalistic explanation is a matter of faith, not blind superstition, but one that is allowed by reason.[12]

Bhikhu Parekh, while not fully endorsing Tagore's position, is extremely critical of Gandhi's defense. Gandhi's key "belief in the unity of matter and spirit or the natural and moral worlds rests on the assumption that the universe is a single and tightly knit whole whose parts are all necessarily interrelated." Gandhi's only basis for such an assumption is "his innermost conviction, too feeble a foundation on which to build a general view of the world. One can argue with equal, even greater, cogency that we live in a pluriverse, made up of different and in some cases autonomous orders of being and levels of reality." Parekh continues that Gandhi's other arguments are just as unconvincing. For example, central to Gandhi's defense is the claim that God would not kill and destroy so many at the Bihar earthquake or at other natural disasters without divine purpose which could only be "just retribution for our sins." But how can we make sense of, accept, or have faith in a mysterious divine purpose that punishes the innocent and guilty alike, is so disproportionate in its killing and destruction to the actual sins committed, and is so indiscriminate and unfair that it fails to meet Gandhi's own tests of verifying and falsifying his experiments with truth and his moral commitment to criteria of justice?[13]

We commented, after noting Gandhi's intemperate claims about technology and other features of modern civilization from *Hind Swaraj*, that these seemingly reactionary, anti-modern, irrational, and dogmatic assertions are sometimes remarkably insightful and relevant to contemporary India and the world. This is also true of some of Gandhi's seemingly unscientific and morally and religiously unconvincing claims about the Bihar earthquake and other natural disasters. In the last section of this chapter, "The Future Significance of Gandhi's Approach to Technology," we use the example of contemporary debates and approaches to the crisis of climate change by modern scientists and engineers, economists, environmentalists, and others.

These modern thinkers reject their earlier, narrow, technological, naturalistic reductionist approaches as now inadequate. They incorporate more complex, interactive approaches recognizing the major part human beings contribute to dangerous levels of fossil fuel emissions, global warming, melting ice caps, destruction of species, and threats to humans. Rarely going so far as to accept key features of Gandhi's moral and spiritual imperative for the need for a radical paradigm shift, these modern thinkers have increasingly begun to address some of Gandhi's moral concerns: our ego-driven desires and attachments to possessions, wealth, and power; our greed and lack of concern for the well-being of others and for future generations; the need to lower our levels of consumption, live more simply, and with more meaningful value-based lives. In short, without using Gandhi's religious terms of sin and evil, they accept that humankind's immoral, violent intentions, priorities, policies, and actions have profoundly negative consequences on our natural world crises of climate change, including recent humanly-caused "natural disasters." We must change our values and actions if we are to respond to the extreme urgency confronting us with unsustainable climate change crises.

Nevertheless, after reading the claims about technology, modern medicine, hospitals, doctors, railways, natural disasters, and other extreme assertions in *Hind Swaraj* and other writings, one can appreciate why so many have dismissed Gandhi's approach as hopelessly ignorant, radically anti-modern and anti-technology. Such passages seem completely irrelevant when dealing with our contemporary economic, social, and political world with its worship of technology, growth, and development and its expressions of violence, terrorism, war, injustice, inequality, and environmental destruction. Even many who are sympathetic with Gandhi's moral, social, political, and environmental insights prefer to ignore *Hind Swaraj* and its approach to technology as embarrassingly simplistic, ill-informed, and irrelevant.

In fairness, Gandhi qualifies and revises many of these rather dogmatic, oversimplified, and harsh judgments about technology in the decades after *Hind Swaraj*. In 1924, in words that are even more relevant today than when Gandhi expresses them, he writes:

> What I object to, is the *craze* for machinery, not machinery as such. The craze is for what they call labour-saving machinery. Men go on "saving labour" till thousands are without work and thrown on the open streets to die of starvation. I want to save time and labour, not for a fraction of mankind, but for all. I want the concentration of wealth, not in the hands of the few, but in the hands of all. Today machinery merely helps a few to ride on the backs of the millions. The impetus behind it all is not the philanthropy to save labour, but greed. It is against this constitution of things that I am fighting with all my might.

In words that express our contemporary crises of unsustainable growing economic inequality and environmental destruction, Gandhi then asserts, "scientific truths and discoveries should first of all cease to be the mere instruments of greed. The laborers will not be over-worked and machinery instead of becoming a hindrance will be a help. I am aiming, not at the eradication of all machinery, but limitations."[14]

Upholding his central humanism, Gandhi concludes with the following powerful formulation that addresses how appropriate limited technology, free from the machine craze, can be invaluable for overcoming economic exploitation and human alienation.

> It is an alteration in the condition of labour that I want. The mad rush for wealth must cease, and the labourer must be assured, not only of a living wage, but a daily task that is not a mere drudgery. The machine will, under these conditions, be as much a help to the man working it as to the State, or the man who owns it. The present mad rush will cease, and the labourer will work ... under attractive and ideal conditions.... Therefore, replace greed by love and everything will come right.[15]

The above-mentioned citations are not an isolated aberration, but are consistent with many of Gandhi's post-*Hind Swaraj* formulations over the decades on the need for swaraj technology. For example, Gandhi asserts, "We have to concentrate on the village being self-contained, manufacturing mainly for use. Provided this character of the village industry is maintained, there would be no objection to villagers using even the modern machines and tools that they can make and can afford to use. Only they should not be used as a means of exploitation of others." He writes, "I would favour the use of the most elaborate machinery if thereby India's pauperism and resulting idleness be avoided."[16]

In her book on the remarkable Gandhian Branwasi Seva Ashram, Elizabeth Hoddy takes the opposite approach to those who claim that Gandhi's view of technology, as seen in *Hind Swaraj*, is anti-modern, irrational, and completely irrelevant in the contemporary world. She acknowledges, "Many influential Indians consider Mahatma Gandhi to be an anti-technology, anti-development traditionalist, irrelevant to the needs of the modern world. Others disagree. They point out that he did not advocate a primitive, back-to-the-land life. Rather he was a firm believer in technology as one of the means to improve the lives and livelihoods of Indians." She dramatically concludes that Gandhi

> favoured technology with a human face, working to build a society where people were masters, not slaves. Indeed, some believe that Mahatma Gandhi's insights on technology, economics and governance may be the most valuable source of the wisdom India needs to survive into the 21st century. In other words, he is the only man who has not lost his relevance in an age of irrelevancies.[17]

At this point we may question those who claim that Gandhi has an approach to technology that is extremely insightful and desperately needed in contemporary India, the USA, and world, as to why Gandhi, in his most important work on technology, *Hind Swaraj*, makes absolute assertions that are so bizarre, ignorant, and dogmatically anti-modern and anti-technology. Without minimizing the observation that Gandhi, in my view, is sometimes ill-informed, irrational, and superstitious when it comes to his understanding of science, technology, medicine, and many other modern developments, I shall briefly suggest several ways of reading *Hind Swaraj* so that one need not simply dismiss Gandhi's approach to technology.

The key to such a reading of *Hind Swaraj* is to contextualize Gandhi's formulations in terms of very complex, often contradictory, highly contested, historical, political, social, economic, and cultural structures and variables. Some of this was noted earlier in this section, as in the dialogue between the Reader and the Editor and the distinction between Moderates and Extremists. *Hind Swaraj* has to be contextualized and approached as complex, multidimensional, and understood on many levels of expression and interpretation of meaning. Its formulations on technology are not to be taken literally and then subjected to criteria of empirical, historical, and scientific verification.

Providing substantial support for such a multidimensional, complex, contextualized approach to *Hind Swaraj* and technology is the fact that Gandhi, both in his writings and in his personal life, fully realizes that what he expresses, if taken literally and dogmatically, is oversimplified and sometimes false. Gandhi's absolute claims are often extremely insightful when it comes to understanding the immorality, violence, and untruthfulness of modern civilization, but he knows that as literal and dogmatic expressions, they cannot be verified historically and culturally. In fact, the anti-modern and anti-technology Gandhi sometimes contradicts such absolute formulations in his own life.

For example, long before writing that he could not think of any good point with regard to machinery, Gandhi introduces the printing press at his first ashram, his Phoenix Settlement in South Africa.[18] For the rest of his life, the printing press remains an invaluable technology for Gandhi to express his views, raise consciousness, mobilize his satyagraha movements of resistance, and organize his constructive program alternatives. He may dogmatically dismiss modern hospitals and modern medicine as evil, but he goes to the modern hospital when faced with life-threatening appendicitis.[19] He may dogmatically dismiss railways, but no one uses railways more than Gandhi to promote his values and energize the masses.

Even more significant, throughout *Hind Swaraj*, Gandhi makes dogmatic claims about premodern Ancient Indian civilization and the traditional village, as expressions of the Kingdom of God and the God of Love, as always moral and nonviolent and truthful, and as diametrically contrasted with Modern Civilization, equated with the Kingdom of Satan and the God of War. However, Gandhi certainly knows that these sweeping claims cannot be read literally and verified historically and culturally. In thousands of pages, he writes critically of how traditional ancient Hindu and Indian civilization and traditional villages have been unjustly hierarchical, exploitative in class relations, casteist in oppressing Dalits and lower castes, patriarchal in oppressive gender relations, and disregard basic hygiene and necessary cleanliness. In sum, when contextualized historically, culturally, socially, religiously, and environmentally, traditional civilization and its traditional villages, far from serving as absolute unqualified paradises and exemplary models for today, need to be critiqued, reformed, purified, and developed.

What this means is that *Hind Swaraj*, with Gandhi's absolute assertions about technology, must be read and interpreted symbolically, with the recognition of complex, overt and hidden, multidimensional similes, metaphors, allegorical expressions, and mythic narrative structures. As was analyzed in Chapter 4, the better-known illustration involves Gandhi's seemingly bizarre claim that his favorite text, the Bhagavad-Gita, is a gospel of nonviolence. Taken literally, the Gita seems to be about Krishna justifying war and killing if one does this with a spirit of renunciation, fulfilling one's duty as a member of the warrior caste and with no ego-attachment to the results of one's action. As commentators have frequently noted, Gandhi often asserts that we should interpret this text symbolically, allegorically, and not take it literally as justifying war and violence. Thus, it should be read as symbolically expressing the inner struggle between good and evil within each of us. Less recognized and even more significant hermeneutically, the Gita is not an absolute, decontextualized, closed text for Gandhi, but he regards it and we can regard it, as a gospel of nonviolence because we can re-read it, re-interpret it, reapply it, purify and develop it in creative ways that relate to our contemporary world of so much violence, war, immorality, and untruthfulness.

Similarly, *Hind Swaraj* and its assertions about technology must not be approached as some historically decontextualized, unchanging, closed text that Gandhi authored in 1909. His understandings of his *Hind Swaraj* as his key text on technology were open to many changes after 1909, especially after his return to India from South Africa, his ashram experiments, his constructive work experiments, and his other practical engagements with modern and traditional technologies. In this sense, *Hind Swaraj* must be approached symbolically and as an integral part of a dynamic, open-ended text, first constituted by Gandhi in 1909 and now inviting us to reconstitute its insights and meanings for the twenty-first century India, the USA, and the world. For a deeper and more adequate Gandhi-informed reading and interpretation of meaning, we can approach *Hind Swaraj* as a dynamic, open-ended, contextually formulated and applied text in which we reread, reinterpret, reapply, and develop Gandhi's formulations of technology in ways that speak to our contemporary world and its age of technology.

What this also means is that Gandhi's formulations in *Hind Swaraj* are an integral part of a highly symbolic, mythically structured, abstracted, and essentialized political narrative. His abstracted, largely decontextualized narrative is aimed at uncovering the key features of contrasting ancient (Indian) civilization and modern (British, Western) civilization. His essentialized narrative is aimed at demystifying and delegitimizing the British, colonial, Modern absolute values, worldview, and attitude of civilizational Enlightenment, technological progress, and Western superiority. His political narrative is aimed at Indian swaraj, in which Indians do not worship the West and its technology, have pride in what is morally, spiritually, and culturally remarkable in their own premodern traditions, and in which Indians are empowered and empower themselves in the struggle for political, personal, social, and cultural self-rule.

Such an abstracted, decontextualized narrative is insightful symbolically, mythically, economically, culturally, and historically, but it cannot be read and interpreted literally, or adequately subjected to modern, empirical, historical, economic, cultural, and technological, contextualized criteria of understanding and justification. The controversial assertions on technology, at times revealing certain moral and mythic and symbolic truths, may be necessary, but not sufficient for addressing the specific contemporary contextual formulations with their variables and structures.

In conclusion, what primarily concerns Gandhi in his *Hind Swaraj* and its approach to the machine (technology) is not technology per se, but modern technology and the machine craze as an integral part of modern civilization. Modern civilization, with its presuppositions, values, priorities, worldview and worship of technology, is the real problem. In this regard, Gandhi's symbolically formulated contrast between ancient civilization and modern civilization and his attempt to contextualize his analysis in more complex, dynamic, open-ended ways best provide the framework for more developed and adequate approaches to the negative and also positive understanding of technology in India, the West, and the contemporary world.

Modern Civilization and Technology

As has been seen, Gandhi structures much of the dialogue of *Hind Swaraj* in terms of diametrically opposed conceptions of civilization:

modern (British, colonial) civilization and ancient (Indian, village-based) civilization. It is not always clear or consistent as to how Gandhi arrives at his sweeping formulations and what he intends by his abstract, universal, essentializing formulations of modern (British, Western, industrialized, technological, violent, unsustainable, Satanic, evil) civilization and the diametrically opposed Ancient (Indian, nonviolent, peaceful, harmonious, moral, God-like, spiritual) civilization.[20] As the Editor, he consistently offers a radical critique of the positions embraced by a wide variety of Indians who identify with features of modern civilization. Such positions are far more prominent today as embraced in India and by Indians in the USA and elsewhere in the West. To realize why Gandhi is so critical of modern civilization, one must understand what he means by "civilization."

"Civilization" is a broad term with a variety of meanings. Most often, as seen in major dictionary definitions and in writings that influence Gandhi, "civilization" identifies a high level or the most advanced level of cultural development. This is a stage of culture marked by human development, typically characterized as developed with regard to technology, science, literacy, social organization, and as more refined, enlightened, and indicating human and social progress. This is evident in dominant British and other colonial attitudes of cultural superiority toward Indians and other backward and uncivilized people, where colonial dominators were civilizing and bringing the benefits of civilization to the natives.

In the case of India, the British civilizing process includes the introduction of railways and other modern technology, a colonial education system including literacy in English, and the study of the required canon of essential Western writings, integration of semi-feudal peasants and newly created wage-laborers into modern capitalist economic relations, and missionary work to convert idol-worshipping Hindus and other primitive religious beings to more civilized, developed Christianity. It is against such attitudes of superiority and views of cultural and civilizational development that Gandhi reacts so strongly in his critique of modern civilization.

In *Hind Swaraj* and throughout his writings, Gandhi submits that civilization has to do with our conduct, our way of actually living in the world. Civilization does involve a worldview, but consistent with his emphasis on practice and not on abstract detached theory,

Gandhi focuses on how such a worldview is actualized through assumptions, priorities, and values on our conduct and how we actually live in the world. In his focus on civilization as conduct, Gandhi insists on dharma, the moral and spiritual basis of civilization. This is why Indians should not accept their cultural civilizational inferiority and worship modern civilization and technology, since its culture and the ways its people actually live their lives reveal a modern conduct, lacking the moral and spiritual basis of any true or developed civilization.[21]

What are the central characteristics of modern civilization that is the dominant global view of civilization in the contemporary world? This is the dominant post-medieval, modern, post-Enlightenment, Industrial Revolution, scientific and technological orientation that defines the major economic, political, social, and cultural approaches with relations toward one's self, other selves, other sentient beings, and nature. As formulated by a wide variety of Western anti-modernists and post-modernists, central in the writings of leading Western Romanticists and other influential critics of the Enlightenment orientation, and as critiqued by existentialists and phenomenologists, this dominant modern approach embraces the view that the ends justify the means.

Because I shall use the term "instrumental rationality" to analyze Gandhi's approach and critique of modern culture and civilization with its view of technology, it is important to clarify how the term will be used. There is a general meaning of "instrumental rationality" or "instrumental reason" as a form of practical rationality in which one identifies a problem, an end, and then identifies the most effective means for solving the problem and achieving that end. As analyzed later in this chapter, one using instrumental reason would formulate the best fossil-fuel technological means for achieving the corporate capitalist goal of maximizing profit and capital growth without reflecting on the value of the end, the cultural and moral dimensions, or the questions of environmental and economic sustainability. Gandhi's critique is most significant in this regard.

There is also a vast literature of highly technical, philosophical research and debates that focus on "instrumental rationality" or "instrumental reason." For example, is instrumental rationality identical with practical rationality? Does this mean that it is not irrational for the person using instrumental reason, using the best fossil-fuel and technological means for achieving the goal of maximizing profit and capital growth, to act immorally since moral means would not be suitable to achieve one's end?[22]

There is another influential philosophical approach, identified with Continental Philosophy that focuses on instrumental reason and, in many ways, shares more with Gandhi's orientation. Most influential is Martin Heidegger's *The Question Concerning Technology*, first published in 1954. Many similar criticisms of modernity and its technology are developed by those identified with the Critical Theory of the Frankfurt School, as seen in Max Horkheimer's analysis in "On the Critique of Instrumental Reason" and "Means and Ends" and works by Theodor W. Adorno.

Special mention may be made of another member of the Frankfurt School, Herbert Marcuse and his *One-Dimensional Man*. Marcuse critiques modern "technological rationality," the triumph of "instrumental rationality" with its technology. Such a technological, instrumental rationality is one-dimensional, a limited view of calculating effective means-ends rationality, and a basis for a dialectic of domination, alienation, and other crises of modern life. With the focus on modern culture and the critique of modern technology as integral to modern domination, we open up space for struggle, resistance, and liberation. This requires a qualitative transformation in our view of culture, society, and its technology. This involves going beyond the limits of technological rationality, instrumental rationality with its narrow focus on efficiency and means-ends practical rationality, to raise descriptive and normative concerns about moral, social, economic, political, and environmental dimensions and consequences of culture, rationality, and our mode of existence.[23]

In what follows, Gandhi's swaraj approach to culture and technology will be formulated as a radical critique of the modern ends-means civilizational approach that adopts a specific, limited, cultural view of reason, as instrumental rationality, in which one uses reason as a means to achieve one's ends. For example, the modern economic approaches use the analysis of ends-means instrumental reason to create and apply relations of exploiting natural resources and human labor power to maximize profit and achieve the end of economic wealth, domination, and power. For example, the modern political approaches use reason as a means to achieve, maintain, and develop relations to achieve the objective of political power and domination. In such a civilizational approach to technology, modern technology is viewed as a thing, the machine, reified and fetishized as something autonomous, and worshipped as central to our "machine craze." Why are moderns so obsessed with their technology? Because it is viewed as something powerful that we can use as a means to allow us to achieve the desired ends of wealth, status, power, happiness, and a higher standard of living.

As repeatedly formulated by Gandhi, this modern civilization is reductionistically "materialist," denying, ignoring, and deemphasizing the moral and the spiritual basis of cultural civilization. In its materialistic cultural perspective, it emphasizes material consumption as developed in British urbanized life after the Industrial Revolution, and as developed through the colonial culture of the British Empire. Maximizing material consumption provides the assumed criteria for civilizational development, progress, and standard of living. In its materialistic cultural perspective, Gandhi emphasizes that modern civilization focuses on the body and not on our moral and spiritual nature. By maximizing material consumption, we are told that we can fulfill our bodily needs. Gandhi submits that even in this limited civilizational perspective, modern civilization is blatantly unsuccessful in meeting our bodily needs, as British and other moderns are driven by undisciplined, insatiable needs, and exhibit so much physical and mental disease, dissatisfaction, and alienation.

All civilizations embrace dominant views of self that are varied in their cultural expressions, whether expressing the nature of a worldly self, individual self, social self, higher Self, what it is to be a human being, the person, the nonself, and so on. As formulated in *Hind Swaraj*, modern civilization adopts a dominant cultural view of the self as the separate, autonomous, I–me, ego-defined and ego-driven self. It is the individualistic ego-self, driven by its ego needs, desires, and attachments, that uses instrumental rationality as a means to achieve its ends of maximizing material consumption, fulfilling bodily needs, and realizing economic wealth, political power, social domination, status, and happiness. In this civilizational orientation, modern ego-selves have maximized modern technology as an essential means for realizing these desired ends. As will be seen, Gandhi provides a radical critique of such a modern self-perspective, radically inverting the dominant terms of modern civilization, by submitting that the modern ego necessarily expresses the false, violent, amoral and immoral, unspiritual self that lacks the sustainable harmonious integration of the mind–body–heart self.

Gandhi's View of Civilization and Technology

In this section, I shall not develop Gandhi's comprehensive interpretation and analysis underlying his approach to true civilization and its dharma culture. In other writings, I have attempted to do this by focusing on Gandhi's two key principles of satya and ahimsa, the integral relation between Truth and Nonviolence, the moral basis of his means-ends analysis, and his ontological view of the primary unity and interconnectedness of reality.[24] Instead, I will focus on the absolute essentialized formulations in *Hind Swaraj* of Gandhi's view of true civilization as formulated in his rejection of the previously delineated characteristics of modern civilization. Such a civilizational, cultural approach reveals Gandhi's contrasting view of a swaraj civilization with an appropriate swaraj technology.

In a developed moral and spiritual civilization, in which human beings actively engage in conduct expressing truthful, nonviolent, harmonious, sustainable living, we develop self-discipline to control and limit our materialistic, bodily consumption desires, needs, and attachments. In a developmental model, this involves increasing levels and degrees of self-rule, self-discipline, and self-sacrifice. Although sometimes misinterpreted, Gandhi does not intend this to be masochistic in extreme self-denial. He is just the opposite: he believes it is key to the process of true self-realization. What is controlled and sacrificed is the undisciplined, untruthful, violent, ego-driven, modern construction of the self, allowing us to experience the deeper Self that really exists and is an expression of Reality.

This Gandhi-informed process of self-realization, as expressing developed conduct of advanced civilization, involves a radical inversion of the modern privileging of one's own individual self.[25] While acknowledging notable exceptions, the dominant post-Cartesian philosophical orientation has usually consisted in the privileging of one's individual self as separate, autonomous, rational, certain, or at least the best-known foundation and starting point of one's philosophical project. The modern philosophical project is largely consisted in the very varied analysis of how one can respond to epistemological scepticism, to the threat of individual self/ego solipsism, to the challenge of unlimited subjective relativism, and justify claims to objective knowledge of other minds, the external world, nature, God, and so on.

In his most frequent, cultural, social, relational formulations, Gandhi radically inverts this modern orientation and establishes asymmetrical self-other relations as essential to the dynamic process of self-realization and civilizational development. It is the experiential other that is privileged, especially the other with the greatest needs, with the greatest bodily and mental and spiritual suffering, and with the least freedom. As Gandhi repeatedly submits, it is when I discipline, control, and sacrifice my ego-driven self, when I identify with the needs of the suffering and unfree other, that is when the deeper, nonviolent, truthful self/Self, God, Reality, and so on, are revealed and become an essential part of my process of self-realization.

While maintaining a realistic recognition of the overwhelming dominant power and influence of modern civilization, Gandhi expresses optimism about the possibilities for such a radical process of self and civilizational transformation. Using his medical image in *Hind Swaraj*, Modern Civilization is characterized as a diseased condition. However, this is a curable disease. As with a cancer, only after acknowledging and becoming fully aware of the origin, nature, and functioning of the disease and then responding with the appropriate treatment can we transform and finally overcome the disease. Only then can we realize the healthy culture and developed civilization that is moral, nonviolent, truthful, and that expresses swaraj, self-realization, and the morally and ontologically interconnected world transformation and development.[26]

In developing his approach to the need for creating the dharma civilization with its swaraj technology, Gandhi often focuses on his famous means-ends analysis. Gandhi's primary emphasis on the ethical basis of this relational analysis is usually recognized. Unlike modern civilization, with its dominant perspective upholding the position that the ends justify the means, Gandhi affirms that our means must be as pure, moral, nonviolent, and truthful as our ends. Impure, ego-driven, immoral, violent, and untruthful means necessarily shape and result in immoral, violent, untruthful ends. One cannot use violence to realize the end of nonviolence, war to achieve the goal of lasting peace, exploitation and oppression to create justice, happiness, and the well-being of all. In his primary ethical orientation, Gandhi often asserts that in their dynamic, integral, relational expressions, means and ends are convertible, two sides of the same coin. Thus, not only do our means necessarily shape our sustainable or unsustainable ends, but also our pure, moral, nonviolent, truthful, and sustainable ends shape and result in our use of moral, nonviolent, truthful means.[27]

As previously analyzed, what is usually unrecognized is Gandhi's emphasis on the ontological basis of this relational means-ends analysis. Gandhi embraces an organic, holistic approach to satya (what is Real, Being, God, Self) that upholds the primary unity and interconnectedness of harmonious, sustainable, moral, and spiritual Reality. Not only do immoral, violent, hateful, unjust, ego-driven means result in immoral ends, but they also violate and are inconsistent with the underlying moral and spiritual nature of Truth or Reality. When I express violent feelings, thoughts, and actions toward the other—whether as caste or class other, gender or racial other, ethnic or communal other, religious or national other, and so on—my existential orientation reveals the primary presupposition and perspective that the other, the target of my violence, is essentially, primordially, ontologically other. As a primordial category, the Dalit, the exploited worker, the woman, the Muslim, the Jew, and so on is essentially different from me. Throughout history, this rejection of the basic unity and interconnectedness of all of reality leads to cultural civilizational means for protecting the purity of myself and self-group, taking violent means for defending us against the threats of the impure, immoral, violent other, and justifying the use of violent means to dominate, control, exploit, and kill the other who has been devalued, dehumanized, and regarded as less human.

In his means-ends ontological analysis, Gandhi submits that nonviolence, love, compassion, and selfless service are the means for experiencing the end of Self-realization, God-realization, Truth, and Reality. Nonviolent-force, love-force, and soul-force are the moral and spiritual forces that bring us into meaningful, interconnected, sustainable relations; that allow us to realize that what unites us is more fundamental than what divides us as integral relational parts of unities with a respect for differences. In short, nonviolent moral means not only lead to greater nonviolent moral ends, but they also are the means for experiencing what is Truth and Reality.

This perspective informs Gandhi's approach to nature and his radical critique of modern technology as emphasized in modern civilization. In modern civilization, nature has no inherent value and serves as a valueless object, a resource, a nonhuman other, for us to control, dominate, and exploit for our own, human, instrumentally-defined ends. Modern technology is the glorified means for exploiting nature. In Gandhi's swaraj, dharma civilizational approach, nature has value, allowing us to experience and constitute integral, meaningful, harmonious, sustainable relations with the other, and in realizing our unity and interconnectedness with reality. Nature, as other, is an integral relational part of our process of self-realization, self-transformation, and world-transformation. As integral interconnected parts of nature, when we relate violently and exploit and destroy nature, we are in reality destroying our self and the necessary conditions for self-development. Where does this leave Gandhi's view of swaraj technology?

On the one hand, technology should not be worshipped as some powerful means that can be used to dominate, control, and exploit other human beings, other sentient beings, nature, and all of reality. This is violent and unsustainable. On the other hand, technology should not be worshipped as some powerful, autonomous, fetishized end in itself that then defines us in nonhuman, passive, objectified, immoral, and untruthful relations. This is also violent and unsustainable.

Instead, limited, human-centric, moral-centric, controlled technology has its place as appropriate for self-development, civilizational development, and realizing the well-being of all. In this sense, granting that Gandhi most emphasizes his extreme rejection of modern technology, and especially the modern machine craze, technology is not absolutely good or absolutely bad. We must always ask whether limited technology, as one of numerous limited historically and contextually relevant means, is appropriate for living a moral life of ahimsa, of loving kindness and compassion, of self/ego-sacrifice and selfless service, for living truthful and meaningful lives in which we experience the unifying, harmonious, sustainable relations of reality.

In this regard, many modern thinkers, both those hostile to Gandhi's civilizational concerns and alternative values, but also some who are sympathetic, often formulate the following sharp either-or dichotomy: contemporary human individuals and cultures have the choice between modern civilization, which necessarily features development, progress, technology, and a much higher standard of living, or Gandhi's moral and spiritual utopian vision of civilization, which necessarily features less development, less progress, an anti-technology approach, and a much lower standard of living? Are you, as a privileged modern American or Indian, willing to give up your technological benefits, your material comforts, your consumerist culture, your ego-defined pursuits, so that others, especially the most impoverished and least free, can live better?

Given this typical formulation of such an either-or choice, there can be no doubt that most modern human beings, especially those with great privilege, status, and power, will opt for the progress, development, glorified technology, and higher standard of living of modern civilization. This is true even of most of those living with some regret or with a somewhat guilty conscience. Given such a dichotomy in the real, contextualized, contemporary India, the USA, and world, the Gandhian alternative civilizational alternative with its swaraj technology has very limited or no chance of future transformative success.

What cannot be overemphasized, and what is far more significant today than when Gandhi was writing *Hind Swaraj*, is this claim: this is a false dichotomy! Yes, Gandhi is opposed to the key terms as defined by modern civilization in the above modern formulation of the either-or dichotomy. However, he is in favor of real progress, real development, appropriate technology, and raising the standard of living of all. It is not accurate to assert dogmatically that Gandhi is against development as such, when he actually embraces sustainable self-development and civilizational development that is human-centric, moral-centric, and addresses the interconnected mind–body–heart unity of the full human being.

As expressed in many hundreds of passages, Gandhi favors a civilization of human beings who are culturally and socially developed, intellectually developed, economically developed, religiously developed, and ecologically developed. Such a civilization has the greater knowledge and more morally developed approach to technology. In rejecting the false standards of progress of modern civilization, this alternative civilizational approach, with its nonviolent, sustainable, swaraj technology and qualitatively different sense of development, more adequately expresses moral and truthful standards of real progress.

Most frequently, Gandhi's modern critics uphold the either-or dichotomy, and easily dismiss his civilizational and technological alternative by citing one of Gandhi's major claims: his insistence on simple living. For most moderns, simple living obviously entails a way of life without modern complexity and diversity, ego-defined desires and attachments, unlimited choices, individualized goals, comforts, technologies, freedoms, rights, development, progress; in short, with a much lower standard of living. Gandhi grants none of this, and he, remarkably, claims just the opposite!

Gandhi repeatedly claims that simple living is high living! As is often cited, when Gandhi is asked to describe an ideal life, he responds: "Simple Living and High Thinking." The "simple living" affirmation is not surprising. Simplicity is invariably listed as one of Gandhi's major virtues. "Live simply so that others may simply live" is one of his best-known quotations. It is important to clarify a common misconception that Gandhi romanticizes and idealizes all simple living. He is not extolling the value of forced and involuntary simple living as seen in the deprivation of contemporary peasants, city slum-dwellers, and others as a result of the concentration of wealth, power, and control of technology and growing inequality of industrialization, globalization, and financial capital. Such forced, unfree simple living expresses a mode of living as in involuntary poverty in which others cannot even meet their basic minimal needs. Gandhi's virtuous simple living, by way of extreme contrast, expresses voluntary simplicity, greater freedom and self-empowerment, with no ego-attachment to wealth, power, technology, and other complex, endless desires and objects of modern civilization.

The "high thinking" affirmation may be more surprising, especially to many with anti-modern and anti-science stereotypes and misconceptions about Gandhi's approach to reason and critical thinking. Although he upholds the view that the total, integrated, mind–body–heart/spirit human being is more than a rational animal, he tells us that we should never accept what is irrational or violates critical thinking, even when one is told that this is divine revelation and in the fundamental scriptures. Critical thinking is essential to what allows human beings to evolve and develop their human potential as self-realized, self-transformative, and world-transformative beings. Without denying that Gandhi is sometimes irrational, his most developed philosophical, moral, and spiritual position is that the total, harmoniously integrated, mind–body–heart human being necessarily includes the rational as well as the nonrational, as distinguished from the irrational. In fact, to reduce the total human being and reality to the rational alone, devaluing or completely ignoring the emotional, imaginative, pre-reflective dimensions of being human, is reductionistically irrational.

How can Gandhi justify his claim that simple living is high living? As we have seen, Gandhi tells us not to accept uncritically, or worship values and the way of living of modern civilization, even when we take seriously its own objectives and rationales. Yes, modern living promotes maximizing ego-desires, attachments, and material consumption as the means for best realizing bodily comforts, physical and mental well-being, and a higher standard of living. But when we actually examine modern living, it fails abysmally in realizing its objectives. With their endless unmet cravings, attachments, and obsessive needs for material consumption, their dependence on medical and other drugs and other forms of addictive behavior, modern life is characterized by its overwhelming sense of dissatisfaction, alienation, violence, immorality, and lack of physical and mental well-being. Why would one accept this as high living when it really expresses a level of low living?

In his claim that simple living is high living and that modern civilization's emphasis on bodily materialistic needs is actually low living, it is important to reject a common misconception that the moral and spiritual Gandhi is not interested in or rejects basic bodily and material needs. First, as analyzed in this chapter, Gandhi claims that such self-disciplined simple living best meets our real, bodily needs as integrated body-mind-heart selves. Second, Gandhi repeatedly asserts that when one relates to another person who is living under extreme poverty, suffering, and lack of freedom, one's first obligation is to act to serve those basic bodily and material needs. In such conditions of extreme involuntary suffering and deprivation, it is both contextually irrelevant and also immoral to preach swaraj, satyagraha, and other lofty ideals. Instead, one should focus on providing nutritious food, safe water, adequate clothing and housing, needed medical care, and the opportunity for basic education and life-affirming labor free from drudgery and exploitation.

What is Gandhi's contrasting alternative for a swaraj self and swaraj civilization that uphold simple living as high living? Such Gandhi-informed individuals exercise greater self-discipline, self-control, and self-sacrifice of their ego-desires and attachments as they attempt to engage in egoless action to serve the needs of other suffering and unfree beings. Such swaraj individuals, engaged in simple living in a swaraj culture, exercise far greater self-rule, self-determination, and real freedom. They are not rendered passive and powerless; not overwhelmed by the objectification and commodification of dominant relations of financial capital and capitalist exploitation, with the endless seemingly inevitable proliferation of unmet desires, needs, attachments, and goals.

Through simple living, they are able to simplify their mode of existence so that they can better understand and focus on which needs, desires, and goals actually allow them to live healthier, more morally satisfying and more spiritually fulfilling lives; what actually allows them to fulfill their real bodily needs, to develop morally and truthfully, and to live more meaningful, value-based, and sustainable lives. With greater self-control, self-discipline, self-knowledge, self-rule, and self-determining freedom, such simple living is indeed high living.

What does simple living as high living mean for a swaraj approach to technology? As we have seen, such a swaraj individual, engaged in a swaraj culture will not be overwhelmed by the modern glorification, fetishization, objectification, and worship of modern technology. Instead, simple living allows for greater self-discipline, self-control, and self-knowledge, including greater understanding and focus on what technology is really appropriate for fulfilling our real bodily needs, physical and mental and spiritual desires and goals. This allows for greater understanding of what technology really allows for our body-mind-heart's harmonious development and meaningful sustainable existence.

In such a Gandhi-informed perspective of active engagement in becoming contextually situated within a developing swaraj civilization, one with simple living is better able to understand and focus on which self-controlled and limited technology is most appropriate as one of numerous means for expressing real, human-centric, moral-centric, value-based, dynamic, interconnected relations. For Gandhi, such a developmental understanding of how a swaraj technology could be situated and applied to historically and contextually defined India and the world could not be deduced from some abstract philosophical theory. Instead, it developed from dynamic, complex, contested, theory-practice relations and through engaged practical experiments in truthful, nonviolent, sustainable living. We are then able to develop our understanding and focus on which relations best allow for highly decentralized, more egalitarian, more democratically empowered, more sustainable and meaningful living. Such simple living, with its approach to limited appropriate technology, expresses high living.

The Future Significance of Gandhi's Approach to Technology

Today and for the future, a selectively appropriated and reformulated Gandhi-informed approach to technology is far more significant—and even absolutely necessary—than when he wrote *Hind Swaraj* for addressing our most threatening contemporary crises. As noted in the first section of this chapter, a consensus of environmental scientists, a growing number of major economists and others now recognize that their modern models and approaches may be economically, technologically, and environmentally unsustainable. This recognition is best evidenced in the awareness that we are now at the "tipping point" at which the humanly-caused destructive consequences of climate change, and the economic consequences of modern technological development and levels of consumption threaten future life on this planet.

With regard to the threats of climate change, rapidly increasing levels of fossil fuel emission and alarming global warming, many environmental scientists have undergone a radical transformation in recent years. Modern science and technology have assumed a paradigm with its scientific approach in which humans are empowered and capable of dominating, controlling, and exploiting valueless, objectified, nonhuman nature as a means to realize our objectives. Until recently, many modern scientists, still functioning within the paradigm of modern civilization, upheld the position that there was a modern technological fix or solution to the crises of climate change. All that was needed was better science with innovative, creative, modern technologies. Today there is widespread recognition that modern technology, by itself, is not sufficient, that modern human-created and imposed fossil-fuel technology is the major cause of the crisis, and that we need a basic paradigm shift with different values and approaches. This includes more focus on alternative solar power, wind power, and other sources of energy that do not leave the same carbon footprint and are more sustainable.

Environmental scientists debate whether we have already gone beyond the catastrophic "tipping point" or whether we still have a short window of opportunity if we now take major action; whether the fossil fuel and other climate change consequences are already irreparable, or if we can gradually undo these consequences with strong alternative policies, technologies, and applications. In promoting the need for alternative technologies, many of these environmental scientists and other modern thinkers increasingly present very pragmatic arguments.

With little or no recourse to a Gandhi-informed perspective on a swaraj technology within a morally, nonviolently, and truthfully developed civilization, it is argued that we must be concerned about fossil-fuel emissions and other consequences of climate change, since we care about our future and we care that our children, grandchildren, communities, and nation be left with a decent and liveable existence. For very practical reasons, we care about the alarming increase in air pollution and drastic environmental disasters; the alarming melting of glacial ice masses, the rise in ocean temperatures, with the prospect that large heavily populated coastal areas will be submerged under the rising waters; the inevitable prospect of hundreds of millions of displaced refugees desperately trying to cross borders, creating impossible economic and security crises and feeding the threat of global terrorism.

In their rather narrow, pragmatic consideration, these modern thinkers greatly concerned with the disastrous consequences of climate change, rarely address Gandhi's key criteria for a swaraj technology and culture.[28] For example, they rarely focus on the key criterion of the need for us to significantly lower our level of consumption. For most of them, this would be tantamount to asking privileged Americans and others to drastically lower their standard of living, and that has no chance of acceptance and practical success. In addition, since so many of the modern environmental researchers maintain integral relations with big corporate capitalist funding interests, asking people to consume less, to buy far less of the capitalist products and greatly reduce corporate profit, is not seen as a practical option.

Equally threatening, and with some of the same catastrophic consequences, is the growing, widespread recognition that our dominant models are economically and technologically unsustainable. In India, there has been rapid, modern, capitalized, technological, economic growth, with the creation of large numbers of new billionaires and multi-millionaires, and with hundreds of millions of modern Indians with raised standards of living, using fossil fuel and other new technologies, and living with rapidly increasing levels of consumption. As has been conclusively shown, for historical, economic, environmental, contextual reasons, it is impossible for India to replicate the past model of development in the USA and the West without catastrophic, unsustainable consequences for India and the world.

At the same time, and as integral to the growing modern economic growth, India has experienced a rapidly growing class inequality. The overwhelming majority of rural India, along with other impoverished, exploited, and oppressed Indians, have little or no place in the modern economic model, priorities, and policies of a modern corporatized and capitalized India. What is to happen to these many hundreds of millions of Indians and others worldwide? Can moderns expect them to accept their growing inequality and deterioration of their mode of existence, despair, and hopelessness, as seen in the alarming increase in suicides in recent times, and to accept passively the privilege, power, domination, and lifestyle of modern Indians?

What is far more likely, and really inevitable, is that the hundreds of millions of exploited and oppressed Indians, with both increased awareness and also desperation, will not suffer and die passively. They will be motivated and driven to act, organize, protest, struggle, and resist, both nonviolently and violently. As the overwhelming, largely uncontrolled majority, this will challenge the modern status quo and create economic, political, and social disorder and chaos. This not only describes the diverse, chaotic, violent and nonviolent, local, national, and global future scenarios, but it also describes what has already been increasingly occurring throughout India, Brazil, and other parts of the world.

What is the likely response from modern India? Predictably, once again really inevitably, modern India, with its commitment to the technology and the standards of living of modern civilization, will use its economic, political, legal, military, police, state, media, and technological power to put down the resistance and protect its privileged relations of domination and its privileged mode of existence. This may include dictatorial measures, demagogic appeals, military and other anti-democratic coercive actions, and violent responses to destroy the class struggle.

Just as predictably, the overwhelming majority of exploited, oppressed, and desperate Indians will not accept this repression and violence passively. Depending on specific contextual situations, they will resort to a wide range of tactics and strategies. This may involve mass mobilizations, protests, boycotts, other forms of noncooperation, armed struggles, and more Gandhi-informed, nonviolent resistance and struggle, including the use of decentralized swaraj technologies. The responses and the leadership may take a more Gandhian development and expression, not to be identified with some recent attempts to use seemingly Gandhian language and limited tactics without embracing an overall Gandhian philosophical, moral, and truthful framework. But the responses and leadership may also express non-Gandhian and anti-Gandhian approaches and values.

For such a Gandhian framework and approach, and embracing a swaraj technology, we would need a radical paradigm shift, and Gandhi's complex and dynamic approach to human nature is significant in this regard. Gandhi does not deny that modern civilization taps into human nature. He identifies this as our lower nature in which we are motivated by ego-driven desires and attachments and focus on our bodily needs. If we are socialized to embrace a modern paradigm, culture and civilization, moderns will be attracted by the machine craze, modern technologies, and other means that are offered for realizing their ego-driven desires, needs, and goals. Any Gandhian technological or other alternative will be seen as irrelevant, utopian, and impractical.

However, Gandhi submits that we can also tap into our higher nature in which humans exert self-control over their ego-driven needs, desires, and attachments through self-sacrifice, and engage in selfless actions to serve the needs of others. This is not some utopian flight of the imagination or some unrealistic impractical demand. Throughout history and throughout India and the world today, countless human beings live lives expressing egoless care for the suffering of others, loving kindness, compassion, nonviolent moral and truthful living. This tapping into our higher moral and spiritual nature is what allows us to develop as human beings, as families, communities, and other interconnected social relational expressions.

What is the place and function of swaraj technology within such a radical paradigm shift in which we tap into our higher nature as integrated body-mind-heart beings within the context of swaraj culture and civilization? Such a Gandhi-informed approach greatly appreciates the insights and values of traditional technologies, but it does not seek uncritically to romanticize them in decontextualized abstracted essentialisms. It also does not seek simply to replicate such traditional technologies in formulating and applying alternative technologies to our contextualized contemporary world.

Contrary to modern critique, swaraj technology is not opposed to creative innovations. Moderns extol innovative creative technology as part of what is really a very limited modern perspective. A swaraj paradigm, culture, and civilization will allow for heretofore unimagined and unrealized human potential for creativity, innovation, and swaraj technological development. It will appropriate what is valuable in traditional technologies, and it will also appropriate what is valuable in modern technologies and not be limited by the modern paradigm of modern civilization. Such traditional and modern insights and developments will be appropriated, integrated, and reformulated as swaraj technologies within a qualitative different, innovative, and creative swaraj paradigm. Such a swaraj philosophy and approach to technology will actualize greater self-rule, be highly decentralized, be more egalitarian and democratic, allow for more harmonious relations with nature, and be sustainable. Within such a radical paradigm shift, swaraj technology will be recognized as having its limited but invaluable place as an integrated relational means for developing our true, nonviolent, human, moral, and spiritual potential and for living sustainable lives of value and meaning.

In this chapter, I have emphasized Gandhi's insights and the invaluable contributions of a Gandhi-inspired swaraj technology that can easily lead to misinterpretations and false conclusions. In focusing on contemporary crises and the role of technology today and in the future of India, the USA, and the world, Gandhi does not have all of the answers, and there are no simple solutions. Mentioned previously, but not emphasized, is the fact that with respect to technology, Gandhi is sometimes ill-informed and embarrassingly ignorant, irrational, and reactionary. Although he becomes more flexible in some of his later engaged experiments and writings in reformulating some of his abstract, nonhistorical, decontextualized, dogmatic, polemical assertions in *Hind Swaraj*, he never fully appreciates the value of some modern contributions and the full value of technology in a swaraj civilization.

We are faced with the challenge of how to apply Gandhian and complementary non-Gandhian insights, values, and contributions with respect to technologies informed by a radical paradigm shift to a contemporary contextualized world dominated by modern technologies, corporate capitalism, financial capital, state power, military and other violent forces, and other values and structures of modern civilization. How, for example, do we actualize Gandhi's insightful, highly polemical, dialogical, essentialized formulations in *Hind Swaraj* so that they are situated within the real contexts of contemporary India, the US, and the world? This often involves complex situations, full of contradictions, without clear applications, and with the need for ongoing experiments, resistance, struggles, and difficult transformations.

In such a complex, dynamic, contextualized perspective and approach to technology, we do not worship and fetishize technology with its machine craze. We do not allow technology overwhelmingly to define us and our mode of existence. Instead, informed by Gandhi's moral and ontological analysis of the value-laden and meaningful interconnectedness of life and reality, we create and appropriate technology as dynamic and relational and as having a limited but invaluable place in acting to create a swaraj, creatively nonviolent, and sustainable culture and civilization.

Using our two contemporary crises cited early in this section, we recognize the dynamic, complex, often contradictory, open-ended contextualization of our analysis and application. We recognize that different formulations of environmentally informed technologies express human relations that are not inherently good or bad, moral or immoral, nonviolent or violent, just or unjust, but which may result in greater economic inequality or more egalitarian and self-empowering swaraj relations. Similarly, in such a dynamic, contextualized, interconnected perspective, we recognize that different formulations of economically informed technologies express human relations that may result in greater environmental destruction and unsustainability, or in more harmonious sustainable swaraj relations with nature.

As relevant to earlier observations with regard to India and the USA in this concluding section on the future significance of Gandhi's approach to technology, the complexity, contradictions, and open-ended nature of contemporary contexts is illustrated by responses to the Paris Agreement (the Paris Climate Accord) in June 2017. President Donald Trump, exploiting his campaign rhetoric of appealing to his angry, America-first, jobs-over-environment political base, pulled out of the Paris Agreement, becoming only one of three nations to reject the Accord. At the same time, as best exemplified by Rex Tillerson, Trump's former secretary of state and the former CEO of the huge oil corporation ExxonMobil, major fossil-fuel and other corporate and political leaders wanted the USA to remain as the most powerful force in shaping the Paris climate change accord. It is not as if these wealthy and powerful corporate leaders are now committed to Gandhi-inspired, egalitarian, and economic relations. Rather, in the globalized, competitive world, they want to use their wealth and power to shape and control profit-driven capitalized solar and other future technologies.

At the same time, with the US withdrawal from the Paris Agreement, India, China, and the European Union stepped up to fill the leadership void. Prime Minister Modi made environmentally encouraging proclamations about lessening dependency on fossil fuels, with India's greater commitment to solar and other technologies, including electric cars. Once again, it would be a mistake to assume that the Indian economic and political elites, determined to provide leadership and control over new, more environmentally friendly technologies, are now committed to rejecting their top-down hierarchical privilege and power, to resisting their ongoing manipulation and distraction of the angry and exploited and oppressed masses, and to achieving Gandhi-inspired, egalitarian, economic relations with egalitarian determined and empowered technologies.

In conclusion, this chapter has attempted to demonstrate in numerous ways why Gandhi's approach to technology is not irrelevant in our modern age of technology. Indeed, Gandhi's approach to technology, as selectively reformulated, contextualized, and integrated with other complementary approaches, will be one of our most significant resources for creating and applying appropriate technologies that will allow for a meaningful, more nonviolent, and more sustainable future.

Notes

1. M.K. Gandhi, *Hind Swaraj and Other Writings*, ed. Anthony J. Parel (Cambridge: Cambridge University Press, 1997). Hereafter cited as Parel, ed., *Hind Swaraj*. *Hind Swaraj* is published in M.K. Gandhi, *The Collected Works of Mahatma Gandhi*, vol. 10 (New Delhi: Publications Division, Ministry of Information and Broadcasting, Government of India, 1963), pp. 6–68. Earlier writings on these views appear in many articles in Gandhi's *Indian Opinion*.
2. This is how we ended Chapter 5 after considering changing readings and evaluations of *Hind Swaraj*.
3. Savarkar, who coined the term "Hindutva," wrote the ideological pamphlet *Hindutva: Who Is a Hindu?* (Bombay: S.S. Savarkar, 1969 edition), which was originally published in 1923 under the title *Essentials of Hindutva* and later retitled *Hindutva: Who Is a Hindu?*
4. See "Gandhi, Contemporary Political Thinking, and 'Self-Other Relations'," in *Gandhi's Experiments with Truth*, ed. Richard L. Johnson

(Lanham, MD: Lexington Books, 2006), especially "Contemporary Political Thinking: Rejection of Gandhi," pp. 306–10, and "Contemporary Political Thinking: Gandhi's Alternative," pp. 310–13.

5. Parel, ed., *Hind Swaraj*, pp. 149–51, 152–4, and 154–6, reproduces letters between Gandhi and Nehru that appear in Jawaharlal Nehru, *A Bunch of Old Letters*, new edition (New Delhi: Penguin Books, 2005). Nehru writes at length about his views of Gandhi in his *Toward Freedom: The Autobiography of Jawaharlal Nehru* (Boston: Beacon Press, 1961) and his influential *The Discovery of India* (New York: The John Day Company, 1946). For a selection of Nehru's writings and speeches on Gandhi, see Jawaharlal Nehru, *Nehru on Gandhi* (New York: The John Day Company, 1948).

6. "Curzon Wyllie's Assassination," *Indian Opinion*, August 14, 1909, reprinted in *CWMG* 9 (1968): 302–3.

7. Parel, ed., *Hind Swaraj*, pp. 27–8.

8. Parel, ed., *Hind Swaraj*, pp. 107, 110, 111.

9. See Parel, ed., *Hind Swaraj*, chap. 12, pp. 62–5.

10. For an excellent summary of the six main points in Tagore's article attacking Gandhi and then Gandhi's defense, see Bhikhu Parekh, "Gandhi-Tagore Debates," in Parekh's *Debating India: Essays on Indian Political Discourse* (New Delhi: Oxford University Press, 2015). The section "Bihar Earthquake" is on pp. 82–7. For his information, Parekh relies primarily on R.K. Prabhu and Ravindra Kelekar, eds, *Truth Called Them Differently* (Ahmedabad: Navajivan Publishing House, 1961).

11. Similar moral and theological questions are raised in my Chapter 5 on Gandhi's approach to the Bhagavad-Gita when, for example, Gandhi claims that God, the divine, Krishna, or the Absolute is responsible not only for all that is good, but also for all that is evil, terrifying, and destructive of life. Citing such Gita passages, as Robert Oppenheimer did, does this mean that it is the divine purpose and that God is the creator of and responsible for the creation and application of the atomic bombs that immediately killed hundreds of thousands of human beings in Hiroshima and Nagasaki in August 1945?

12. Gandhi's position is presented as "Bihar and Untouchability," in *CWMG* 57: 86–7 (*Harijan*, February 2, 1934). He sends an initial "Letter to Rabindranath Tagore," in *CWMG* 57: 95 (reprinted from a photostat) and then includes "Rabindranath Tagore's Statement" criticizing Gandhi's claim that the Bihar earthquake is a result of the sin of untouchability as Appendix I in *CWMG* 57: 503–4 (*Harijan*, February 16, 1934). Gandhi's response to Tagore defending his position

is presented as "Superstition v. Faith," in *CWMG* 57: 164–6 (*Harijan*, February 2, 1934).
13. Parekh, *Debating India*, pp. 85–7.
14. *Young India*, November 1924, reprinted in *CWMG*, 25 (1967): 251–2.
15. *Young India*, November 1924, reprinted in *CWMG*, 25 (1967): 251.
16. Parel, ed., *Hind Swaraj*, pp. 153, 157.
17. Elizabeth Hoddy, *The Banwasi Seva Ashram in Gandhi's Footsteps* (Govindpur, Sonbhadra, UP: Banwasi Seva Ashram; New Delhi: Gandhi Peace Foundation, 1999), pp. 164–5.
18. Gandhi founds his Settlement outside Durban in 1904, where he uses the printing press at his ashram to publish his weekly *Indian Opinion* that he started in 1903. He also uses the printing press to publish his first book, *Indian Home Rule* (Hind Swaraj). Some scholars have noted that with the introduction of his best-known technology, the *charkha*, the spinning wheel, as a symbol of swadeshi (self-sufficiency), satyagraha, and the swaraj independence movement, the anti-technology Gandhi first makes an exception and sees positive value in "the machine." The printing press is one of several examples showing that this is not completely accurate. See Isabel Hofmeyr, *Gandhi's Printing Press: Experiments in Slow Reading* (Cambridge, MA: Harvard University Press, 2013).
19. Although Gandhi repeatedly attacks modern Western medicine, doctors, and hospitals and rejects recommended modern medicine for his wife, children, and himself, he makes significant exceptions. For example, on January 12, 1924, after serving two years in prison, in a dramatic life-saving operation in which the electricity goes off and use is made of a hurricane lamp, Gandhi has modern British Colonel Maddox operate on him for acute appendicitis at Sassoon Hospital, Poona.
20. In his contrasting civilizational formulations, Gandhi attempts to abstract from particular contextual variables to reveal essential foundational truths and realities. As one of many examples of Gandhi's ambiguity and possible inconsistency, see Gandhi's letter to Nehru in Parel, ed., *Hind Swaraj*, pp. 149–51 and also William L. Shirer, *Gandhi: A Memoir* (New York: Simon and Schuster, 1979). In Parel, ed., *Hind Swaraj*, p. 73 and elsewhere, Gandhi seems to present a romantic, idealized, utopian formulation of traditional Indian villages as historically accurate by maintaining that such a swaraj culture and civilization is not a dream but can be realized in contemporary India. In his letter of October 5, 1945, he thus reasserts that he "stands by his system of Government envisaged in *Hind Swaraj*" (written almost 36 years earlier). However, in the very next paragraph of the letter, Gandhi writes that he is not "envisaging our village life as it is today" and that this is the "village of my

dreams still in my mind," but it is essential for him to have a picture of the ideal village if he is to engage in the contemporary transformative process.
21. See chap. 6 "Civilisation" and chap. 13 "What is True Civilisation?" in Parel, ed., *Hind Swaraj*, pp. 34–8, 66–71. I attempt to formulate Gandhi's views of civilization, ancient (Indian) civilization, and modern (Western) civilization in "Modern Civilization, Religion and a New Paradigm," in Douglas Allen, *Mahatma Gandhi* (London: Reaktion, 2011), pp. 131–54.
22. See "Instrumental Rationality," *Stanford Encyclopedia of Philosophy* (2013).
23. See Herbert Marcuse, *One-Dimensional Man: Studies in the Ideology of Advanced Industrial Society* (Boston: Beacon, 1964). Marcuse's critical theory introduces many key concepts that could be related to Gandhi's approach, such as technological rationality, one-dimensionality, the dialectic of domination and liberation, the Great Refusal, repressive tolerance, repressive desublimation, radical democratic struggle, and nonhierarchical social relations. As with the other Continental philosophers, applying such Marcusean concepts would be insightful in bringing out both similarities and differences with Gandhi's approach. An obvious difference, for example, in Marcuse's integration of Marx and Freud, can be seen in Marcuse's *Eros and Civilization: A Philosophical Inquiry into Freud* (Boston: Beacon Press, 1955) in which Marcuse privileges a non-Gandhian/anti-Gandhian Eros. Marcuse's analysis and especially his influential *One-Dimensional Man* have shaped scholarship for over 50 years and continue as central to much contemporary debate over modern technology, instrumental means-ends rationality, ideology, and the domination of capital. See "Special Issue Refusing One-Dimensionality," *Radical Philosophy Review* 19, no. 1 (2016), especially the section "Critical Technology," pp. 85–172. See also, "Special Issue Refusing One-Dimensionality," *Radical Philosophy Review* 20, no. 1 (2017).
24. See chap. 6 "Gandhi's Philosophy: Truth and Nonviolence," in Allen, *Mahatma Gandhi*, pp. 105–30, which contains citations from Gandhi's writings. My analysis of Gandhi's philosophy of truth and nonviolence in the aforementioned chapter is based on my previous writings, including "Gandhi, Contemporary Political Thinking, and Self-Other Relations," in *Gandhi's Experiments with Truth*, ed. Richard L. Johnson (Lanham, MD: Lexington Books, 2006), pp. 303–29, and "Mahatma Gandhi's Philosophy of Violence, Nonviolence, and Education," in *The Philosophy of Mahatma Gandhi for the Twenty-First Century*, ed. Douglas Allen (Lanham, MD: Lexington Books, 2009), pp. 33–62 and *The Philosophy of Mahatma Gandhi for the Twenty-First Century* (New Delhi: Oxford University Press, 2009).

25. For my more developed analysis of Descartes's orientation and the modern Western privileging of the individual ego-self and of Gandhi's radical inversion of the self-other relation, see "Social Constructions of Self: Some Asian, Marxist, and Feminist Critiques of Dominant Western Views of Self," in *Culture and Self: Philosophical and Religious Perspectives, East and West*, ed. Douglas Allen (Boulder, CO: Westview Press/Harper Collins, 1997), pp. 3–26, and the section "Self-Other Relations: A Radical Inversion," in "Gandhi, Contemporary Political Thinking, and Self-Other Relations," in *Gandhi's Experiments with Truth*, pp. 320–4.

26. Gandhi's powerful medical image, simile, and metaphor in *Hind Swaraj* of modern civilization as diseased, but not as suffering from an uncurable disease, shows that technology per se is not his major focus, but rather technology as expressive of a deeper cultural and civilizational orientation.

27. See, for example, the following writings by Gandhi: *CWMG* 26, p. 224; *CWMG* 33, p. 452; *CWMG* 37, pp. 348–9; *CWMG* 38, pp. 404–5; *CWMG* 48, p. 404; *CWMG* 84, p. 229; *An Autobiography or the Story of My Experiments with Truth*, trans. Mahadev Desai (Ahmedabad: Navajivan Publishing House, 1957, first published in two volumes, in 1927 and 1929; 14th reprint), pp. xi–xii, 503; *From Yeravda Mandir: Ashram Observances*, trans. V.G. Desai (Ahmedabad: Navajivan, 1957 ed.), pp. 12–13; *Truth is God* (Ahmedabad: Navajivan, 1990), p. 28. See Bhikhu Parekh, *Gandhi: A Very Short Introduction* (New York: Oxford University Press, 2001), pp. 56–9, 62, 94.

28. In noting this modern "pragmatism," when giving "practical" arguments for why engineers, scientists, environmentalists, economists, and others must respond to climate change and other contemporary crises, this should not be equated with "Gandhian pragmatism." Although one cannot neatly classify Gandhi's approach according to the modern theories of truth, one notes that Gandhi is a "pragmatist," with his emphasis on the primacy of practice and his criteria in his experiments with truth that actions, even with the best of intentions, are falsified if one fails to achieve the desired results. However, Gandhian pragmatism is very different from the noted modern pragmatic arguments in which one maintains the basic assumptions, values, and framework of modern civilization.

7

Terrorism and Violence
Gandhi after 9/11 in the USA and 26/11 in India

Ever since the tragedy of September 11, 2001, terrorism and security have been at the center of US political and military policies, media coverage, and public concerns. It is not as if terrorism is something new to US history. After all, blatant terrorism marks the history of the genocide of Native Americans (American Indians), the history of the enslavement of Africans and slavery of African Americans, and such terrorism continues in many forms to the present. Nevertheless, such histories of American terrorism have traditionally been omitted or revised and marginalized in standard US history narratives. In India and other parts of the world, terrorism, of course, has been part of the daily discourse and policies long before 2001. For geographical, economic, political, military, and other reasons, the USA has for the most part been sheltered from the terrorism experienced by much of the world.

On September 11, 2001, approximately 3,000 people were killed as civilian airliners were transformed into weapons of mass destruction, and two planes were crashed into the World Trade Center in New York, another plane was crashed into the Pentagon in Washington, DC, and a fourth plane was crashed in rural Pennsylvania. Al Qaeda and its leader, Osama bin Laden, had planned and took credit for

9/11. The USA responded with its "war on terrorism" that was used to justify the invasion and infliction of "shock and awe" terror on Iraq, which had nothing to do with the terrorist attacks, and later, the war in Afghanistan. To this day, key US political figures repeatedly justify violent policies and the curtailment of civil liberties by maintaining that "everything changed with 9/11."

On November 26, 2008, 10 Pakistanis associated with the group Lashkar-e-Taiba (LeT) launched terrorist attacks throughout Mumbai. 164 people were killed during the four days of attacks at the Chhatrapati Shivaji Terminus, the Taj Mahal Palace and Tower Hotel, the Oberoi Trident Hotel, the Leopold Café, the Chabad Nariman House, the Cama Hospital, and several other locations. Nine of the attackers were killed, and the lone survivor, Mohammed Ajmal Kasab, was later tried and then executed in 2012. Although India is used to frequent terrorist attacks and the 26/11–29/11 terrorism does not approach 9/11 in terms of the level of violence and the economic impact, this Mumbai terrorism shocked the nation and the world. Part of the shock arose from the fact that the terrorism was so carefully planned over a long period of time, it continued for four days with nonstop media coverage, the Indian response was so inept, and there was overwhelming evidence that the attackers were trained in Pakistan and even had handlers in Pakistan throughout the terrorist attacks, as directed by LeT leader Zaki ur-Rehman Lakhavi.

Since 9/11 and 26/11, I have given many lectures in the USA, India, and other parts of the world, focusing on Gandhi's analysis of violence and nonviolence, terror, and terrorism. Audiences always seem curious, fascinated, and even sympathetic. When it comes time for the question and answer session, the first question is usually some variation of the following: what would Gandhi have done about the terrorists? When asking such questions, the audience members are not interested in the analysis of long-term preventive measures, which may be significant in getting at economic, cultural, religious, political, and other root causes and in transforming the conditions and causal determinants that give rise to the terrorism. They are focusing on the situation in which 9/11 or 26/11 terrorists were about to slaughter innocent human beings by crashing airplanes or shooting other people. What would Gandhi do to stop them?

Numerous examples can be given from overt, blatant terrorism, such as the terrorist killings in Brussels, Paris, Nice (France), London, Manchester, San Bernadino (California), Orlando (Florida), Somalia, Egypt, Afghanistan, Iraq, Syria, and other parts of the world. US news coverage in 2018 has often been dominated by the epidemic of terrorist killings at the Marjory Stoneman Douglas High School in Florida and other schools, churches, and public gatherings. Once again, what would Gandhi's nonviolent approach do to stop such terrorism?

Questioners usually seem confident that Gandhi has nothing relevant to offer the contemporary world when it comes to 9/11, 26/11, and other major illustrations of certain kinds of violence, terror, and terrorism. Indeed, the questioners often express a kind of contemptuous smugness when asking what Gandhi would do to stop the terrorists, as if they already know that they have demolished any possible Gandhian response. At best, Gandhi, in his extreme commitment to nonviolence and pacifism, is naïve and completely irrelevant. At worst, Gandhi is complicit in furthering terror and terrorism, and is culpable as he opposes the very violent measures necessary to deal with post-9/11 and post-26/11 terrorist crises that threaten to destroy us.

My position is that Gandhi is very insightful and relevant in serving as a gadfly and a catalyst, challenging dominant immoral and unsuccessful positions. He challenges us to rethink our views on violence and nonviolence, terror and terrorism, insecurity and real security. When interpreted and applied selectively and creatively, Gandhi provides a radical critique of dominant, contemporary, political, economic, social, cultural, and religious priorities and policies. He provides invaluable insights and positive directions allowing us to reformulate our views about terrorism, violence, and our relations to others. Gandhi does not have all of the solutions, but Gandhian analysis, when integrated with other complementary approaches, offers real hope for dealing with contemporary terrorism, and with the billions of human beings now being defined, devalued, and destroyed as "the other."

What Is Terrorism?[1]

"Terrorism" is a difficult term to define. A "terrorist" to some is often a "freedom fighter" to others. From perspectives of British colonialists, many eighteenth-century American or twentieth-century Indian revolutionary "freedom fighters" could be classified as terrorists. In the 1980s, Dick Cheney, later vice-president under George W. Bush, and other key policymakers in Washington repeatedly described the anti-apartheid African National Congress as a terrorist organization and its leader, Nelson Mandela, as a terrorist who should not be freed from imprisonment on South Africa's Robbin Island. In fact, Mandela remained on the US terrorist list until 2008, even while he served as president of South Africa's first multiracial democratic government and was probably the most admired human being in the world.

An examination of the literature shows that there is not one, universally accepted definition of terrorism. There is a wide range of definitions, with some overly narrow in their specificity and others overly broad in their vague generality. This range of diverse definitions usually reflects how they are filtered through the perspectives of the individual scholars, the particular disciplines, the specific government or governmental agencies, or the United Nations and other international organizations. The definitions often reflect the biases, self-interests, and self-justifications of those formulating the definitions. Various definitions emphasize that terrorism expresses a violent force that is "illegal," thus seemingly excluding by definition that the policies of the German Nazi regime, the South African Apartheid regime, or US slave and segregation states in the South can be classified as terrorism. Various other definitions formulate terrorism as "international," thus excluding the domestic terrorism of national governments and domestic religious and ethnic hate groups.

For example, according to the US Code of Federal Regulations (CFR), terrorism includes "the unlawful use of force and violence against persons or property to intimidate or coerce a government, the civilian population, of any segment thereof, in furtherance of political or social objectives" (28 CFR Section 0.85). Does this mean not only that the lawful use of violent force cannot be defined as terrorism, but also that terrorism cannot have economic or religious objectives? Similarly, in Joint Publication 3-07.2, *Antiterrorism* (24 November 2010), the US Department of State grants that although there is no universal definition of terrorism, "the Department of Defense (DOD) defines it as the unlawful use of violence or threat of violence to instill fear and coerce governments or societies. Terrorism is often motivated by religious, political, or other ideological beliefs and committed in the pursuit of goals that are usually political." Does this mean, once again, not only that the lawful use of violence cannot be terrorism, but also that terrorism, while it may have religious, racial, ethnic, economic, and other motivations, has goals that are political ("usually political"), even when terrorists claim the opposite?[2]

In formulating a more adequate definition, I would begin by defining terrorism as always involving explicit violence or the threat of violence. As defined by *Webster's Revised Unabridged Dictionary* and other standard dictionaries, violence has two major meanings. First, definitions emphasize that violence is a quality or force that is intense, immoderate, fierce, and rough. In this sense, violence is not necessarily a negative force, and many proponents submit that it is necessary in bringing about positive results, such as peace, wealth, development, and justice. Second, many definitions emphasize that violence is a negative force that involves aggression, infringement, assault, oppression, and injustice. Most violence does not involve terrorism. Terrorism is a specific kind of violence.

Terrorism always involves the infliction or threat of terror, a specific kind of violence. Terror involves extreme fear and anxiety and the experience of violent dread. Perpetrators of terrorism certainly intend to create great fear in the direct victims and other targets of their terror. In addition, conditions of terror breed certain kinds of terrorists. People who live under daily conditions of terror, who experience humiliation, domination, and hopelessness, sometimes find messages of terrorists appealing, or at least, they see no alternatives.

Nevertheless, terror can be distinguished from terrorism. Most terror does not involve terrorism. Human beings, who experience terror, when confronting their own mortality or other existential crises, rarely transform their sense of terror into any form of terrorism. Even most people living under humanly caused, socioeconomic, and political forms of terror, do not turn to terrorism. Their sense of hopelessness and despair resulting from such terror frequently leads to withdrawal and passivity in which they accept oppressive conditions as overwhelming, natural, inevitable, or eternal. Human beings living under terror often turn their feelings of hopelessness and powerlessness on themselves, turning to alcohol and drugs. In different situations, human beings turn the rage they feel at their powerlessness and humiliation against family members and others most vulnerable who are not the real causes of their oppressive conditions and consequent feelings of terror. They may engage in imaginary escapist fantasies that do nothing to change the objective conditions that oppress and terrorize them. They may turn to religious messages of divine or supernatural retribution and of a better life in the next world. Only under certain conditions do a minority of people, who are terrorized and living under conditions of terror, turn to terrorism as a means for expressing their sense of humiliation and rage.

What then is this specific form of violence utilizing terror that can be considered "terrorism"? My definition of terrorism, consistent with Gandhi's approach to violence, is the following: "Terrorism" consists of policies and actions, usually intentional, that use explicit violence or implicit forms of violence and threats of violence—economically, militarily, psychologically, politically, culturally, religiously—primarily directed against civilian populations to terrorize or inflict extreme fear and insecurity as the means to achieving political and other objectives. Discussions of terrorism are invariably linked with demands for "real security." I use the term "security" as freedom from danger and risk and involving a well-founded confidence.

As is evident in the above definitions, I (and Gandhi) use such terms as terror and terrorism, violence, and insecurity and real security, in much broader ways than one finds expressed by politicians, business leaders, and media figures. The usual, much narrower uses are oversimplified, inadequate, self-serving, and used to obfuscate and justify ideologically questionable policies and actions of dominant power interests. Consistent with our definition, 9/11 hijackers, 26/11 attackers, suicide bombers, and small terrorist organizations certainly perpetuate terrorism. However, US, Indian, Pakistani, and other military and economic forces can also be seen as actively creating, funding, supporting, and benefiting from policies and actions of terror and terrorism. In addition, our definition also points to much of terrorism as rooted in the violence of the status quo. One can speak of corporate and state terror and terrorism and of policies of terror and terrorism formulated by dominant, "respectable," powerful, economic, political, and military forces.

Terrorism and Intentionality

Critics have challenged the component of my definition claiming that terrorism is usually "intentional." Certainly, those involved in planning and carrying out the terrorist attacks of 9/11 and 26/11 intended the terrorism. It is granted that individual terrorists and terrorist groups usually calculate and intend the devastating consequences of their actions, but this cannot be said of dominant economic, political, and military interests and the violence of the status quo. Some critics working on terrorism in political science and other disciplines adopt definitions of terrorism that exclude the possibility of military terrorism or corporate terrorism, intentional or unintentional. Some critics submit that the devastating terrorism of such corporate, state, and military policies and actions—if one is willing to grant that this is terrorism—is usually unintended.

Although this criticism has merit, it seems of value to retain the intentional component of terrorism, and there are several possible responses to such criticism. First, I would submit that justifications for dominant policies and actions are too apologetic. Multinational corporate chief executive officers, military officers, and political leaders are not so naïve or uninformed about the likely terrorism resulting from their priorities and decisions. They usually are very aware of such destructive consequences, but they either do not care or they have other priorities that overrule such concerns. One thinks, for example, of political and military leaders who employ weapons of mass destruction, and more recent drone attacks with the predictable death and suffering inflicted on innocent civilians, and then cover this up or rationalize this as unintended "collateral damage." Similarly, one thinks of war profiteers, private weapons' contractors, and other corporate leaders who do best when selling profitable weapons of mass destruction and when exploiting conditions of insecurity, fear, violence, war, and terrorism.

Second, there certainly are cases in which those perpetrating terrorism may be completely unaware of the consequences of their policies and actions. Even Gandhi, who did not promote terrorism and focused on the nonviolent moral will and good intentions, often wrote of how he had been uninformed, or misjudged situations, and how his actions then produced unintended violence and other negative results. Much of this he learned from unintended consequences, from failed experiments in truth.

Gandhi gradually realized through his support of the savage British response to the Bambatha Rebellion in 1906, as an aftermath of the Anglo-Boer War against the Zulus, his shock at the slaughter of Indians at Jallianwala Bagh in Amritsar in 1919, and many other painful experiences that much of his earlier faith in noble British intentions and in British law had been misinformed.

Particularly alarming are Gandhi's writings, support for, recruitment of Indians for, and participation in the British terrorism against the Zulu uprising (the Bambatha Rebellion, also known as the Second Zulu War). For example, in violation of his key means-ends analysis, Gandhi is willing to support the British war effort, using the Zulus as a means, to achieve his ends of challenging the British stereotypes of inferior Indians, impressing the British with Indian courage and loyalty, and moving the British toward granting greater Indian freedom from colonial domination. Gandhi's silence in the face of atrocities committed against the Zulus, his embrace of colonial racist views, and his promotion of Indian patriotism and loyalty to the Empire are shocking. *The Collected Works of Mahatma Gandhi* contains many questionable writings with Gandhi supporting the British war of terrorism against the Zulus.[3] Gandhi's complicity and participation in the British terroristic war blatantly violate his ideals of truth, nonviolence, and other moral and spiritual values we have formulated in previous chapters.

In fairness, in his 1927 and other writings, Gandhi strongly rejects his earlier support, justification, and participation in "just war," as part of his larger rejection of British civilization. In this and many other cases, we can observe both that Gandhi is a flawed human being and also that he has an admirable capacity for critical self-reflection and for learning from his past errors and failed experiments in truth.

We may highlight this by briefly mentioning Gandhi's radically changing views and engaged positions in his approaches to war that often reveal his changing positions toward violence and terrorism. In the historical narrative of Gandhi's development, he experiences and responds to many war situations. These start with his understandings, intentions, and participation in support of the British in the Boer and Zulu wars in South Africa, extend through his recruitment for the British war effort in World War I and his changing views by 1919, his controversial views and advice to Czechs and Poles invaded and occupied by Germans, the British being bombed by the German air forces during the Battle of Briton, German Jews and other Jews facing Nazi genocide, and others in the 1930s and 1940s, extend to his positions at the end of World War II after the use of modern weapons of mass destruction, and may include his controversial support for India's military action in Kashmir after Partition.

In all such war situations, Gandhi claims to uphold his personal philosophy and practices of ahimsa. Nevertheless, his views change significantly with regard to his deeper understanding of violence and nonviolence and the unacceptability of justifications for war. We see changes in Gandhi's intentions, means, and goals, ranging first from his narrow primary concern with the contextualized internal situation of the Indian community in South Africa and extending later to a more developed, wider, and broader focus on how war and violence are untruthful, immoral, and unsustainable.[4]

In terms of intentionality, Gandhi had underestimated the violent nature of British colonialism and of modern civilization. In his satyagraha campaigns in India, the well-intentioned Gandhi later realizes that he has sometimes misjudged the lack of moral and spiritual values and commitment of other satyagrahis. In these failed nonviolent experiments, some Indians reveal that they are not sufficiently committed to nonviolence or lack the courage necessary to submit to brutal violence and self-suffering. In short, in numerous examples, Gandhi later acknowledges that his involvement with violence was not intentional, desired, or even willingly undertaken in terms of conscious awareness and choice.

Returning to those cases in which the perpetrator of terrorism is unaware of terrorist consequences, in which there is no intentional terrorist structure of consciousness, we may respond as follows. It is usually possible to reconstruct the intentionality of a rationally informed consciousness with the reasonable requirement that one will attempt to understand the objective situation and likely consequences resulting from one's policies and actions. In such cases, ignorance is no excuse. If one sells powerful weapons to brutal dictators, who have known records of repression and human rights violations, one cannot rationalize that the resulting predictable terror and terrorism are completely unintended. If corporate leaders, in their exclusive focus on fiduciary responsibility and maximizing profits, maintain high prices and thus deny supplies of medicine to poor people, they cannot rationalize that the resulting, predictable terror, suffering, and death of millions of human beings is completely unintended.

Third, in some examples, seemingly lacking a human intentional component, there is indeed, devastating terror but not terrorism. One thinks of human beings being terrorized as a result of natural disasters, of terrifying experiences with animals, or of many relations with those with power and authority to make life and death decisions affecting one's survival. In such cases, there is often terror, but usually no sense of terrorism.

In such cases of terror when relating to those with power and authority, it may be claimed that structures of terrorism are not present. For example, in the Abu Ghraib prisoner scandal in Baghdad revealed in 2004, US authorities granted that Iraqi prisoners were subjected to all kinds of abuses involving terror, including waterboarding, degrading sexual practices, and defenselessness before vicious dogs. The defense was that these were isolated acts of terror inflicted by a few soldiers and civilian contractors. However, it seems more likely that these acts of terror were part of a policy of terrorism in which prisoners were intentionally terrorized in order to obtain information and achieve certain objectives as part of the Iraq war and the so-called war on terrorism.

This possibility of terrorism is evident in many cases of economic, political, and military power relations, but it also extends to illustrations such as educational relations. A teacher, for example, in cases illustrating violent relations and extreme brutality, may intentionally use texts, pedagogical methods, grades, and other hierarchical power relations to shame, humiliate, control, and inflict terror on students in ways that satisfy all of the conditions in our definition of terrorism.

It may at first seem to trivialize a serious treatment of terrorism by including such educational examples in light of clear, overt examples such as the 9/11 and 26/11 terrorisms. Gandhi himself writes of the terror he experienced as a student. In the larger framework, the hierarchical authority and control, the educational priorities and values, and the shame and terror experienced by traditional Indian students, were part of the British colonial educational system. Colonial education, ideologically justified as "the white man's burden" and bringing culture and civilization to the backward natives, was intentionally and integrally related to British colonial, political, economic, and military domination that reveals terror and sometimes terrorism. Gandhi's broad approach to educational terrorism is evident in examples in which Indian and US students are educated, or Gandhi says "miseducated," to fulfill their roles in systems of state-military-corporate-educational complexes of violence, exploitation, and terrorism.[5]

Finally, and perhaps challenging my inclusive formulation most seriously, there are economic and other impersonal structures of power domination that seem to function completely independent of any human agency, with its intentional structure of consciousness. Marx tells us that capitalism, as a structural system of economic relations, consists of foundational principles—such as the centrality of exchange value, the extraction of surplus value, and laws of capital accumulation—that function regardless of the intentional consciousness of individual human beings. Structuralists are also correct in maintaining that one cannot understand objective reality, including contemporary terrorism, by reducing it to the functioning of intentional consciousness of subjects with intended consequences.

We may grant that such structures, including those of the violence of the status quo that can result in terrorism, do, to some extent, assume a life of their own, independent of intentional consciousness with its intended consequences. There is a real world of objective structures and relations that exists independent of what I intend, and that determines, to a great extent, the limits and possibilities of my human existence. Nevertheless, it is a mistake to analyze such structures in completely impersonal terms as if they are totally detached from human agency. Human beings have constituted, continue to reconstitute, and maintain and develop these structures, such as those disclosed in the dynamics of terrorism. What may seem to be completely impersonal is in fact an intentional structure that is disclosed as being for human consciousness, and one that is contingent and open to our dynamic reconstitution.

Gandhi's Different Approach to Violence and Terrorism

Gandhi's most important contribution toward understanding terrorism is seen in his lifelong attempt to redefine, broaden, and deepen our understanding of violence. In radically transforming our understanding of violence, both quantitatively and qualitatively, Gandhi transforms our approach to those forms of violence classified as terror and terrorism.

In most discussions of violence, including contemporary terrorism, contexts and meanings of "violence" are restricted to expressions of overt physical violence. For example, terrorism is evident in 9/11 as terrorists crashing their planes into the twin towers of the World Trade Center, and in 26/11 as terrorists killing unarmed Indians in the CST railway station or the Taj and Trident five-star hotels. Gandhi also devotes a lot of attention to such physical violence, sometimes expressing physical acts of terror and terrorism, as seen in wartime acts of death and destruction, killings and acts of domestic physical abuse directed at family members, acts of physical terror directed at those of oppressed classes, castes, religious and ethnic minorities, and so forth.

However, for Gandhi, such important acts of overt physical violence and terrorism are only a small part of overall violence and terrorism. In his attempt to broaden and deepen our sensitivity and awareness of violence, Gandhi claims that most of us who profess to stand for peace and nonviolence and oppose terrorism are actually very violent. For example, Gandhi always emphasizes internal violence as well as external violence. Love, often identified as ahimsa, is nonviolent, whereas hatred is violent. I may not kill you or inflict direct violence on you, but if I have a violent will, if I am full of hatred, then I am a violent person and my violence will be manifested in violent relations toward myself and toward others. In some cases, my hatred for others may contribute to and justify acts of terrorism directed at the terrorized other.

As presented in earlier chapters formulating Gandhi's insightful analysis of violence, he broadens and deepens our approach to violence, and hence to terror and terrorism, in two significant ways. First, he emphasizes the diversity, multidimensionality, complexity, and interactional nature of overt and subtle forms of violence that sometimes lead to and perpetuate terrorism. Second, his approach to such complex multidimensionality of expressions of violence is especially insightful in emphasizing the usually neglected structures of the violence of the status quo. Such violence of the status quo is part of our normal daily life, part of business as usual, and it is usually not even recognized as violent or as sometimes incorporating forms of terror and terrorism.[6]

For example, from the Gandhian point of view, much of the popular, seemingly nonviolent methods of conflict resolution and of nonviolent therapy, often promoted by those with power as useful in prisons, in universities and other educational systems, and in corporations, consist of identifying "dysfunctional" acts of individual behavior or overt conflicts, and then attempting to transform the "antisocial" persons so that they are harmoniously integrated into the structures of the dominant status quo. Unlike Gandhi, those promoting such nonviolent therapy and conflict resolution usually do not challenge how the dominant normal status quo expresses violent relations and often accepts forms of military, economic, political, and religious terrorism.

In addition to acts of overt physical violence, Gandhi primarily emphasizes multidimensional foundational structures and diverse kinds of violence: economic violence, psychological violence, linguistic violence, political violence, social violence, cultural violence, religious violence, educational violence, and so on, that are sometimes expressed as multidimensional terrorism. It is inadequate to restrict our attention and approach to overt acts of suicide bombers and other individual terrorists. We must primarily focus on the many dimensions of violence that are at the foundations, are the root causes and key determinants of terrorism, and that continue to fuel terrorism. Not only must we come to terms with these diverse kinds and structures of violence, but we must also recognize that they cannot be understood and approached as separate, isolated expressions of violence. They mutually interact and reinforce each other as integral parts of a violent whole, sometimes as integral physical, psychological, economic, political, cultural violent parts of a terrorism whole.

For example, the 9/11 terrorists and Al Qaeda, as well as the 26/11 terrorists and LeT, use violent language, often presented in violent jihadist formulations. To understand such holy war language, with its classification of others as infidels and its language of victimhood and martyrdom, one has to understand the underlying historical, economic, psychological, cultural, and religious conditions that both fuel such violent language and provide it with an ideological appeal and justification for millions of human beings. To the extent that it takes hold, such violent language has a profound effect on redefining and reinforcing interconnected economic, political, cultural, religious, national, gender, and other violent relations.

From Gandhi's perspective, the very same observations can be made with respect to the Bush administration's violent language, extending to the Trump administration's blatantly violent language, often presented in post-9/11 formulations of the war on terrorism. To understand these dominant versions of this holy war language, in which God (Truth, Goodness) is on our side (our nation, our economics, our military, and so on), and the others are evil (Muslims, immigrants, economic others, racial others, and so on), one has to understand the underlying historical, economic, political, cultural, religious, racial, and other conditions that provide the contexts and ideological appeal and justifications for such a violent worldview. Such violent language, often promoting and justifying terrorism, then reinforces and furthers the relations of the permanent war economy, justifies doctrines of might makes right and the need for pre-emptive war and nuclear superiority, appeals to American exceptionalism with its political and Christian evangelical ideological justification, and promotes relations with "friendly" dictators who act in the US interest, as defined by certain power interests, even if they terrorize their own populations.

Violence and Suffering

A Gandhi-informed approach is the most important contribution to our understanding of violence and the transformative potential of creative nonviolence for our world of Gandhi after 9/11. As seen in Chapter 4 in his interpretations of the Gita's path of karma-yoga and the emphasis on self-purifying yajna, self-sacrifice and self-suffering are essential for Gandhi's philosophy of ahimsa, satya, satyagraha, sarvodaya, swaraj, aparigraha, morality, spirituality, and sustainable living. Nevertheless, Gandhi's extensive writings relating violence, nonviolence, and suffering are sometimes confusing and are often misinterpreted.

Stated briefly, Gandhi places the highest value on the self-purifying, nonviolently transformative effects of suffering, but this is overwhelmingly in contexts of active self-disciplined, self-sacrificing voluntary suffering. Gandhi is not glorifying all suffering, the vast majority of which includes the examples of involuntary suffering. Suffering is not an absolute good. Widespread involuntary suffering from poverty, starvation, other dimensions and structures of dominant economic exploitation, dominant globalization, dominant hierarchical racism and sexism and casteism, or dominant ideological socialization and control has little or no value in the positive nonviolent transformative effects of suffering.

As has been seen and will be analyzed in Gandhi's approach to violence and war, cowardice and bravery and dharma, satyagrahas, constructive work, religious and communal violence, wealth, trusteeship and other topics, Gandhi remarkably opens up our potential for tapping into our individual and social creative forces of transformative nonviolence, However, he sometimes overestimates the transformative effects of self-sacrifice and self-suffering.

As Gandhi himself sometimes concedes, this leads to his miscalculations and blunders. He miscalculates that if Indians in South Africa show loyalty to the British Empire and self-sacrifice and suffer as contributing to the British wars against the Boers and the Zulus, the British will reward them. Gandhi mistakenly hoped that the British would then treat Indians with dignity as equals and would enact reforms leading toward India's freedom and independence. A second example of such miscalculation is seen in various Gandhi formulations on how the self-sacrifice and self-suffering of India's impoverished and exploited suffering workers will have significant nonviolent transformative effects in touching the hearts of the wealthy capitalists and other land owners, so that they will voluntarily give up their possessions and private property and accept nonhierarchical, egalitarian relations. One can give other examples, such as some of Gandhi's advice to suffering *harijans* (untouchables) as to how their self-suffering will have transformative effects touching the hearts of Brahmins and other upper-caste Hindus so that they will voluntary renounce their violent caste privileges and power.

This overestimation of the transformative effects of self-sacrifice and suffering not only leads to historical contextualized positions in which Gandhi may have been naïve, but also to positions in which he certainly miscalculated. Most serious to his remarkable analysis of suffering and transformative nonviolence, I would submit that several of his positions are shockingly immoral and involve complicity, even if unintentional, with the perpetuation of violence, oppression, exploitation, and injustice.

Perhaps the most frequently cited example, usually raised by anti-Gandhians but also by sympathetic interpreters including myself, is some of Gandhi's advice to European Jews and others facing violent Nazi occupation, brutal domination, and genocidal violence. On moral and other grounds, it strikes most of us as a completely inadequate and immoral response to advise those facing extermination to self-sacrifice, respond with self-suffering and not with hatred and violence, and have faith that their voluntary suffering will touch the heart of Hitler and the Nazis, as if this were a Gandhi-led satyagraha campaign. It is of little comfort to those exterminated to know that they have retained their self-sacrificing nonviolent dignity and honor.

What complicates and renders Gandhi's approach more controversial are Gandhi's frequent formulations that the creative, transformative nonviolence of the satyagrahas, noncooperation, and sometimes civil disobedience, ashram vows, and other expressions is "solely for the good of the wrong doer."[7] Does this contribute to unacceptable patience and tolerance of ongoing suffering, miscalculations, and complicity with the multidimensional and structural violence and suffering imposed by the evil doers? Is Gandhi telling Dalits, Adivasis, peasants, wage laborers, African Americans, Jews, and others practicing creative nonviolence that what they are doing is solely for the good of the evil-doing Brahmins, capitalists and feudal land owners, white supremacists, and anti-Semites?

In my view, these serious concerns are not fatal to recognizing the unlimited potential of Gandhi's approach to widespread contemporary violence and transformative creative and sustainable nonviolence for our world of Gandhi after 9/11. In fairness, Gandhi often learns from his miscalculations and his complicity in perpetuating violence. He removes many of his inconsistencies. He reformulates some of his earlier positions on voluntary self-sacrifice and self-suffering, such as earlier advice to rape victims and others suffering patriarchal violence or earlier advice to Dalits and workers suffering from class and caste violence. He reformulates nonviolent positions that occasionally allow for moral and spiritual violent resistance. Fortunately, as evidenced in other formulations by Gandhi, my Gandhi-informed interpretation is that he is concerned not solely with the good of the evil doers, but with sarvodaya, the well-being and good of all, and with his primary solidarity with and focus on the well-being and good of the victims of wrong doing.

Nevertheless, this cautionary section on violence and suffering shows that just as Gandhi struggles with Hindu–Muslim–Sikh and other communal violence, untouchability and other caste violence, poverty and inequality, and other issues in the Gandhi before 9/11 world, we also must experiment and struggle to find desperately needed and more creatively nonviolent responses to our modern violent and unsustainable crises.

Economic Violence: An Illustration

Gandhi's different approach to violence and terrorism can be seen in one of his major concerns: economic violence. It is easy to recognize Gandhi's emphasis on some other kinds of violence, such as psychological violence, with his focus on ego-driven feelings and thoughts, selfishness, greed, hatred, and other motives and inner states of consciousness. However, it is also easy to devalue the emphasis of the "spiritual" Gandhi on economic conditions and economic violence. India has a long history of revered spiritual teachers and philosophies that have largely devalued, ideologically justified, or completely ignored economic violence. Such economic violence, primarily manifested through the normal structures and relations of the dominant status quo that express hierarchical relations of power and domination, is usually overlooked or deemphasized by others in their approaches to spiritual liberation and to violence and terrorism.

Unlike many others who share Gandhi's emphasis on the need for a spiritual and ethical approach, and as sometimes misinterpreted by those who idealize him as the larger-than-life saintly Gandhi, he emphasizes the importance of economic and material causes and conditions in shaping our lives. Gandhi tells us that it is only when one has focused on basic material necessities of life and dealt with basic human needs necessary for survival dominating the lives of starving and impoverished human beings that one can address swaraj, freedom, and "higher" ethical and spiritual values.[8] Gandhi sometimes writes about poverty as the worst form of violence. In most of his uses, economic violence is synonymous with exploitation. Although Gandhi resists personalizing the struggle against violent oppression, thus keeping open the possibilities for personal reconciliation, he repeatedly identifies with the plight of peasants, workers, and others who are disempowered. In his approach to violence, Gandhi is always attentive to unequal, asymmetrical, violent power relations in which some, who possess wealth, capital, and other material resources, are able to exploit and dominate those lacking such economic power.[9]

A Gandhian approach to violence, terror, and terrorism today emphasizes the following kinds of economic violence. The economic violence of the status quo is expressed domestically and globally through the concentration of wealth and power defined by the domination of the ruling class, multinational corporations, and the military–industrial complex. It is expressed through the growing inequality between the powerful economic elite and the working class and impoverished masses. True nonviolence, security, and democratic empowerment are only possible under more egalitarian economic conditions free from terror and terrorism, with structures of a more decentralized, more equitable control and distribution of economic resources and power.

The economic violence of the status quo is expressed through the permanent war economy which removes vital resources that could be used to meet human needs and which flourishes most under conditions of terror, insecurity, violence, and war. The economic violence of the status quo is also expressed through dominant economic power relations, both globally and domestically, in which indigenous and local self-sustaining economic relations are destroyed. Food, water, medicine, and other necessities of all human life are increasingly commodified, produced, and distributed on the basis of profit for the least needy and more privileged and powerful who can afford them.

The main concern for Gandhi, in all such economic violence, is that it involves humanly-caused exploitation, domination, and suffering. Gandhi goes so far as to tell us that if my neighbor is impoverished or suffering in other ways and if I could change the conditions and help alleviate the suffering, but I choose not to get involved, then I am complicit in the violence and terror of the status quo. As Gandhi learned from the Bhagavad-Gita, inaction is a kind of action. If I do nothing about economic exploitation and refuse to serve the needs of other suffering human beings, I perpetuate and am responsible for the economic violence of the status quo that sometimes expresses terrorism and sometimes leads to violent reactions against the status quo that express terrorism.

If we want to understand and confront contemporary terrorism, Gandhi challenges us to examine economic violence. Otherwise our understanding is limited and our approach inadequate, self-defeating, and dangerous. Providing such an explanation, trying to understand terrorism, in no way justifies terrorism. As Gandhi repeatedly emphasizes, if we want to combat and overcome the threat of violence and terrorism, we must understand and then eliminate the root causes and oppressive conditions that give rise to and perpetuate terrorism. Otherwise short-term actions will do little to overcome long-term insecurity and repetition of tragedies at home and abroad.

Only by understanding such economic violence can we understand the suffering, humiliation, hopelessness, rage, terror, and violence of those committing overt violent acts of terrorism and of those supporting or not opposing terrorism. It is only by understanding such economic violence that we understand how those with dominant economic power, as expressed through the multidimensional violence of the status quo, create and maintain conditions of exploitation, domination, and terror and exercise their own forms of terrorism.

A common refutation to such an economic analysis of 9/11, especially by those representing dominant US power interests, is the obvious objection that Osama bin Laden was extremely wealthy. He did not grow up suffering poverty and economic exploitation in Saudi Arabia. Therefore, bin Laden and his Al Qaeda terrorism have nothing to do with any experience of those suffering economic violence. Indeed, Saudi terrorists, Pakistani terrorists, European terrorists, and others often do not come from the most impoverished, exploited, and oppressed classes of their societies, but tend to have personal backgrounds reflecting a privileged education and standard of living.

This objection misses the strength of Gandhi's analysis. In focusing on economic violence, Gandhi is not a simple, reductionistic, economic determinist. Violence is multidimensional, has multiple causes, and religious, cultural, psychological, ideological, and other causal factors sometimes become major determinants. This also includes various privileged leaders of terrorism in India, the USA, and other countries, who sometimes manipulate those who are oppressed and exploited through racism, sexism, xenophobia, and other means in order to obscure and maintain their own economic privilege and power. In addition, in avoiding a one-dimensional, simple, economic determinism, we affirm that the fact that bin Laden was personally wealthy does not mean that he was not motivated by claims about economic exploitation, oppression, and humiliation of Islamic societies.[10] Most important for our analysis, Gandhi's emphasis on economic violence is very significant for understanding why so many millions of human beings were receptive to bin Laden and continue to be receptive to the many terrorist messages in Iraq, Afghanistan, Syria, Libya, Somalia, Sudan, Palestine, Israel, Pakistan, India, Europe, the USA, and other parts of the world.

Gandhi and Terrorists

One might submit that Gandhi was naïve and uninformed about terrorism because he lived long before the New York and Mumbai terrorisms and did not have to address our contemporary world so defined by terrorism. Such a response is greatly uninformed. Gandhi lived through and responded to the horrific violent acts of terror and terrorism leading up to and continuing after Partition and Independence in 1947. Before that, extending over a period of at least 50 years, Gandhi experienced, responded, and wrote about terror and terrorism.

In this regard, Gandhi was very aware of Indian terrorists, their arguments, and their refutations of his position. Indeed, throughout his life, he attempted to engage in dialogue with terrorists in order to understand their positions and to attempt to persuade them of the greater morality and even the greater effectiveness of nonviolence. *The Collected Works of Mahatma Gandhi* contains numerous writings on terrorism and terrorists, often addressed to Extremists, anarchists, and revolutionaries.[11]

Gandhi's *Hind Swaraj*—written in only 10 days in November 1909 while on a ship returning from England to South Africa—may be his most important single work for grasping the fundamental principles of his life and his philosophy.[12] Gandhi formulated *Hind Swaraj* as a dialogue between a newspaper Editor, representing Gandhi's views, and a Reader, representing the contrasting views of "modern" Indians, including expatriates he had met in London. These Indian expatriates included those who accepted violence and terrorism as legitimate means in the struggle for independence from British colonial rule.[13]

Particular mention may be made of Savarkar (1883–1966), who lived in London during 1906–10 and was an influential figure among the Indian expatriates. The revolutionary Dhingra (1887–1909), who came under Savarkar's influence, assassinated Sir William Curzon-Wyllie, the aide-de-camp to Lord Morley, the secretary of state for India, on 1 July 1909, a few days before Gandhi arrived in London.[14] The same Savarkar also had a great influence on the assassination of Gandhi on January 30, 1948. The assassin, Nathuram Godse, was a Savarkar follower.[15] Many passages expressing Gandhi's views on Krishnavarma Shyamji, Savarkar, Dhingra, and terrorists or those justifying violence and terrorism can be found throughout *The Collected Works of Mahatma Gandhi*.

Although Gandhi sometimes asserts that Dhingra and other terrorists act in a cowardly manner, since they are willing to inflict violence on others without suffering the violence themselves, such a simple impression can be misleading. Gandhi's approach is very different from that of President George Bush and his administration after 9/11. Unlike Bush, who repeatedly described the terrorists as cowards, who simply envy and resent our freedom, Gandhi acknowledges that terrorists are often patriots who act with courage and are willing to die for their cause.

Gandhi's contrasting approach is even clearer when it comes to President Donald Trump's unqualified violent tweets attacking all terrorists as cowards who are "losers." Using our expanded meaning and application of terrorism, Gandhi would be alarmed by the Trumpian violent and terroristic words, practices, and the US political, military, and corporate practices of terror and terrorism. He would submit that those with dominant power, who terrorize the innocent and oppressed others, do act in a cowardly manner. However, his primary nonviolent approach to these terrorists is not to personalize the attacks on their political, corporate, and militaristic terrorism, but instead to attempt to engage them through dialogue and nonviolent resistance in order to transform their terrorism in the direction of greater peace, real security, and human relations free from terrorism.

With regard to Gandhi's approach to some of the Indian terrorists, his position on terrorism is similar to a position on violence that he expresses in numerous passages.[16] Some soldiers and other perpetrators of violence have high ideals, are brave, and are more courageous than the cowardly response of so-called nonviolent people who are passive and refuse to get involved in resisting oppression and injustice. Gandhi prefers courageous violence to cowardice. However, he usually adds a third alternative, that of the satyagrahi, the nonviolent peace and justice activist, who expresses the most moral and spiritual position. This is the bravest position that requires the greatest courage in voluntarily accepting self-sacrifice and self-suffering without inflicting violence on others.[17]

Gandhi strongly refutes the terrorist position. First, although some terrorists are brave, there is a morally and spiritually superior position that requires far more courage: that of nonviolent resistance in which I refuse to inflict violence, suffering, and terror on others. Second, Gandhi repeatedly claims that Indian expatriate terrorists and other proponents of "modern civilization" actually imitate the worst features of colonial and other oppressors. Indians, as victims of British terror and terrorism and who then accept the legitimacy of terrorism, are linked with the violence and terrorism of the modern civilization of the British oppressor. Violence and terror, if successful in driving out the British, will lead to a false independence, not real swaraj, in which Indian violent oppressors simply replace British oppressors and inflict terror and terrorism on other Indians. Third and most importantly, expanding the second objection, Gandhi repeatedly introduces his famous analysis of the integral relation of means and ends.

Gandhi's Means–Ends Analysis

Gandhi rejects utilitarianism and many other contemporary positions, including various justifications of terrorism, which maintain the dominant view of "modern civilization" that the ends justify the means. In relating to violence and terrorism, we must emphasize both means and ends and their integral, mutually reinforcing relations. On the whole, Gandhi places even more emphasis on means, avoiding means that express terrorism, because he tells us that we often have much greater control over our means, whereas ends may be unattainable because of unintended consequences or because they express ideals free from all violence and terror that are beyond our power of realization.

Regardless of short-term benefits, Gandhi repeatedly emphasizes that we cannot use violence to overcome violence and achieve nonviolence. He would emphasize that India and Pakistan, from 1947 to the present, should have learned that they cannot use terrorism and counter-terrorism that uses terrorism in order to create Indo-Pakistani relations of real security, free from terrorism. The USA, since 2001, and even long before going back to terrorist policies in Vietnam, Central America, and elsewhere, should have learned that it cannot use terrorism as a means to defeat anti-American terrorism and create US relations free from terrorism. We cannot use terror and terrorism to overcome terrorism and achieve real sustainable security free from terror. If we use violent and impure means, these will shape violent and impure ends, regardless of our moralistic self-justifying slogans and ideology about our war on terrorism.

In language similar to formulations of the law of karma, Gandhi repeatedly warns us that violence leads to more violence, terror leads to more terror, and we become entrapped in endless vicious cycles of escalating violence and terrorism. For Gandhi, as it was for the Buddha, most of violence has a moral character and involves intention and choice. It is this moral character of volitional karmic intention and choice that binds us to the vicious cycles of violence and suffering. The only way to move toward more nonviolent ends, free from terror and terrorism, is to introduce nonviolent causal factors through the adoption of nonviolent means. Such nonviolent factors will begin to weaken the causal factors that produce violent chain reactions and will undermine the mutually reinforcing causal relations that keep us trapped in destructive cycles of violence and terrorism.

Gandhi's warning and critique can be illustrated by any of the contemporary sites of overt terrorism. In the Middle East, more powerful Israeli governments and their military forces have spent decades inflicting terror and terrorism on Palestinians in order to break the Palestinian will of resistance and achieve security for Israel. For decades, less powerful Palestinians have attempted to inflict terror and terrorism on Israelis in order to break the Israeli will and achieve Palestinian objectives. The result has been mutually reinforcing, escalating cycles of violence and terrorism with no real security for either Palestinians or Israelis.

The most obvious illustration, at the center of the Bush administration's post-9/11 war on terrorism, is the US war in Iraq, more accurately described as the war on Iraq, that began in March 2003. Through pre-emptive war and the overwhelming use of means of terror, including actions and policies of terrorism that involved larger regional and global objectives, the USA would overcome terrorist threats and be more secure. Instead, the USA has found itself drained economically and militarily, trapped in a quagmire of escalating violence and war without end. Before March 2003, Iraqis had been terrorized by the brutal Saddam Hussein dictatorship, but there was no evidence of Al Qaeda or other terrorist links or weapons of mass destruction threatening the US security. Following Gandhi's approach, we can better understand how US terror and terrorism has not only trapped the USA in destructive cycles of violence; it has created and conditioned new groups and forms of anti-US terror so that Iraq did indeed become a center of terrorism. Indeed, US terrorism in Iraq, linked with Shia politicians and militias, led to Sunni terroristic resistance, new terrorist groups that included ISIS in Iraq, and the spread of new Sunni terrorist groups in Syria. Such massive US violence has made the USA much more vulnerable to terrorism and much less secure.

Although President Barack Obama was more aware of the complexities and dangers of such an American approach to terrorism, the policies of the Obama Administration continued the anti-Gandhi pattern in Iraq, especially in Afghanistan and Syria, and in other parts of the world. There may have been more of a reluctance to employ US ground troops and massive US bombing as counterproductive in defeating Muslim terrorists, but pre-emptive strikes and pilotless drones have been terror operations, inflicting collateral damage on innocent civilians, and breeding ISIS and other anti-American terrorism.

As this chapter was being completed, Donald Trump had become the US President. His campaign rhetoric, as well as his continuing rhetoric as president, usually expressed through simplistic, violent, racist, anti-Muslim, xenophobic sound-bites and tweets, has insisted that he knows how to defeat ISIS and other "Islamic terrorism," that he will do it quickly, and that it will be easy. He transparently and ruthlessly upholds the doctrine of "winning" by any means necessary, including his endorsement of waterboarding and other torture, banning Muslim immigrants, and increasing the US nuclear arsenal. He approaches the complex issues of terrorism the way he ran his business and his Reality Television program, The Apprentice, in which his best-known refrain was "You're Fired," and he had the absolute power to impose his violent will. In terms of Gandhi's approach, the Trump administration policies are terroristic, will breed more terrorist responses, will be self-defeating, and will entrap the USA and the world in relations of less security and greater terrorism.

In many respects, Gandhi's means-ends analysis is similar to the Buddha's formulation of his Doctrine of Dependent Origination (*pratitya-samutpada*).[18] Through his formulation of the 12 links or factors, Buddha analyzes how we become imprisoned in this cyclical world of existence (*samsara*), the world of suffering (*dukkha*). Samsara is the world of dynamic, impermanent, interdependent, relative, causal relations. There is not one, independent, absolute cause to our entrapment in this world of suffering. Each relative and contingent factor is conditioned as well as conditioning; caused by antecedent causal conditions and is itself a causal factor shaping future conditions. The Buddhist path involves identifying these causal factors and gradually weakening the causal links that keep us trapped in cycles of ignorance and suffering by introducing more ethical and spiritual causal factors.

Gandhi's means-ends approach to violence, terror, and terrorism shares much with this particular Buddhist orientation and other Indian orientations. Violence, terror, and terrorism are not independent, inevitable, eternal, or absolute. They exist within a violent phenomenal world of impermanent, interdependent relativity. Terrorism and other forms of violence are caused and conditioned, and they themselves become causes and condition other violent consequences that then become new violent causal factors. The path and goal for Gandhi involves focusing on the means that allow you to decondition such violent causal factors and conditions that give rise to and perpetuate terror and terrorism, by introducing nonviolent causes and conditions free from terror and terrorism. That will lead to more nonviolent results that will then become new causal factors moving you closer to your nonviolent ends of a relational world of real security free from terrorism. The means-ends relation involves mutual interaction, since the adoption of nonviolent anti-terrorism ideals as ends will also have a causal influence on shaping appropriate means free from terrorism.

In this way, one aims at transforming the causally connected, means-ends, interdependent whole, of which you are an integral part, from one constituted through ignorance, violence, terror, terrorism, and suffering to a more moral and spiritual relational whole. This very process of means-ends causal transformation, by which one transforms relations with others in order to serve their needs, is the very process by which one transforms one's own self toward greater freedom and self-realization necessarily grounded in relations free from terror and terrorism.[19]

Gandhi's Preventative Approach to Terrorism and Short-Term Violence

The tremendous contribution of Gandhi's approach to 9/11 and 26/11 terrorism and to violence lies not in any insights about how to respond when terrorists are about to strike, but rather about what to do beforehand. Gandhi's major focus is always on preventative measures that we must take in order to transform and remove the violent conditions and causes before they reach the point of exploding into terror and terrorism.

This emphasis by Gandhi on the larger picture and the need for preventative approaches should be evident from previous sections, especially formulations of Gandhi's deeper and broader analysis of violence and terror, including economic violence, and his analysis of means-ends relations in terms of a larger framework for getting at root causes and conditions underlying violence and terrorism. As Gandhi repeatedly warns us, if we do not understand and respond to the larger framework of complex, multidimensional, interrelated structures and relations of violence, if we do not address the root causes, conditions, and dynamics of violence, then our short-term responses will not be sufficient for dealing with escalating current and future violence, terror, and terrorism.

This is why Gandhi, in his approach to violence and nonviolence, devotes so much time and effort to a radically different model of education, with emphasis on character building and moral and spiritual development.[20] This is why he is preoccupied with expanding our psychological awareness and analysis of how we constitute and must decondition ego-driven selfishness and greed, defense mechanisms responding to fear and insecurity, hatred, aggression, and other violent intentions and inner states of consciousness. This is why Gandhi is so attentive to political, cultural, social, economic, linguistic, religious, environmental, and other aspects of our overall socialization that contribute to, ignore, tolerate, reward, and justify violence, terror, terrorism, and unsustainable living.

A frequent response to such a Gandhian nonviolent approach to terrorism is that it may have value for long-term preventative measures, but what do we do about the short-term threat of terrorism? Unfortunately, we cannot wait for long-term educational and other preventive measures gradually to reconstitute our human relations in more nonviolent, ethical, truthful, sustainable ways when responding to the post-9/11 or post-26/11 terrorisms. We live in a contemporary world of terrorists who are intent on inflicting terrorism on us right now.

As will become apparent, Gandhi does agree that we must actively respond to immediate threats of violence and terrorism, and we cannot wait for long-term solutions. In attempting to interpret and apply Gandhi's significance for our contemporary world of terrorism, it is important to emphasize that Gandhi's preventive measures are intended not only for the gradual long-term changes that are most important for dealing with violence, terror, terrorism, and unsustainability. His preventive nonviolent approach also has profound short-term benefits, and, in some extreme cases, may even necessitate a short-term violent response.

If I relate to someone intent on inflicting short-term violence, there are many Gandhian responses that may be effective in preventing the violence, terror, and terrorism. If I manage to limit my own ego, achieve a larger perspective, and empathize with feelings and intended actions of the terrorist, even if I find them immoral, horrific, and dangerous, this may allow for dialogue, and for creating nonthreatening relations with the other. In addition, as Gandhi repeatedly emphasizes, while intellectual approaches with rational analysis and arguments often have no real transformative effect on the other, approaches of the heart involving deep personal emotions and feelings often have profound, transformative, relational effects. If I refuse to strike back and am willing to embrace self-sacrifice and self-suffering, this can touch the heart of the other, can disrupt the expectations of the violent other, and can lead to a decentering, reorienting, and defusing of an extremely violent situation. Throughout his writings on satyagraha and other methods for resisting and transforming violence, Gandhi proposes numerous ways for relating to short-term violence and terrorism and moving toward conflict resolution and reconciliation, grounded in truth and creative nonviolence.

Nevertheless, we must acknowledge that Gandhi's nonviolent proposals are sometimes completely ineffective in preventing certain kinds of short-time violence and threatening terrorism. I would submit that non-Gandhian proposals are also usually ineffective in completely preventing such violence. What does one do about the terrorists about to crash airplanes in New York on 9/11 or the terrorists engaged in shooting people in Mumbai on 26/11? What does one do about the suicide terrorist about to explode a bomb? What does one do about the pilot about to drop napalm on innocent civilians? What does one do about the determined rapist as the victim is being raped? What does one do about the mentally unhealthy person in a state of deep depression and rage as he is killing students in their school?

The major difficulty with these and related examples, often presented as refutations of Gandhi's approach to terrorism, is that there is no opportunity for empathy, communication, changing causes and conditions and human relations, or any of the other preventative measures that are the strength of Gandhi's short-term, and especially long-term orientation. The violence and terrorism are at the explosive stage and beyond our nonviolent preventative interventions. The violence, terror, and terrorism are also often expressed through completely impersonal structures and relations in which there is no possibility for constructive, personal, nonviolent interaction.

It may surprise some readers to learn that Mahatma Gandhi, the best-known twentieth-century proponent of peace and nonviolence, sometimes concludes that violence is a necessary response. This is the case, for example, in his many writings on what to do about "menacing monkeys." To understand on what grounds Gandhi allows for violent preventative intervention in certain extreme situations, such as acts of terrorism, we must turn to his key distinction between absolute truth and relative truth.[21]

Absolute Truth, Relative Truth, and Terrorism

As we have seen, Gandhi sometimes conveys the impression of a rather simple, rigid absolutist with respect to violence, nonviolence, and other ethical and spiritual concepts and values. This is not only about how many critics interpret Gandhi in their criticisms of what they take to be Gandhi's dogmatic, oppressive, and inadequate positions, but one also finds evidence of such rigid absolutism in some of Gandhi's own writings about his reactions and relations with his wife and his sons, satyagraha campaign developments, and other controversial issues. A more comprehensive and adequate examination reveals a Gandhi who is much more nuanced, and recognizes the complexity and difficulty in sorting out and resolving conflicts and contradictions in human relations.[22]

It is true that Gandhi is firm in upholding ideals of absolute truth, love, and nonviolence. In terms of such absolutes, he resists many contemporary views of complete subjectivism or unlimited facile relativism. Gandhi would never agree that the infliction of terror and terrorism may be wrong for him, but it may be right for the terrorists in New York or in Mumbai. On a descriptive, phenomenological level, the terrorists may think that what they are doing is right on political, economic, religious, or other grounds, but they are wrong.

What is often overlooked by those focusing on passages of Gandhi's commitment to absolute truth is the recognition that Gandhi also repeatedly emphasizes that he and others exist in this world as relative finite beings of limited embodied consciousness. Our knowledge is conditioned and perspectival. As Gandhi repeatedly tells us, he at most has "glimpses" of absolute truth and nonviolence. Since we have partial truths, we should be tolerant and open to other points of view; others have different relative perspectives and glimpses of truth that we do not have. As relative finite beings with limited knowledge, we often misjudge situations and even misjudge our motives. That is why we must learn from our errors in the movement toward greater truth and nonviolence.

While upholding ideals of ahimsa, nonviolence and benevolent harmlessness, and the moral and spiritual judgment that terrorism is never justified, Gandhi can even acknowledge that we can learn partial truths from the perspectives of at least some terrorists. For example, the perspectives of some terrorists can challenge us to understand and respond to the objective contextual causes and conditions under which such terrorism can arise, be ideologically embraced, and be violently practiced, or at least not resisted, by others.

In defining terrorism and formulating Gandhi's anti-terrorism approach, we previously emphasized Gandhi's focus on intentions as essential to good will, and his rejection of utilitarianism and consequentialism. It is also an error to classify Gandhi's approach with the emphasis on intentions as Kantian or purely deontological. One must focus on both intentions and results, as seen in Gandhi's emphasis on both means and ends. Gandhi emphasizes the primacy of practice, and there is something very pragmatic about his approach to violence and terrorism. Even with the best of intentions, our experiments in truth may be failures because of unintended violent consequences. Sometime Gandhi assesses and reconsiders his own motives and intentions based on later negative consequences. In short, in understanding contextually-situated relative truths and relating them to absolute ideals, Gandhi's approach includes the importance of both intentions and consequences and how they are often dialectically and integrally connected in contextually complex and at times contradictory ways.

Our ethical and spiritual path is to move from one relative truth to another greater relative truth. One of the most arrogant and dangerous human moves is to make what is relative into an absolute. This is the move of those inflicting terrorism, whether emanating from Al Qaeda, IS and other militant Islamists, or from militants in Washington and the military-industrial complex, who act as if they possess the absolute truth, and all the others are absolutely evil. Such absolutists pose the greatest challenge to Gandhi's approach to violence, terror, and terrorism: how does one deal with others who reject the relative-absolute distinction and Gandhi's inclusivistic, tolerant approach and framework? If you adopt an exclusivistic, rigidly dichotomous approach, in which you claim to possess absolute truth and goodness and regard the other as representing total untruth and pure evil, you may have no interest in dialogue, mutual understanding, and nonviolent reconciliation. If your goal is to establish absolute truth and goodness, your intention and relevant means may be directed at destroying the others as evil. This is easily recognized in the ideological rhetoric of certain Islamic leaders and groups that meet the criteria as terrorists, but it is also true of the ideological rhetoric of Donald Trump in his election campaign and his presidential tweets and policy directives and of other violently nationalistic, anti-foreigner, white supremacist, Islamophobic, Western politicians.

How does the absolute-relative distinction guide Gandhi in approaching the most difficult cases we have cited: those challenges in which the terrorists or perpetrators of violence reject Gandhi's inclusive tolerant approach, claim that they possess the absolute truth, and are at the explosive point of inflicting terror and extreme violence? Unlike some critical interpreters, I do not think that Gandhi is rendered passive. He is not reduced to inaction, simply allowing terrorist acts to take place.

In extreme cases with no nonviolent options with any possibility of success, Gandhi suggests that we may use necessary violence in the cause of nonviolence. We act, using violent means if necessary, to prevent the terrorism, because that is the least violent, effective response possible. Consistent with other responses in his writings, Gandhi would tell us to use violent means if necessary in order, say, to stop the 9/11 terrorists, the 26/11 terrorists, or the "lone wolf" suicide bomber about to kill many innocent human beings.[23]

It is essential that we distinguish such a Gandhian response from the usual, dominant, violent actions and policies endorsed as necessary in the war on terrorism and for dealing with other forms of crime and violence. First, Gandhi would only advocate such violent means as a last resort, when preventative measures have failed and there are no remaining nonviolent alternatives. Gandhi, for example, could never support the US "doctrine of pre-emptive war," used to justify the invasion and war in Iraq and other violent policies. In such a situation—in which there were no Iraqi weapons of mass destruction, no Iraqi links with Al Qaeda or 9/11, and no evidence of an Iraqi imminent threat to the USA—Gandhi would view such a doctrine, justifying war in order to prevent some potential future threat, as an early resort, not the last resort. For Gandhi, most of the time when we resort to violence, justifying these as necessary anti-terrorism acts, there are nonviolent options and means that we have overlooked or are unwilling to consider.

Second, even in those extreme cases in which we have exhausted nonviolent options and in which we are forced to use violent means to avoid much greater terrorist violence, Gandhi's approach is radically different from usual anti-terrorism proponents of such violent means. Even when we are engaged in relative violence, we must always uphold the absolute truth, the ideal of absolute nonviolence. We must never glorify violence, even when it is necessary and we have no nonviolent relative options. When we use violence, even against real terrorism, what we do is tragic and is a terrible thing. It may be necessary, but it is not really moral. That we live in a world of violence, terror, and terrorism is an indication of human failure. That we are forced to use violence is also an indication of human failure; that we have failed to create preventive nonviolent structures, relations, and conditions free from terrorism, and to take nonviolent actions that could have avoided the need for such violent anti-terrorism. Rather than extol and celebrate such violence, we should be saddened, seek forgiveness, and work toward reconciliation.

Third, by maintaining the absolute ideal of nonviolence, we approach the use of necessary violence in reacting to terrorism with an attitude, intention, and goals informed by a commitment to nonviolence. This means that we severely limit the need for violence and restrict to a minimum the intensity and duration of such relative violence. This means that when we engage in such tragic relative violence, we then do everything possible to change the economic, political, cultural, and other conditions and human relations constituting the specific forms of terrorism to avoid the repetition of our necessary violence. This is the only way to confront extreme terror and terrorism and transform ourselves and our world toward greater nonviolence, truth, and sustainable living.

Relating to the Other

Ever since René Descartes's well-known formulation of his process of methodological doubt, resulting in the conclusion that the only thing of which he could be absolutely certain was the existence of his own ego, Western thought has increasingly focused on the primacy of the self.[24] The modern focus on the primacy of the I–me self or ego, with its focus on self-interest, individual realization, and an ideology of individualism, is reflected in our socialization, our economic system, our educational system, our legal system, our culture, and all aspects of our life. In this sense, nationalism often appeals to a kind of collective ego; the nation is ideologically presented as embodying and expressing the essence of the individual self of its citizens as distinguished from the self-essence of the others who are not part of the nation. As Descartes established, with such a focus on the primacy of one's self, one is constantly confronted with the possibilities of solipsism and various forms of self-alienation. This dominant modern Western orientation renders problematic any meaningful relations with the other. This is especially the case when the other is othered as violent, untruthful, immoral, evil, backward, terroristic, and threatening; in short, as radically opposed to our self-nature, our values, our nation, our religion, and our civilization.

In a such a dominant, modern, ego-defined self-orientation, it is a major challenge when Gandhi implores us to empathize with, understand, and serve the needs of the other. This is obviously a much greater challenge when instructed to serve the needs of those we have identified as integral to terrorism. Such a post-9/11 and post-26/11 challenge in no way negates the Gandhi-informed analysis in previous sections, such as the claim that our authentic response to terrorism involves resistance, not a kind of empathetic passive acceptance, and that, in extreme cases, it involves violent resistance to terrorist actions.

Gandhi not only disagrees with the modern focus on the primacy of the ego, but he also advocates a radical inversion of this self-other relation.[25] As with the Buddha, Gandhi maintains that the construction and focus on the primacy of one's self leads to illusion, unhappiness, selfishness and greed, violence, war, terrorism, and lack of ethical and spiritual development. Gandhi, in complete contrast to dominant Western modern orientations, proposes that we focus on the primacy of the other, by striving as much as possible to reduce our self to a state of egoless consciousness, and by directing our attention toward serving the needs of the other, including those who are terrorized and those who may commit or accept acts of terrorism.

Ever since 9/11, with the overwhelming emphasis on terror and terrorism, there has been an increasing anti-Gandhian focus on the primacy of self, with the devaluation of the other as the enemy and as evil.[26] This, of course, is true of those who planned, perpetrated, and supported the terrorism of 9/11, but it is also true of those in charge of the US led "war on terrorism."

This may at first seem to be a surprising claim. It is certainly true of certain militant Islamists directly involved in the terrorism of 9/11, but what about the neo-conservatives ("neocons") in charge of Washington's "war on terrorism"? If one reads the policy positions of those identified with the Project for a New American Century and other neoconservative policymakers in the 1990s, the same pattern emerges. We are in possession of truth and goodness, and as the world's only superpower, we have both the capacity and the moral duty to ensure that our absolute values are applied globally. Iraq comes first as we use our power, including extreme shock and awe violence, to remake Iraq in ways consistent with our model of truth and goodness. Then Iranians, Syrians, Lebanese, Palestinians, and others, in awe of our determination and capacity to use terrifying violence, will be receptive to such radical restructuring according to our need to control oil and other resources, our neoliberal economic and political values, and our other national, corporate, and cultural interests.[27]

In our attempt to remake the region and the world, you can join us and be part of the coalition of truth and goodness and progress, or you can oppose us or refuse to join us, in which case you support or tolerate terrorism and forces of evil. If you do not follow our position, you may be a short-term problem, but you are of no long-term consequence. You will become dysfunctional and eventually extinct, since our position alone defines truth, goodness, progress, prosperity, and the future.

This dominant orientation has been revised and updated since 2001 through neoliberal globalized corporate capitalism, innovative militarized and politicized technologies, and other policy reformulations. It has defined the ill-informed, arrogant, ineffective policies and relations as they have extended to Iraq, Afghanistan, Libya, Syria, and other nations, with the terroristic war on terrorism and the creation of new hotbeds of terrorism. Through it all, the basic anti-terrorist, violent and terrorist approach has not changed, as seen in the policies and priorities of the Trump administration.

Both those who planned the 9/11 terrorism and also those in charge of the US war on terrorism view the world in rigid, dichotomous, Manichean terms. We are good and the other is evil. You are either with us or you are with the enemy. For Osama bin Laden and Al Qaeda, the USA and those aligned with it are infidels, an evil enemy that must be terrorized through policies and acts of terrorism. For the neoconservatives, within the Bush administration and as part of the Project for a New American Century and other conservative think tanks shaping Washington's policies today, militant Islamists and others resisting US truth and goodness are evil, enemies that must be destroyed through violence and terrorism.[28]

This pattern has continued to the present. One can present the same pattern of positions and relations by focusing on the IS and its leader Abu Bakr al-Baghdadi and President Donald Trump. Bakr al-Baghdadi and other ISIS leaders transparently present in dichotomous black-and-white terms: we are the warriors and martyrs, defending the pure absolute truth of Islam against the American and other Western anti-Islamic infidels and their false Islamic allies as we restore the glorious Caliphate. Similarly, Donald Trump and his reactionary xenophobic populist and corporate neoliberal policymakers present in equally dichotomous black-and-white terms: we are the defenders of American exceptionalism with the unique US values of truth and goodness, and we shall use any means necessary, including extreme terrorizing violence and torture, to annihilate the terrorist forces of radical Islam that are pure evil.

In the Gandhian approach I have presented, George Bush and Osama bin Laden, Donald Trump and Abu Bakr al-Baghdadi are closer to each other than either is to Mahatma Gandhi. From Gandhi's point of view, each is sometimes the mirror image of the other. Each serves as the evil enemy and as the other necessary for one's self-definition as upholder of absolute truth and goodness. Since each refuses to recognize the limited relativity of their partial truths and refuses to privilege the real needs of the other, each becomes trapped in arrogant self-assertions and escalating cycles of ignorance, violence, and terrorism.

There should be no confusion about Gandhi's position on the immediate terrorism of 9/11 and 26/11: he would speak out unequivocally on how such terrorism is unjustified and must be opposed. But he would also maintain that refusal to understand the basic conditions, causes, and dynamics of escalating cycles of violence and terror, insistence that ends justify means, and refusal to relate to the needs of the other and the need for a long-term nonviolent preventative approach will guarantee failure in dealing with the real problems of insecurity, unsustainability, violence, terror, and terrorism.

Notes

1. A much earlier version of this chapter appeared as "Mahatma Gandhi After 9/11: Terrorism and Violence," in *Comparative Philosophy and Religion in Times of Terror*, ed. Douglas Allen (Lanham, MD: Lexington, 2006), pp. 19–39. In this chapter, I shall not provide extensive documentation from Gandhi's writings. Most of my analysis from Gandhi, such as his focus on truth (satya), violence (himsa), and nonviolence (ahimsa), can be found in the 100 volumes of CWMG (New Delhi: Publications Division, Ministry of Information and Broadcasting, Government of India, 1958–91). I attempt to provide documentation of major aspects of Gandhi's philosophy in many writings, starting with my "Philosophical Foundations of Gandhi's Legacy, Utopian Experiments, and Peace Struggles," *Gandhi Marg* 16, no. 2 (July-September 1994): 133–60; "Gandhian Perspectives on Self-Other Relations as Relevant to Human Values and Social Change Today," in *Human Values and Social Change*, Vol. I, ed. Ishwar Modi (Jaipur and New Delhi: Rawat Publications, 2000), pp. 283–309; "Gandhi, Contemporary Political Thinking, and Self-Other Relations," in *Contemporary Political Thinking*, ed. B.N. Ray (New Delhi: Kanishka Publishers, 2000),

pp. 129–70, and extending through more recent books and articles cited later in this chapter.
2. Soon after the September 11, 2001 terrorist attacks, using my knowledge of Gandhi, King, and other sources, I attempted to formulate my own definition and analysis independent of the specific recent literature on terrorism. Since 9/11, a huge literature on terrorism has emerged from different disciplines, such as political science, sociology, and security studies, as well as from governmental agencies, think tanks, and international bodies.
3. M.K. Gandhi, *The Collected Works of Mahatma Gandhi*, Vol. 5 (New Delhi: Publications Division, Ministry of Information and Broadcasting, Government of India, 1961), contains many writings from 1906 in which Gandhi expresses his view of the duty of Indians as members of the South African colony to support the British military action against the Zulu Uprising. Especially revealing are pages 281–2 ("The Natal Rebellion"), pp. 311–12 ("Indian Volunteering"), and pp. 361–2 ("Indian Volunteers"). See also pp. 134, 252, 291, 293, 353, and 373. For a detailed documentation of Gandhi's writings with regard to the Zulu Uprising and other controversial positions while he was in South Africa, see Ashwin Desai and Goolam Vahed, *The South African Gandhi: Stretcher-Bearer of Empire* (Stanford: Stanford University Press, 2015).
4. After completing my book manuscript, I came across the excellent historical narrative formulated by George Paxton, "Gandhi's Wars," *Gandhi Marg* 39, nos 2–3 (July–December 2017): 135–55. In making sense of Gandhi's developing views about war, his strengths and also some weaknesses, and his apparent inconsistencies, Paxton insightfully introduces Gandhi's complex framework of multiple changing perspectives: Gandhi's own changing personal preferences with regard to war and nonviolence and his support of the perspectives of others who may not share his views of war and nonviolence. Interestingly, this kind of framework of multiple perspectives is consistent with what I introduce in Chapter 1 under the relevance of Gandhi's approach to truth and which informs my analysis in many chapters on topics such as violence and nonviolence, terrorism, diverse approaches to the Bhagavad-Gita and *Hind Swaraj*, capitalism and socialism, modern technology and swaraj technology, and economic and environmental sustainability.
5. See Henry A. Giroux, *America's Addiction to Terrorism* (New York: Monthly Review Press, 2016). Giroux is very insightful in analyzing the violent and terrorizing impact of US and global capitalism on all areas

of life, the need for a critical pedagogy, and especially "academic terrorism" and the assault on public education and on higher education.

6. In my writings, I have emphasized these two ways that Gandhi broadens and deepens our approach to violence: the multidimensionality of violence and the violence of the status quo. I could easily include a third way: the ideological acceptance and justification of violence. Gandhi always emphasizes how we are socialized through the dominant cultural, economic, political, religious, and educational systems to accept uncritically and to provide justifications for our violence through constructed views of human nature, of "the other," of sin and evil, of means-ends rationality, of technology, of progress, and of nonhuman nature.

7. See Vinit Haksar, "*Satyagraha* and the Right to Civil Disobedience," in *The Philosophy of Mahatma Gandhi for the Twenty-First Century*, ed. Douglas Allen (Lanham, MD: Lexington Books, 2009), pp. 63–97. Haksar's analysis appears in his recently published *Gandhi and Liberalism: Satyagraha and the Conquest of Evil* (New Delhi: Routledge, 2018).

8. See, for example, *Young India*, March 18, 1926, in *CWMG* 30: 133; Ronald J. Terchek, *Gandhi: Struggling for Autonomy* (Lanham, MD: Rowman and Littlefield Publishers, 1998), pp. 111–12.

9. For many relevant citations from Gandhi's writings, see Chapter 8, "Gandhi and Socialism."

10. One can make the same observation of the need to avoid a kind of one-dimensional, simple, economic, reductionistic determinism with regard to Gandhi's own life and message. One cannot understanding Gandhi's moral and spiritual philosophy, practice, and identification with the plight of the most exploited and unfree others by reducing his orientation to his relatively privileged economic caste background as a member of the Vaishya caste, and, more particularly, as a member of the *Bania* (merchants, bankers, money-lenders, with the name "Gandhi" referring to grocers) caste grouping. In focusing on dominant economic violence, Gandhi was shaped by, but even more importantly, rejected much of the contextualized multidimensional and status quo violence and terrorism of his economic caste Hinduism. Similar anti-reductionist observations can be made with regard to how one cannot understand the Buddha and his teachings by reducing them to his background as an economically and politically privileged member of the Kshatriya (warrior) caste.

11. See, for example, "My Friend, the Revolutionary" (*Young India*, September 4, 1925), in *CWMG* 26: 486–92, with Gandhi's assertion

that "I do not regard killing or assassination or terrorism as good in any circumstances whatsoever"; "Letter to Lord Ampthill" (October 30, 1909) in *CWMG* 9: 508–10; "Speech at Plenary Session of Round Table Conference" (London, December 1, 1931), in which Gandhi addresses how "the page of history is soiled red with the blood of those who have fought for freedom" and "I hold no brief for the terrorists" or those who "would encourage terrorism" (*CWMG* 48: 356–68, especially 358–9).

In this chapter, I do not consider the most controversial case of Bhagat Singh, who is a socialist revolutionary and is hanged by the British on May 23, 1931 at the age of 23. Bhagat Singh emerges as a folk hero of the Freedom Movement for Independence, and remains to this day an honored national hero, often promoted as an anti-Gandhi heroic figure, especially admired by many Indian youth. The continuing Gandhi-Bhagat Singh controversy arises from the fact that Gandhi fails to secure the commutation of Bhagat Singh's execution sentence. Critics sometimes strongly condemn Gandhi as responsible for or complicit with the execution. Gandhi supporters, while acknowledging that Gandhi opposes Bhagat Singh's policy of violence and violent terrorism, argue that he nevertheless intervenes unsuccessfully, in attempting to save Singh's life.

12. Swaraj means "self-rule" and "independence." In *Hind Swaraj*, Gandhi gives *swaraj* two interconnected meanings: "Indian Home Rule," Gandhi's title for his English translation of the work, and individual self-rule. Highly recommended is the edition, M.K. Gandhi, *Hind Swaraj and Other Writings*, ed. Anthony J. Parel (Cambridge: Cambridge University Press, 1997) with Parel's excellent introduction.
13. For a more detailed formulation and interpretation of Gandhi's *Hind Swaraj*, see Chapter 6, "Is Gandhi's Approach to Technology Irrelevant in the Modern Age of Technology?" See especially the first section "*Hind Swaraj*: The Text and Some Historical Background," which also contains some background on Savarkar. See also Chapter 5, "Personal Reflections on Reading *Hind Swaraj* and Indian Reactions."
14. See Parel's edition of *Hind Swaraj*, pp. xiv–xviii, 77–8, 95n, 118.
15. In his *Rediscovering Gandhi* (London: Century, 1997), Yogesh Chadha devotes considerable time to reconstructing the hatching of the plot and the assassination of Gandhi and the debate over whether Savarkar was directly responsible for Godse's killing of Gandhi. There is a vast literature on the assassination of Mahatma Gandhi, including Nathuram Godse's justification of *Why I Assassinated Mahatma Gandhi* and writings by his many supporters and by those critical of his philosophy, approach, and act of assassination. There is a lively

contemporary literature debating key issues, including interpretations of why Gandhi did not allow security measures to be taken and whether he welcomed the possible assassination as a desperately needed act of transformational martyrdom. For a more recent, creative interpretation, see Makarand R. Paranjape, *The Death and Afterlife of Mahatma Gandhi* (London and New York: Routledge, 2014). There is a much wider growing literature on Savarkar, who, in many respects, has been rehabilitated and revered by the militant, Hindutva nationalists. See Chapter 6 in this book.

16. There is a crucial difference in Gandhi's attitude toward violence as distinguished from violent terrorism. Gandhi grants that some people perpetrating violence and some violent terrorists may have high ideals and show courage. In passages in which the only choice is between cowardice and courageous violence, Gandhi advocates the latter. However, he never advocates terrorism. With regard to war, where there is often a lot of bravery, Gandhi changes his view about "just war." Although he supported the British war efforts against both the Boers and the Zulus in South Africa, he later rejects any view of a just war, starting with the end of World War I.

17. There are numerous formulations throughout Gandhi's writings on the relations of cowardice, violence, and nonviolence. See, for example, "The Doctrine of the Sword" (*Young India*, August 11, 1920) in *CWMG* 18: 131–4; "Hindu-Muslim Tension: Its Cause and Cure" (*Young India*, May 29, 1924) in *CWMG* 24: 140–2; "Has Non-Violence Limits?" (*Young India*, August 1, 1926) in *CWMG* 31: 292; "Non-Violence v. Cowardice" (*Young India*, October 10, 1929) in *CWMG* 42: 73. Although one can appreciate Gandhi's reaction against cowards who only pretend to be nonviolent and one can understand why he thinks that the brave proponents of violence are closer to his courageous satyagrahis, some of his advice is troubling. In some cases, I would prefer the inactive and perhaps even cowardly person to the brave person, incapable of courageous nonviolence, who is advised by Gandhi to exert violent force, especially when this results in the death and suffering of many innocent human beings. My only defense of Gandhi in such passages is that he certainly knows that history is full of brave and violent people who have caused great suffering and that he must be assuming an unacknowledged moral and spiritual approach and framework. In other words, the brave violent person, while not at the ethical and spiritual level of the truly nonviolent person, will only use violent force consistent with ethical and social dharma and other positive values.

18. The Doctrine of Dependent Origination (*pratitya-samutpada*, Pali *paticca-samuppada*), also known as Conditioned Genesis, found in *Samyutta-nikaya* xxii. 90, appears in many translations, including Sarvepalli Radhakrishnan and Charles A. Moore, eds, *A Source Book in Indian Philosophy* (Princeton: Princeton University Press, 1957), pp. 278–9. See also the translation of Dependent Origination, found in *Visuddhi-magga* xvii, in Radhakrishnan and Moore, eds, *A Source Book in Indian Philosophy*, pp. 279–80.

19. Here and in so many other ways, it is important to note that Gandhi, while deeply influenced by Hindu, Buddhist, and Jain approaches and analysis, is not a "traditional" Hindu or Indian. He is an original, creative thinker who often rejects dominant, traditional, Indian approaches and reconstitutes positions in new ways. To use the present illustration, Gandhi accepts the rather traditional Indian approach of viewing the *karmic* world of illusion in terms of causally-connected relations of ignorance, violence, bondage, and suffering. However, unlike the approach of much of traditional Indian philosophy that views worldly existence as imprisonment in vicious causal cycles and has the spiritual goal of freeing oneself from such worldly involvement, Gandhi places a much higher value on our human relations in this world. An essential part of his moral and spiritual path is the transformation, rather than the transcendence of such violent human relations. See Chapter 3 for an analysis of this as applied to the question of whether Gandhi is a Vedantist.

20. I develop this analysis at length in "Mahatma Gandhi's Philosophy of Violence, Nonviolence, and Education," in *The Philosophy of Mahatma Gandhi for the Twenty-First Century*, ed. Douglas Allen (Lanham, MD: Lexington, 2008), pp. 33–62.

21. Although Gandhi's distinction of relative and absolute truth resembles classical formulations of the "doctrine of two truths" found in Indian philosophy, Gandhi's approach is significantly different from that found in Shankara's Advaita Vedanta or Nagarjuna's Madhyamika Buddhism. For the difference in Gandhi's approach to relative and absolute truth, see the analysis in Chapter 3.

22. See Chapters 2 and 3 for a more developed analysis of the complex relations between relative truth and absolute truth in Gandhi's approach.

23. In several previous publications, I formulate such an interpretation of Gandhi's approach, consistent with his description of himself as a "practical idealist." In such an interpretation, Gandhi recognizes and struggles with the specificity and complexity of relative contextual situations, and he is much more nuanced, flexible, and relevant than some

uncompromising, rigid, "pure," absolute Mahatma. See "Gandhi's Challenge to the Paradigm of Justifiable Violence," pp. 13–26, in Bart Gruzalski, *On Gandhi*, by Bart Gruzalski (Belmont, CA: Wadsworth, 2001), pp. 13–26.

24. See René Descartes, *Meditations on First Philosophy* (Cambridge and New York: Cambridge University Press, 1986). For a more developed formulation of Descartes's orientation, as well as alternative non-Cartesian perspectives, see Douglas Allen, "Social Constructions of Self: Some Asian, Marxist, and Feminist Critiques of Dominant Western Views of Self," in *Culture and Self: Philosophical and Religious Perspectives, East and West*, ed. Douglas Allen (Boulder, CO: Westview Press/Harper Collins, 1997), pp. 3–26.

25. For a much more detailed treatment of Gandhi's analysis of self and self-other relations, see Allen, "Gandhi, Contemporary Political Thinking, and Self-Other Relations," pp. 129–70, especially "Self-Other Relations: A Radical Inversion," pp. 152–7, and "Key Questions Regarding the Self and Self-Other Relations," pp. 157–65. Gandhi usually endorses a dynamic, social, relational view of self in which there is no ethical and spiritual self without the other, and the other is an integral part of who I am as self. However, there are other writings in which Gandhi emphasizes "the inner voice" of an autonomous, nonsocial, individual self that is distinguished from and contrasted with any relational other. There are still other writings in which Gandhi accepts a deeper, ultimate, metaphysical, spiritual self (or Self), often identified with the Hindu, Upanishadic, nondualistic Atman, but also capable of other formulations in Gandhi's inclusivistic approach. These self and self-other formulations are often complementary, but they also express ambiguities, tensions, contradictions, and unresolved philosophical problems and issues. In Chapter 3, I developed more analysis of Gandhi's diverse, complementary, and perhaps contradictory approaches to self and self-other relations.

26. In this brief concluding section on relating to the other, I will present my formulation through the illustration of anti-American terrorism and the US war on terrorism. Similar points could be made by focusing on major terrorist and ideologically justified anti-terrorist terrorist forces and policies within and between India and Pakistan.

27. It would be a mistake, based on my examples, to conclude that the values, formulations, and justifications of US terror and terrorism are restricted to conservative (neoconservative) positions. There is a long history of US "liberal" politicians and economic elite, going back long before the Vietnam/Indochina War of terrorism, who have embraced

terror and terrorism in achieving their goals. President Bill Clinton and his administration in the 1990s put into practice many domestic and international policies using terror and terrorism. More recently, as secretary of state under President Obama and as presidential candidate for the Democrat Party in 2016, Hillary Clinton identified with Wall Street interests, was an aggressive militaristic hawk, and advocated many priorities and policies of US terror and terrorism.
28. See "Gandhi and Osama bin Laden: Is a Dialogue Possible?" in Bhikhu Parekh, *Debating India: Essays on Indian Political Discourse*, ed. Bhikhu Parekh (New Delhi: Oxford University Press, 2015), pp. 270–91.

8

Gandhi and Socialism

During the Indian movement for independence from British colonial rule, the term "socialism" is commonplace. Indian leaders often identify themselves as socialists.[1] More precisely, many Indian nationalist leaders increasingly identify themselves as socialists starting in the 1920s. They identify with a wide range of diverse socialist positions, from reformist to revolutionary, and some leaders identify themselves with communist, Marxist, and atheist positions. In the last decades of his life, Gandhi often engages in dialogue with J.P. Narayan, M.N. Roy, Rammanohar Lohia, Nehru, and other leaders, as they are sometimes influenced by Gandhi and change their positions and as Gandhi himself changes his positions. Indeed, consistent with my interpretation found throughout this book, I submit that the Gandhi, in the last period of his life, develops his deepest understanding and his most consistent revolutionary theory and practice with regard to socialism, capitalism, class, caste, trusteeship, nonviolence, and sustainability.

The most influential leader of the Indian freedom movement, Gandhi, often identifies himself as a socialist, and his followers often identify themselves as Gandhian socialists. Major Indian thinkers and activists, such as Rammanohar Lohia and Jayaprakash Narayan, are part of this rich, dynamic, and innovative tradition of Gandhian socialism. Jawaharlal Nehru, the second most influential person in the freedom movement and the dominant figure after Independence, is a committed socialist who serves as the first prime minister of India from 1947 until his death in 1964. Strongly influenced by a non-Gandhian Fabian socialism and other modern, Western formulations of socialism, Nehru embraces a rather pragmatic, flexible, and open-ended view of a secular, democratic, humanistic, and socialist India.

All of this has changed. Especially in recent decades, with the domination of financial capitalist institutions and big corporate capitalism, the growing world of information technology and globalization, and the emergence of India as a rapidly growing economic power, socialist discourse and identifications have receded or disappeared. It is impossible today to name Indian socialist figures comparable in creativity and influence to earlier luminaries. Does this mean that Indian socialism, including Gandhian socialism, is dead—at best an interesting ossified relic from past history?[2]

The challenge for those who believe that Gandhi's philosophy and practice are not only relevant, but also desperately needed in the contemporary world is to examine the relationship between Gandhi and socialism and to ask what Gandhian socialism might mean today. It is not very helpful to deify or dogmatize Gandhi, as have some rigid, conservative, reactionary devotees. One then repeatedly proclaims and upholds a view that Gandhi would oppose contemporary state–monopoly–military–corporate capitalism, oppose contemporary globalization, oppose contemporary industrialization, and so forth. This may be correct, but we are left with a nonhistorical, non-dialectical, largely irrelevant Gandhi for the contemporary world.

It is also not very helpful simply to proclaim Gandhian socialist slogans or quote Gandhian socialist passages without deeper analysis and explorations of tensions and contradictions in Gandhi's views and their contemporary development and contextual applications. Such slogans and quotations may be accurate in expressing what Gandhi writes, and they often sound revolutionary. However, we are left with a Gandhi, who may be ethically and spiritually admirable, but who is largely abstracted from the historically contextual world within which he struggled and developed his formulations, and we are left with an oversimplified and idealized Gandhi, who is of limited contemporary relevance for engaged practice.

Throughout this book, I have emphasized the integral dialectical relation between Gandhi's philosophy/theory and practice, with his primary focus on engaged practice. It would be necessary to provide a more developed historical narrative for a broader and deeper understanding of how Gandhi developed his dynamic, open-ended, contextually informed philosophical, ethical, economic, social, nonviolent, sustainable, socialist practices. Such a historical narrative is necessary for a fuller understanding of Gandhi's formulations, interpretations, and applications of *Hind Swaraj*, the Bhagavad-Gita, Vedanta, and other topics presented in previous chapters. Especially in this chapter, historical narrative is necessary for a fuller understanding of other formulations of Indian and Western socialism, including their rise and decline, Gandhi's relation to other socialisms and his specific Gandhian features, as well as the post-Gandhi historical contexts that provide the basis for new Gandhi-informed capitalist and socialist reformulations.

In short, one cannot sufficiently understand Gandhi and socialism by focusing exclusively on his philosophy with its abstracted essentialized views of Truth and Nonviolence or by focusing exclusively on his writings. One must include the primacy of Gandhi's engaged *praxis* by including the historical and contextual world that shaped Gandhi and that he shaped through his economic, cultural, religious, educational, and other constructive work and his changing satyagraha and other experiments in truth, nonviolence, and sustainable living throughout his life.[3]

The important challenge in this chapter is to examine Gandhi's writings on socialism and then to determine whether an orientation that embraces Gandhi's basic philosophical and ethical principles, commitments, and practices commits one to some version of Gandhian socialism that is significant and relevant today. After the first section clarifying different forms and meanings of "socialism," the second section presents passages in which Gandhi clearly identifies himself as a socialist and even at times as a communist. In the third section, "Confusion about Gandhi and Socialism," we see that such a simple identification may be misleading, and we examine three reasons for confusion regarding Gandhi's relation to socialism. In the fourth section, we examine "Gandhi's Writings on Socialism" in terms of five general topics. In the fifth, more developed section, "Characteristics of Gandhian Socialism," we delineate and analyze a view of socialism that emerges from Gandhi's writings. In the sixth and seventh sections, "Weaknesses and Confusion" and "Strengths: What Socialists Can Learn from Gandhian Socialism," we analyze in some detail weaknesses and strengths of such a view of Gandhian socialism. In the concluding section, "Gandhian Socialism Today," we examine and assess some of the relevance of such a view of socialism for the contemporary world.[4]

Socialism

In analyzing Gandhi's identification of himself as a socialist and the development of Gandhi-informed socialism, we must recognize that "socialism" is a very broad term that takes numerous forms with many meanings. Diverse forms emphasize economic, social, cultural, ethical, religious or spiritual, and/or environmental dimensions of human existence and reality. For example, for thousands of years, one finds cultural and religious formulations of socialism, often expressing ideal or utopian perspectives and often with transcendent supernatural views of reality. Some forms of socialism, emphasizing economic and historical analysis, regard such religious socialisms as imaginary escapisms and as obstacles to creating real socialist transformations in this world. Conversely, some forms of religious socialism regard such economic and historical formulations as limited, illusory, and always lacking the spiritual sacred foundation of true socialism.

Some forms of socialism are grounded in the modern, Western, Enlightenment, rational, scientific project, while others reject this orientation; some emphasize centralization, while others emphasize decentralization; some emphasize particular grassroots localism, others, nationalism, and still others, universal internationalism; some emphasize nonviolence, while others uphold the need for revolutionary violence; some present a gradual, evolutionary, reformist socialist project within capitalism, while others uphold the need for the qualitatively different, revolutionary overthrow of capitalism. In terms of these and other characteristics of diversity of different socialisms, how do we situate Gandhi and a Gandhi-informed socialism?

In terms of the most admired figures in the world, including the modern West, it is often not acknowledged how many of them identify themselves as socialists. The leading figure, of course, is Mahatma Gandhi. Another example is Albert Einstein, who writes essays on why he is a socialist.[5]

To provide a recent example, in the 2016 US presidential campaign, Bernie Sanders emerges as the most admired and most popular politician. Remarkably, in light of the control of US politics by wealthy capitalists and corporate capitalist interests and the US history in which identifying oneself as socialist frequently meant the destruction of one's life and political career, Bernie Sanders repeatedly identifies himself as a "democratic socialist." This does not have a negative impact on his surprisingly effective campaign and continuing widespread popularity.[6]

The relations between different forms of socialism and Marxism are complex, sometimes complementary, and usually contradictory. Karl Marx usually avoids the term socialism, probably because he rejects other influential thinkers who identify their philosophies as socialist. While Marx formulates the post-capitalist transitional stage as "lower-stage (undeveloped) communism," Engels, in his influential "Socialism: Utopian and Scientific," identifies this as "scientific (or true) socialism." In several writings, Marx and Engels also use the terms socialism and communism interchangeably. It is Lenin who most establishes the meaning of socialism as the transitional stage between capitalism and communism. In this sense, the wide variety of most Marxist philosophies and parties are socialist, in that they analyze the current anti-capitalist struggle as socialist in nature. However, the wide variety of diverse socialist philosophies and parties–institutionalized socialist parties in capitalist states, "democratic socialists," "market socialists," utopian socialists, Gandhian socialists, and so on—are not Marxist and are usually anti-Marxist.

In understanding different forms of socialism in general and Gandhi's socialism in particular, one needs to contextualize these formulations in analyzing their meaning and assessing their significance for the contemporary world. What are the contextual settings, variables, and influences that allow us to understand Gandhi's critiques of capitalism and his formulations of socialism? In terms of the open-ended, dynamic, contextual nature of capitalism and socialism in the post-Gandhi contemporary world, what are Gandhi's insightful critiques and constructive insights and practices, and what is the potential for a Gandhi-informed socialism today?

Consider the central contradiction in capitalism, as formulated by Marx and Engels, and how socialism is theoretically the response to overcoming this contradiction. Any developed economic system, including many thousands of years of pre-capitalism, has a mode of production with class relations. These express the dominant relations of the ruling class who control the means of production (slave owners, feudal land owners, and so on), and the subordinate relations of the working class (slaves, peasant serfs, and so on). Capitalism originates and develops as a modern, post-feudal, economic system, with its capitalist mode of production organized to produce surplus value through the production of commodities that can be exchanged for profit, and increase the accumulation of capital. In most general, asymmetrical, class relational terms, the ruling class under capitalism consists of the propertied capitalists, those who own and control the means of production as capital, and the lower class, the working class of wage-laborers, who create surplus value, but do not own or control the means of production and must sell their labor-power to the capitalists for a wage.

Therefore, the central contradiction in capitalism, which according to Marx is historically and economically grounded and is not some decontextualized imaginary abstraction, is between social production and private and individual ownership, control, and appropriation. In class terms, the social producers are the wage-laborers, the working class, and the individual and private owners and appropriators are the capitalists of the ruling class. This theoretical formulation of this contradiction has explanatory value in analyzing class exploitation, increasing commodification and capitalization of all of life, dehumanization, alienation, growing centralization of wealth and power with growing inequality, and a system based on increasing capital and profit and not on meeting real human needs. Socialism is the response to overcoming this central contradiction and bringing the mode of social control and appropriation in line with the mode of social production.

We have devoted some time to this contradiction because it is instructive in analyzing Gandhi's socialism. As will be seen in the following sections, Gandhi, for the most part, accepts this analysis of the central contradiction in capitalism and the socialist response, but he is not always consistent in this regard in his approach to capitalism, capital, capitalists, labor, and socialism.

Gandhi as Socialist

Did Gandhi consider himself a socialist? This may appear to be an odd or unnecessary question since Gandhi repeatedly identifies himself as a socialist. Indeed, one Gandhi publication is entitled *My Socialism*.[7] Gandhi's personal assertions about his identification as a socialist and even as a communist and his thoughts and feelings about socialism and capitalism are often dramatic, and shed light on his personality, values, ethical and spiritual principles, and engaged practice.

Gandhi asserts: "I have claimed that I was a socialist long before those I know in India had avowed their creed. But my socialism was natural to me and not adopted from any books. It came out of my unshakable belief in non-violence."[8] In a publication late in his life, Gandhi tells us that for him "socialism is a beautiful word and so far as I am aware in socialism all the members of society are equal—none low, none high." Consistent with his basic egalitarian principles of truth, nonviolence, and the interconnectedness of reality, Gandhi goes on to submit that in his socialism, in which everyone is "on the same level," there is a basic unity that overcomes the dualities we find in the world. Such a "pure" socialism cannot be achieved by impure and untruthful means. "Therefore, only truthful, non-violent and pure-hearted socialists will be able to establish a socialistic society in India and in the world."[9]

Although he uses the term "communism" less frequently, Gandhi sometimes relates his socialism to communism and identifies himself as a communist. "I call myself a communist also.... My communism is not very different from socialism. It is a harmonious blending of the two. Communism as I have understood is a naturally corollary of socialism."[10]

In a very dramatic, but also puzzling formulation, Gandhi writes: "I am not ashamed to own that many capitalists are friendly toward me and do not fear me. They know that I desire to end capitalism, almost, if not quite, as much as the most advanced Socialist or even Communist. But our methods differ, our languages differ."[11] In an earlier, similarly puzzling formulation regarding trusteeship, Gandhi writes: "By the non-violent method, we seek not to destroy the capitalist, we seek to destroy capitalism."[12]

From the above citations and numerous other passages, it is clear that Gandhi repeatedly identifies himself as a socialist and considers this an early, "natural" commitment on his part. It is also clear that his writings significantly change until we find Gandhi's position in writings during the last years of his life, what one might call "the mature Gandhi," as a more developed socialist. This late Gandhi writing increasingly begins to attack capitalism and emphasizes the need to destroy capitalism with its inherent evils.

Given this, what is puzzling is why leading Indian capitalists are not only friendly to Gandhi, but also give him financial and other support. There is a wide range of reasons that can be given for this. On the one hand, there are explanations that Gandhi inspires and touches the hearts and souls of many wealthy Indians, who genuinely admire Gandhi and his ethical and spiritual principles and struggles. On the other hand, there are explanations that Gandhi and his engaged socialist experimental practices were perceived as posing no threat to these capitalists, that they could use his successes against British colonialism and premodern communalism for their own Indian capitalist interests, and that they could "support" Gandhi while carrying on their own capitalist objectives.

What is more interesting and puzzling in terms of this chapter is that Gandhi's simple identification with socialism is not as simple as the Gandhi quotations given above might lead one to believe. As we shall see, many of Gandhi's writings about capitalism and socialism are complex, at time contradictory, puzzling, and confusing. We must examine these passages in order to clarify the relation of Gandhi and socialism, including the nature of Gandhi's socialism, its strengths and weaknesses.

Confusion about Gandhi and Socialism

There are many reasons for the confusion about Gandhi and socialism. We shall briefly consider three of the major reasons that have contributed to this confusion.

First, as I have analyzed in Chapter 4 and other chapters in this book, there is the issue of the complex, dynamic relations that hold between texts, contexts, and interpretations. We are concerned with texts by Gandhi and others that are relevant to Gandhi and socialism; the linguistic, historical, economic, and cultural contexts within which Gandhi and others formulate their views and practices; and how Gandhi and others interpret the nature, meaning, and significance of these contextualized texts and practices. For us, every reading of a Gandhi text on socialism, every interpretation, and every formulation is always to some extent a new reading, a new interpretation, and a new formulation, and these are at least partially filtered through our own contextualized horizon of meaning.

In such a hermeneutical approach, our interpretations involve the dynamic process of attempting to fuse or relate two horizons of meaning: that of the contextualized socialist textual formulations and socialist practices of Gandhi and our own, often very different, contextualized textual understandings and formulations of socialist theories and engaged experiments. This means that there is not one, static, correct, essential, and absolute Gandhi view of socialism or of Gandhian socialism. We are always engaged in an open-ended, developing process in which different Gandhian, anti-Gandhian, and non-Gandhian readings and interpretations will present a wide variety of views of Gandhi and socialism, based, at least partially, on different cultural and contextual factors, different methodological assumptions, different principles of selectivity of relevant data and of what is significant, and other historical contextual variables. This unavoidable contingency need not commit us to some completely facile relativism and subjectivism in which anything goes and no interpretation is any better than any other. In interpreting and applying a view of Gandhi and socialism, one must examine the Gandhi texts and practices carefully, be concerned with such criteria as consistency and adequacy, and provide analysis of how Gandhi's views and engaged practices can evolve so that they become relevant and significant when applied to our contemporary world.

Second, as Gandhi informs us, he has left us with no "ism," no Gandhism. What Gandhi offers is an ideal, a vision, a philosophy grounded in principles of truth and nonviolence and sustainable living, along with relative imperfect practical experiments attempting to realize those ideals. But he does not leave us with any formula or any certain way to apply these ideal principles to capitalism, socialism, and other contemporary concerns.[13] Instead, consistent with the title of his autobiography and the way he views his own life, Gandhi left us with "experiments with truth."[14] Even an exemplary ethical and spiritual human being like Gandhi repeatedly confesses in his writings to failed experiments with truth, even "Himalayan blunders." What could one expect of his lesser followers, but a lot of disagreements and confusion? Even his immediate followers, who identify themselves as committed Gandhians, have no clear, agreed upon path to follow, develop so many different constructions of the Mahatma and the preferred Gandhian approach, and formulate so many confused, inadequate, and contradictory views and practices of Gandhian socialism.

Third, and most significant for this chapter, Gandhi himself adds to this confusion. As we will see in the following section, he repeatedly identifies himself as a socialist, but he does not formulate a clear, consistent position on socialism and capitalism. Many of his formulations are strong, clear, and profound, but others are uncritical, undeveloped, contradictory, muddled, and in need of radical revision. Much of the problem with his undeveloped and uncritical formulations of capitalism and socialism can be attributed to the fact that Gandhi has very limited interest in intellectual debates and in developed, critical, intellectual analysis. Throughout his life, his experiments with truth are practical, and his primary concern is moral. When asked about his philosophy, he responds that his life is his message. He wants to be a good human being who lives a moral and spiritual life. This is key to his incredible strengths, but also to some of his confused formulations and limitations.

Gandhi's Writings on Socialism

There are numerous passages by Gandhi on socialism, and I will subsume many of these writings under five general topics: the ancient and Asian roots of Gandhi's socialism; his identification with labor; his emphasis on nonpossession and trusteeship; his striking assertions about capitalists, capital, and labor; and passages where he rejects socialism. Gandhi's relevant views about truth, nonviolence, satyagraha, and other topics will be saved for later sections.

Although he expresses admiration for much of the spirit of Western socialism, Gandhi characteristically reminds his Indian audience that the West does not have all of the answers. He submits that "Real Socialism has been handed down to us by our ancestors" and that a critical study of "our Eastern institutions" will allow us to "evolve a truer socialism and a truer communism."[15] Gandhi often relates his socialist principles to the Bhagavad-Gita and other ancient, Indian sacred texts. Gandhi submits: "Socialism was not born with the discovery of the misuse of capital by capitalists. As I have contended, socialism, even communism, is explicit in the first verse of *Ishopanishad*."[16]

It is certainly the case that there are numerous, significant examples of premodern socialism and communism, as seen in various formulations of "utopian socialism" and "utopian communism," in various religious and spiritual texts and in experimental intentional communities. This is how one may approach the Buddha's values, principles, and practices in organizing the intentional communities of the *sangha* (Buddhist monastic order). The key question facing Gandhi and Gandhians is whether such ancient and premodern socialist formulations can be reformulated in ways that are relevant to the contemporary economic, political, and cultural world.

Throughout his writings, Gandhi clearly identifies with labor, especially the labor of the masses impoverished, dominated, exploited, and oppressed by big feudal landowners, modern capitalists, and others with wealth and power. Simply to summarize, the following are among Gandhi's key assertions on labor: true capital is our physical and mental labor, not gold, silver, or money. Labor is capital, and pure labor is against exploitation. No one should want anything that others cannot have with equal labor. No one should have more land than is needed for dignified sustenance. Labor that is educated and organized can dictate its own terms, and if labor develops its own internal strengths, then exploitation will be impossible.[17] From these and similar statements, one could easily conclude that Gandhi is a strong, determined opponent of capitalism. However, we shall consider other statements that complicate the issue and may produce confusion about Gandhi's position.

Many of Gandhi's strongest statements relevant to capitalism and socialism focus on his commitment to aparigraha, or nonpossession. These statements often express his opposition to private property. For example, after confessing that he has limited understanding of Bolshevism, Gandhi writes: "All that I know is that it aims at the abolition of private property. This is only an application of the ethical ideal of nonpossession in the realm of economics and if the people adopted this ideal of their own accord or could be made to accept it by means of peaceful persuasion, there would be nothing like it."[18] Capitalism is an economic system of private property relations in the form of capital. If Gandhi were so committed to the abolition of private property, it would seem to follow that he would be committed to the abolition of capitalism.

Relevant here are Gandhi's formulations of the controversial doctrine of "trusteeship," which he often presents as an alternative to class struggle and other violent means for abolishing private property and capitalism. For example, Gandhi proposes: "Trusteeship provides a means of transforming the present capitalist order of society into an egalitarian one. It gives no quarter to capitalism, but gives the present owning class a chance of reforming itself." Trusteeship "does not recognize any right of private ownership of property except so far as it may be permitted by society for its own welfare."[19]

Gandhi's writings also reveal many controversial and confusing formulations about labor, capital, and capitalism. For now, we may simply note a few examples. Gandhi tells us that he has always said that his "ideal is that capital and labour should supplement and help each other. They should be a great family living in unity and harmony, capital not only looking to the material welfare of the labourers, but their moral welfare also—capitalists being trustees for the welfare of the labouring classes under them."[20] Gandhi tells us: "I do not fight shy of capital. I fight capitalism." But, unlike Karl Marx, Gandhi then asserts: "Capital and labour need not be antagonistic to each other."[21] In many other passages, Gandhi writes that capital and labor need each other, that capital will always be with us and that he is against capitalism but not against capital or capitalists. These assertions will be analyzed later under weaknesses in Gandhi's position.

Finally, it is important to note that there are many passages in which Gandhi rejects socialism. Although Gandhi is not a rigorous systematic thinker deeply concerned with possible inconsistencies, we can usually remove the apparent inconsistencies between these passages rejecting socialism and Gandhi's frequent identification with socialism. In almost all cases where Gandhi rejects socialism, he identifies "socialism" with modern, Western, materialistic, violent forms of socialism. We may note four major reasons for this rejection. First, in the overwhelming majority of cases, Gandhi rejects such socialism on the basis of his well-known, integral means-ends analysis and how one cannot use violent impure means in order to achieve noble ends.[22] Second, as part of his commitment to decentralization and a minimal state, Gandhi rejects the modern formulations of a centralized state socialism.[23] Third, and often related to his critique of centralized state power, Gandhi rejects an elite, top-down, socialist model of power and embraces a village-based, grassroots, decentralized, self-sustaining, democratic, socialist model of power. He supports a nonviolent revolution from the bottom up. Fourth, Gandhi strongly argues for the ideal of a classless society, but he is against class conflict, class struggle, and class warfare that are part of various Western socialist approaches.[24]

Characteristics of Gandhian Socialism

Raghavan Iyer provides a very impressive formulation of some of the major characteristics of Gandhi's view of socialism:

> When Gandhi advocated non-violent socialism as a wider political and social ideal [wider than his *ashram* experiments], rooted in the philosophy of *yajna* or sacrificial action, *aparigraha* or non-possession and responsible trusteeship, and *sarvodaya* or universal uplift, with a primary emphasis upon the emancipation of the least favoured in society, he could never look to the State as the chief instrument for furthering the socialist ideal. Rather, the masses should be enlightened by the exemplary leadership of the morally committed.[25]

What follows is a delineation of several of the major characteristics of Gandhian socialism that emerges from Gandhi's writings. These key characteristics will be presented with limited analysis.

First, and most important, Gandhi claims that his two major principles, Truth and Nonviolence, are at the foundation of his view of socialism. Since everything significant in Gandhi's philosophy, ethics, and spirituality unfolds from his understanding of these two principles and especially how they may be realized imperfectly through action-oriented practice, it is not surprising that he asserts that true or pure socialism must embody truth and nonviolence. Indeed, this chapter could be entitled "Gandhi's View of Truth, Nonviolence, and Socialism."

Only nonviolence, not violence, can lead to socialism. Only truth, not untruth, can lead to socialism. As Gandhi repeatedly tells us, he uses truth and nonviolence interchangeably. Usually, nonviolence is the means for attaining truth, but truth is also the means for attaining nonviolence. Since Gandhi offers this as essential to his ideal, universal, means-ends analysis, socialism, with its socialistic means and socialistic ends, would illustrate and embody his general formulations. Only nonviolent and truthful socialistic means can lead to the end of a nonviolent, truthful, sustainable socialistic society.

To provide only a few citations, Gandhi claims: "Truth and *ahimsa* must incarnate in socialism." To do this, the socialist "must have a living faith in God. Mere mechanical adherence to truth and *ahimsa* is likely to break down at the critical moment. Hence I have said that Truth is God." Gandhi continues: "This God is a living Force. Our life is that Force." This force resides in us but cannot be reduced to some physical or bodily force. The socialist who denies the existence of this great force denies to oneself "the use of that inexhaustible Power and thus remains impotent."[26]

Note Gandhi's characteristic attempt at inclusiveness. As he frequently does, he offers the more inclusive "Truth is God," rather than his earlier "God is Truth." Truth, as the primary principle of Reality, may be "God" to various religious believers but may be experienced differently by atheists and others equally concerned with truth and morality. Similarly, just as he defines Truth as a Power or Force in different formulations, Gandhi presents "God" in inclusivistic terms as a great force and inexhaustible power. In such a way, a humanistic ethical socialist, who may reject traditional religion, may be able to embrace such a formulation.

Truth and nonviolence are at the heart of Gandhi's formulations on the means for realizing socialism.

One cannot reach truth by untruthfulness. Truthful conduct alone can reach truth. Are not non-violence and truth twins? The answer is an emphatic "no." Non-violence is embedded in truth and *vice versa*. Hence has it been said that they are faces of the same coin. Either is inseparable from the other. Read the coin either way. The spelling of words will be different. The value is the same.[27]

If one has mental or bodily impurity and an impure heart, one has untruth and violence in oneself and cannot attain true socialism. "Therefore, only truthful, non-violent and pure-hearted socialists will be able to establish a socialistic society in India and the world. To my knowledge there is no country in the world which is purely socialistic. Without the means described above, the existence of such a society is impossible."[28]

Second, and next most important, is Gandhi's claim that satyagraha (truth-force, soul-force), the means for expressing truth and nonviolence, is the only means for realizing socialism. Sometimes, satyagraha refers to the narrower meaning of Gandhi's method of nonviolent civil disobedience. However, here and elsewhere, Gandhi is using satyagraha to refer to truth-force with a broad method, the only method that can bring about moral, psychological, economic, social, political, cultural, sustainable socialist transformation. "This I do assert that every worthy object can be achieved through *Satyagraha*. It is the highest and the most potent means, the most effective weapon. I am convinced that socialism will not be reached by any other means. *Satyagraha* can rid society of all evils, political, economic and moral."[29]

Third, as previously indicated, Gandhi primarily identifies with impoverished and exploited labor, and swaraj, or the freedom and self-determination of labor, is key to his socialist commitment. What can be added are Gandhi's strong views about the potential and the complicity of labor. Labor has all kinds of resources, and capital is helpless without labor. Educated, organized, determined, and active, labor can say "no" to its exploitation and can determine its own destiny. Why does it not do this? The masses are their own worst enemy.

Under the hypnotic spell of capital, with capitalists using the desire of labor for capital, labor does not realize its own strength and is complicit in its own oppression and exploitation.[30]

Gandhi's approach here is identical with his analysis of why Hindus and other Indians should blame themselves and not the British for their lack of swaraj, freedom, and self-rule under British colonialism. Gandhi repeatedly admonishes Indians that it is only because they are weak, lack courage, and are complicit in their own condition that the British are able to maintain unjust colonial domination.[31]

Many of Gandhi's similar formulations, that seem to blame the victims of exploitation and oppression for their own condition, can be very controversial. On the one hand, there is the admirable effort by Gandhi to challenge the usual sense of passivity and powerlessness by workers, lower castes, women, colonized Indians, and other victims, so that they become active, self-determining subjects in challenging and transforming their situation. On the other hand, Gandhi's language is often similar to that of the "victim blaming" today, used by the privileged, and perpetrators of imperialism, globalization, classism, sexism, and racism to deflect attention away from and to justify ideologically their exploitation and domination. Thus, it is claimed that we have a hierarchical merit-based system in which the poor have only themselves to blame for their poverty, laziness, lack of skill, depression, addictions, and so on. Some of Gandhi's most objectionable, really anti-Gandhian victim-blaming formulations are blatantly patriarchal and violently sexist, as when he blames the rape victim, claiming that her being raped is an expression and result of her impurity. Fortunately, Gandhi usually revises and rejects such earlier victim-blaming formulations that are insensitive, backward, ignorant, violent, and immoral and antithetical to any developed Gandhi-informed socialism today.

Fourth, throughout his writings on morality, economics, politics, and spirituality, Gandhi focuses on our false ego-constructions and ego-attachments, our endless ego-generated needs and greed, and the illusory and disastrous consequences of ego-defined relations for our self, other human beings, all sentient beings, and nature. This, of course, is an orientation that is central in most of Hinduism, Jainism, and Buddhism. In numerous formulations, Gandhi maintains that it is our ego-structured, ego-driven, and ego-attached experiences and relations that give rise to hatred, anger, lust, and violence; that give rise to the ignorance and illusions that prevent us from realizing the deeper ethical and spiritual Self, Truth, God, and the unifying interrelatedness of all of life. Gandhi asserts that his goal is to reduce his ego-self to "zero." As was analyzed in Chapter 4, Gandhi was drawn to his favorite text, the Bhagavad-Gita, and especially to its action-oriented path of karma-yoga that emphasizes the need to act, fulfilling one's dharma, in a selfless manner with no ego-attachment to the results of one's action.

For Gandhi, if individuals are ego-driven, motivated by greed and attached to wealth, private property, possessions, and power, as they are in capitalism, then true socialism is impossible. The ideal of pure or true socialism for Gandhi is a way of socially, politically, economically, and culturally weakening attachment to ego, transcending the illusions of ego, and nonviolently and truthfully realizing the unity of reality.

This commitment to a selfless service, "sacrificing" one's ego, and working for the welfare of all, especially the most disadvantaged, are integral features of Gandhi's vision of socialism. Such a commitment is integrally connected with Gandhi's emphasis on nonpossession, trusteeship, decentralization, egalitarianism, sustainable living, and other characteristics of Gandhian socialism.

Fifth, in his socialist vision, Gandhi is very concerned with accumulation of private property and wealth and the need to abolish the inequalities that result in the existence of millions of "have-nots" dominated by a small minority of "haves." Economic equality "is the master key to non-violent independence. Working for economic equality means abolishing the eternal conflict between capital and labour." This "means the levelling down of the few rich in whose hands is concentrated the bulk of the nation's wealth on the one hand, and the levelling up of the semi-starved naked millions on the other." A nonviolent government and society are impossible so long as glaring inequality between rich and poor persists. A "violent and bloody revolution is a certainty one day unless there is a voluntary abdication of riches and the power that riches give and sharing them for the common good."[32]

Gandhi offers many strong condemnations of the accumulation of wealth that is usually presented as unethical, violent, and untruthful.

Under his "Vow of Non-thieving" as part of "The Ashram Vows," Gandhi maintains: "If I take anything that I do not need for my own immediate use and keep it, I thieve it from somebody else." This is a universal law of nature: nature produces enough to satisfy our needs, but not our greed, and if we only took enough for ourselves and nothing more, there would be no poverty and no starvation in the world.[33]

If I gain a fair amount of wealth, through inheritance, trade, or industry, "I must know that all that wealth does not belong to me; what belongs to me is the right to an honourable livelihood, no better than that enjoyed by millions of others. The rest of my wealth belongs to the community and must be used for the welfare of the community." Gandhi continues that he presents his view at the time that other socialists with a different theory are considering what should be done with the possessions of the wealthy. The other socialists

> would do away with these privileged classes. I want them to outgrow their greed and sense of possession, and to come down in spite of their wealth to the level of those who earn their bread by labour. The labourer has to realize that the wealthy man is less owner of his wealth than the labourer is owner of *his* own, viz., the power to work.[34]

This approach to wealth leads Gandhi to his view of trusteeship as key to socialist transformation. "The real remedy is non-violent democracy, otherwise spelt true education of all. The rich should be taught the doctrine of stewardship and the poor that of self-help."[35] After asserting that he believes in the nationalization of key industries, but not all of the means of production, Gandhi upholds both private enterprise and planned production. He would therefore allow the capitalist and the large landholder "to keep their factory and their land, but ... I would make them consider themselves trustees of their property."[36]

Under the "Practical Trusteeship Formula"[37] approved by Gandhi, "trusteeship provides a means of transforming the present capitalist order of society into an egalitarian one. It gives no quarter to capitalism, but gives the present owning class a chance of reforming itself. It is based on the faith that human nature is never beyond redemption."

Trusteeship "does not recognize any right of private ownership of property except so far as it may be permitted by society for its own welfare." Under such trusteeship, with legislative regulation of ownership and wealth and with production determined by social necessity, "an individual will not be free to hold or use his wealth for selfish satisfaction or in disregard of the interests of society." Gandhi upholds that there would be a fixed decent minimum living wage, a fixed limit for the maximum income, and the tendency to move toward the obliteration of the difference between such minimum and maximum incomes.[38]

Most twentieth-century socialists, including Marxists, tend to focus on the mode of distribution under capitalism that results in glaring inequalities in income, wealth, private property, and possessions. Marx, by way of contrast, focuses on the primacy of the mode of production. Unequal, asymmetrical class relations of exploitation and domination, rooted in the capitalist mode of production, defined by who owns and controls the capital, are the key to understanding inequalities in income and wealth. From the above passages by Gandhi, it might seem that his socialism, along with that of other contemporary socialists, focuses on the primacy of inequalities in the distribution of income and wealth. However, I would submit that an overall, more critical reading of Gandhi leads to the conclusion that he, like Marx, also emphasizes the primacy of productive relations. On the one hand, only unalienated, free, non-exploited, life-affirming, relational labor, grounded in the principles of truth and nonviolence, can allow for true socialism. On the other hand, unfree, violent, ego-defined, exploited labor results in immoral and untruthful relations, in gross inequalities, and in economic and social relations that make real sustainable socialist development impossible.

Weaknesses and Confusion

As indicated several times in this chapter, some of Gandhi's passages on capitalism and socialism are unclear, uncritical, and in need of clarification, critical analysis, and revision. I will restrict my formulation of weaknesses and confusion in Gandhi's writings, with a small sample of Gandhi passages, to two general, very significant criticisms:

his confused and inadequate analysis of capitalism, and, more surprisingly, his confused and inadequate analysis of violence.

First, there are many confusing passages in Gandhi's writings on capitalism. Without providing extensive quotations, we may note and summarize some aspects of his inadequate approach. Gandhi is very explicit in telling us that he wants to end capitalism and achieve socialism. In some passages, he maintains that he wants to destroy capitalism, but not capital or the capitalist. What does this mean? Gandhi is not simply saying that we should not destroy any human beings, who may be capitalists, but rather that we should not get rid of their identity and function as capitalists. What does it mean to destroy capitalism but have some people continuing to function as capitalists?

Gandhi is very explicit in telling us that he wants to work for a classless society in which there is "no room for classes." In his socialist vision, all members of society are equal, all are on the same level, with no one ruling over another, and there is no distinction in rank. Yet, in other passages, and often in the very same passages, Gandhi also maintains that capital and capitalists will always be with us; that capital and labor are mutually dependent and need each other; that the destruction of the capitalist must mean the destruction of the worker; that there will be no distinction or rank between capital and labor, but the rich will always be with us (ideally as trustees of their wealth); that the wealthy capitalists will voluntarily come down to the level of the laboring masses (while still being wealthy); and that the toiling laborer and the rich capitalist will be regarded as equal and as equal partners.[39]

The first general weakness in Gandhi's muddled account of capitalism arises from the fact that he is a powerful moral idealist, but he has no theory or analysis of history or historical development. What this means is that Gandhi often takes historically and economically specific capitalist categories and he then universalizes and eternalizes them in a nonhistorical, non-contextualized manner: "The rich will always be with us. Capitalists and capital will always be with us." Yes, for thousands of years, there have been different premodern economic systems in which there were rich privileged people, who owned or controlled the means of production and oppressed and dominated workers, who were slaves, serfs, artisans, and so forth.

But before the emergence of capitalism as the dominant economic system, we do not analyze the wealthy as "capitalists," since they did not acquire and maintain their wealth from a capitalist mode of production and exchange, and the basis of their wealth and power was not their "private property" as "capital." Similarly, workers were always laborers but not wage-laborers hired by capital as an investment in capitalist production.

Gandhi throws out the vague, inadequate "labor is capital," as if all labor under any conditions is capital, instead of the more precise and more adequate, "labor is capital" *as wage-labor*, as labor-power purchased by the capitalist under capitalism. Gandhi throws out the vague "the laborer needs the capitalist," as if this is some permanent condition of all labor, instead of the more precise and more adequate "labor needs capital" to meet its basic necessities and survive under capitalist conditions defined by the domination of capital. Gandhi, in passages that have some moral and spiritual force, claims that there are no distinctions, no differences in rank, and no inequalities between rich capitalists and poor toiling laborers under them. They are all on the same level. Is this just sincere confused thinking or something worse? Gandhi clearly maintains that he is "against private property," but he claims that he is not against capital or capitalists. But it does not make any sense to talk about capital but no private property, since capital is based on the ownership and control of private property; and it makes no sense to talk about capitalists without private property, since the "capitalists" are identified as the propertied class that owns and controls the private property, that is, the capital.

Gandhi could make a case for some of these formulations by claiming that this reflects the realities of the contemporary world dominated by capitalist relations and the conditions necessary for the gradual, nonviolent, democratic transformation of capitalism to socialism. In other words, in the transitional period, we need people with technological and other capitalist skills, with knowledge of how to invest existing capital to meet social needs, and so forth. However, unlike Marx's analysis in the "Critique of the Gotha Program," in which a post-capitalist transitional period will necessarily express various capitalist features, Gandhi does not always provide such a specific, transitional, contextualized analysis. Instead, he often offers nonhistorical and non-contextualized formulations about the permanent need of labor and socialism for capital and capitalists.

The second weakness and confusion arises from some of Gandhi's inadequate accounts of violence. This is surprising since Gandhi deserves his reputation as the twentieth-century's greatest proponent of nonviolence. Gandhi is clear that he regards capitalism and its private property relations of domination based on exploitation as violent. He maintains that "what was gained by violence could not only not be defended by non-violence but the latter required the abandonment of the ill-gotten gains." He is then asked: "Is the accumulation of capital possible except through violence whether open or tacit?" He responds: "Such accumulation by private persons was impossible except through violent means."[40] Gandhi, as we have seen, most often rejects modern, Western socialism because it allows violent means for attaining noble ends. So far so good: Gandhi is certainly consistent in rejecting violence. However, other passages such as many of those on trusteeship complicate his approach and open him to my second criticism.

In a dramatic passage "Vow of Non-thieving," we previously noted Gandhi's contention: "If I take anything that I do not need for my own immediate use and keep it, I thieve it from somebody else." If we only took enough for ourselves to meet our basic needs, there would be no poverty or starvation in the world. However, Gandhi continues: "I am no Socialist, and I do not want to dispossess those who have got possessions.... I do not want to dispossess anybody; I should then be departing from the rule of non-violence. If somebody else possesses more than I do, let him." Gandhi then concludes that when it comes to regulating his own life and not committing the violence of dispossessing others of their possessions, he can uphold the position that we "have no right to anything that we really have until these millions are clothed and fed," and this means adjusting our wants and undergoing voluntary privation.[41] What are the implications and unintended consequences of such a position on violence?

This brings us to the second criticism: the weakness and confusion in some of Gandhi's accounts of violence with regard to socialism and capitalism. Gandhi is remarkable for his strong will and determination to avoid violence, including his willingness to sacrifice and absorb suffering rather than inflict suffering on others. Here we see another contrast with Marx. For Marx, the capitalist mode of production, with the basic class relations and the basic laws of capital accumulation, is structurally defined by exploitation, violence, domination, contradiction, and conflict. Gandhi agrees with much of this analysis of capitalism, but he is determined to do everything possible to avoid violent means, class struggle, and class conflict. Yet, I would submit, Gandhi's formulation, as illustrated by the above passage on dispossessing anyone of possessions, reveals complicity, even if unintended, with capitalist structural violence, with capitalist institutional violence, and with the violence of the capitalist status quo.

In his formulations of trusteeship and other writings, Gandhi certainly is aware of huge inequalities, great suffering, and the violence of the status quo, and he wants to convert and transform the capitalists and their relations of domination to more moral nonviolent conditions. This is his intention when he urges the rich, the big capitalists, and the big landholders to voluntarily and freely act as trustees, to meet the social needs of the suffering masses.

But why should the wealthy and powerful have this permanent choice? Why should they be allowed to maintain their violently exploited and accumulated capital, private property, and wealth if they so choose, regardless of the social consequences? Gandhi sometimes regards this as a separate, individual choice and ignores the social consequences. Under certain conditions, dispossessing the wealthy capitalists may do them violence; but not dispossessing them and allowing them to maintain their capital and function as capitalists may do far greater violence to millions of less powerful, dominated human beings.

Gandhi, of course, should be sensitive to all of this. Influenced by karma-yoga of the Bhagavad-Gita, Gandhi knew that "inaction is an action," and it can bring very violent with negative consequences. That is why he is so critical of historical events in which inaction takes the form of cowardly passivity, and this inaction allows for disastrous consequences. What this means is that not dispossessing the powerful and dominating capitalists of their possessions based on violent exploitation, thus allowing the continuation of the unequal power base of the rich capitalists, will result in consequences that will perpetuate the violence of the status quo. Gandhi, of course, also consistently urges laborers, the impoverished, and exploited masses to educate themselves, to mobilize, to resist, and to determine their own destinies and not to sit back passively and allow the wealthy and powerful capitalists, with their possessions, to do what they want.

Nevertheless, Gandhi's philosophy, ethics, and spirituality, including his vision of socialism, are part of a holistic, organic, relational, interconnected, unifying, sustainable worldview. This was previously seen in Gandhi's analysis of how the illusory, divisive ego prevents us from realizing the unifying interconnectedness of all life, and it will be emphasized in last two paragraphs of this chapter. Therefore, it is puzzling that he is not always sensitive to how some of his writings about capital, capitalists, the rich, and possessions have relational consequences that make him complicit with the perpetuation of the violence he opposes.

Finally, there are passages on wealth and possessions in which Gandhi either seems inconsistent with his absolute ideal of nonviolence or, as I prefer to interpret it, renders his position on capitalism, socialism, and violence more adequate and relevant to issues of the contemporary world. For example, in his discussion of capitalism or his preferred trusteeship, Gandhi writes: "I would be very happy, indeed, if the people concerned behaved as trustees; but if they fail, I believe we shall have to deprive them of their possessions through the State with the minimum exercise of violence." He continues that that is why he said at the Round Table Conference in London that every vested interest must be examined and "confiscation ordered where necessary—with or without compensation as the case demanded."[42]

As we analyzed in Chapter 7, especially in the section on violence, suffering, and transformative nonviolence, Gandhi sometimes miscalculates the effects of his advice and practices, and he sometimes is complicit in perpetuating multidimensional structural violence. This is true in many of his approaches to capitalists and his proposals for transformative, nonviolent, egalitarian trusteeship. With several, frequently cited exceptions, most notably Jamnalal Bajaj and also J.R.D. Tata, few of the wealthy embrace some of Gandhi's vision of trusteeship and his proposed transformative practices. The historical narrative of Gandhi before 9/11 shows that the overwhelming majority of powerful capitalists and other land owners continue to maintain and develop their violent hierarchical relations of domination, exploitation, oppression, and injustice.

In fairness and consistent with other interpretations in this book, Gandhi often changes his earlier formulations with regard to caste, class, gender, voluntary trusteeship, and other topics involving multidimensional structural violence and unsustainability. In his later formulations, Gandhi often loses his patience and faith in the voluntary goodness of the wealthy capitalists and others with hierarchical power, calls for dispossessions and confiscations, and develops a more radical approach to class exploitation and the need for class struggle, without renouncing his ideals of transformative nonviolence.

The above Gandhi citations on depriving capitalists of their possessions, dispossessions, and confiscations are examples of a surprisingly large number of passages in which Gandhi, albeit reluctantly and with limited applications, upholds the necessity for some violence. In other writings on violence in general, and on such specific forms of violence as terrorism in particular, Gandhi's position is that in certain extreme unavoidable cases, while maintaining an absolute commitment to ahimsa, we may be required to use necessary relative violence in the cause of nonviolence.[43] We use violent means only when necessary to prevent extreme violence because that is the least violent, most effective, contextualized, relative response possible. In many of these passages, Gandhi is not restricting his analysis to unintentional violence or to courageous violence by those not at the highest ethical and spiritual level of development. He also advocates active intentional violence, including killing, even killing as an act of ahimsa, by ethically and spiritually committed followers who embrace the absolute regulative ideal of nonviolence.

Such extreme cases allowing for our response by violent means include various acts of self-defense and to stop the rapist, the violent lunatic or murderer, Nazis committing genocide during the Holocaust, the 9/11 terrorists in New York or the 26/11 terrorists in Mumbai, as well as life-threatening dogs, monkeys, mosquitoes, snakes, and insects. Always upholding the ideal of nonviolence, Gandhi reluctantly submits that such violence may be necessary but it should not be glorified and is not moral. As analyzed in Chapter 7, such violence should be used only as the last resort, we should restrict to a minimum the intensity and extent of such relative violence, and we should do everything possible to work for nonviolent structures and alternatives that avoid the repetition of such violence.

Once again, this is not to deny that there are inconsistencies in Gandhi's approach to such necessary violence, and he sometimes takes positions that are, at best, uninformed, and, at worst, immoral and violate his basic principles and values. As I have analyzed in previous writings, these include some of the advice he gave to Jews experiencing the Holocaust and to rape victims and others experiencing extreme gender violence. This also applies to some of his approach to caste violence and class violence. In many of these controversial positions by Gandhi, he later changes his views and rejects his earlier writings. In other cases, one can use a Gandhi approach, informed by Gandhi-informed principles and practices, to reformulate a new contextualized Gandhian socialist approach that rejects some of Gandhi's earlier contextualized writings.[44]

This more complex, nuanced, and contextually sensitive approach to violence offers constructive possibilities for a reformulated Gandhian socialism. It offers the potential for transforming some of the weakness and confusion in Gandhi's more rigid, uncritical, inadequate formulations into a more adequate and more relevant socialist position.

Strengths: What Socialists Can Learn from Gandhian Socialism

The above consideration of weaknesses and confusion in Gandhi's formulations of capitalism and of his socialist vision should not minimize the significant contributions Gandhi offers for a more adequate development of socialism. What follows is a list of 10 such contributions without providing the relevant analysis.

First, and in most general terms, Gandhi offers a revolutionary vision of an ideal, ethical, and spiritual socialism and communism that provides valuable criticisms of other forms of socialism and communism. These will be delineated in the following.

Second, Gandhi repeatedly offers an insightful and relevant analysis of the integral relations of means and ends. He is correct in critiquing how other socialists have been too willing to adopt an approach in which worthy ends justify violent, untruthful, unethical means, and we are all aware of the disastrous consequences.

Third, and relevant to the means-ends formulations, Gandhi provides a brilliant, complex, multidimensional analysis of violence and the violence of the status quo: interrelated physical, psychological, linguistic, economic, social, political, cultural, religious, and educational violence; sometimes overtly violent, but often hidden and camouflaged; and expressing a systemic structural violence that is often unquestioned as business as usual, as how the dominant relational system functions efficiently. Other socialists have usually been insensitive to the many dimensions of violence, have not explored preventative nonviolent alternatives, and have too easily resorted to violence, even in ways that subverted their socialist ideals.

Fourth, socialists can learn from much of Gandhi's critique of modernity, even if he is deeply influenced by some modern values, and he often presents his critique in a nondialectical manner that does not adequately recognize the positive achievements of modernity. As shaped by the Western Enlightenment tradition, most modern socialists have too easily adopted values and priorities embracing modern views of science, technology, rationality, and progress.

Fifth, socialists can learn from Gandhi's critique of the dangers and inadequacies of centralized power, as in various forms of state socialism, and of top-down elitist socialist models of power. For socialism to achieve real freedom, real equality, and real democracy, Gandhi has much to contribute, with his emphasis on decentralized power and bottom-up grassroots self-determination.

Sixth, in very general terms, modern socialists can learn much from Gandhi's primary emphasis on morality. For Gandhi, morality is the basis of philosophy and religion, and it must be at the foundation of any socialist experiment, as is clear in his insistence that socialism must embody the primary principles of truth and nonviolence. Gandhi resists modern deterministic reductionisms that do away with morality and spirituality. Too many Western socialists have claimed that their modern scientific, economic, and historical theories have no need of ethical analysis, are "beyond morality," and we have seen the disastrous consequences.

Seventh, Gandhi offers much to modern socialism in his critiques of the construction of the separate, selfish ego with its anti-social ego-desires, defense mechanism, attachments, violence, and illusions. Marx and other socialists, with their focus on class relations, the mode of production, and "external" relations of power, usually do not devote sufficient attention to this. How many socialist experiments, from local groups to nation states, have been subverted and destroyed largely because key individuals have been motivated by their ego-driven needs, attachments, and goals?

Eighth, modern socialists can learn from Gandhi's emphasis on the whole person. Like most modern socialists, Gandhi surprisingly places a very high value on reason and rationality. He even tells us that if God or sacred scriptures command us to do something that violates human experience and reason, we should reject what is irrational in religion. He agrees with Marx that capitalism is fundamentally irrational and socialism is a more rational way of socially and economically structuring society to meet human needs and allow for full human development.

However, unlike some modern socialists, Gandhi does not believe that the real is the rational alone. The whole human being is more than a rational being and includes the nonrational, the pre-reflective, the emotions, and the imagination. True socialism must do justice to the whole person as a harmoniously integrated mind–body–heart (or soul) being. Similarly, as someone with such a lofty ethical and spiritual vision, Gandhi is remarkable in his emphasis on meeting basic body and other needs, and providing food, housing, sanitation, and other basic necessities. But Gandhi, unlike some modern socialists, correctly believes that the whole person is more than a being reduced to increasing basic consumption, and thus meeting bodily needs, and even this false reductionism does not satisfy bodily needs. Total human development, freedom, equality, selfless service, participatory democracy, and self-determination must be part of any socialist experiment.

Ninth, Gandhi offers a valuable cosmocentric view. Most modern, Western socialist formulations have been strongly and exclusively anthropocentric. Many socialists, and even some anthropocentric capitalists, are increasingly concerned with destructive developments that define the contemporary world, and that include questions about the sustainability of human existence on the planet: the threat posed by climate change and other environmental disasters; the increasing gap between the haves and the have-nots; the widespread examples of modern alienation and destructive behavior; and the prevalence of religious, ethnic, and other forms of violence, nuclear weapons, terrorism, and war.[45] Socialists who are critiquing capitalism and looking for socialist alternatives are increasingly realizing that they need to weaken or completely reject some of their anthropocentric entrapments and limitations, and to explore more cosmocentric approaches.

Tenth, in contrast to many modern, Western socialist formulations, Gandhi offers a socialist vision with engaged practice that is holistic, organic, unifying, interrelated and interdependent, and potentially sustainable. The Gandhi-informed socialist vision emphasizes nonegoistic, egalitarian social relations that are grounded in social and moral duties and in promoting individual freedoms and rights. As analyzed previously, as with other features of Gandhi's theory–practice dialectic, this socialist vision and its practices are grounded in Gandhi's ontological structure and framework. This Gandhian ontology unifies, interconnects, and dialectically renders sustainable and meaningful the physical, bodily, mental, psychological, economic, social, cultural, moral, spiritual, and cosmic relations of reality. It challenges the basic assumptions, values, principles, and worldview of "modern civilization" in its capitalist and socialist formulations and practices. In this way, Gandhi's alternative socialism, acknowledging its limitations and weaknesses, can serve as a catalyst, allowing others, including modern socialists, to rethink inadequacies and limitations in their modern formulations and to formulate qualitatively different ideals and engaged practices.

Gandhian Socialism Today

The relevance of Gandhi's socialism for the contemporary world can be seen in the above strengths as well as the above confusions and weaknesses indicating formulations that need to be revised or simply discarded. Such a revision involves the complex dynamic task of relating texts, contexts, and interpretations in which we analyze Gandhi's contextualized writings on capitalism and socialism, attempt to contextualize them in terms of contemporary historical, economic, cultural, and other contextual variables and structural relations, and then determine what remains and what can be reformulated for our interpretation of socialism that has significance and meaning today. Such a socialist project is consistent with Gandhi's own open-ended approach of ongoing, often reformulated, experiments with truth.

In interpreting, reformulating, and applying Gandhian socialism today, it is helpful to distinguish three interconnected and often overlapping levels of analysis in Gandhi's socialist writings. First, when he is considering the highest level of ethical and spiritual development, Gandhi endorses an ideal of pure socialism that he sometimes calls spiritual communism. This is his ideal of his ashram as a self-contained, highly regulated and structured, ethical and spiritual intentional community. This is also the lofty level that he applies to his most devoted and developed satyagrahis, who aim at a pure socialism and are to serve as moral and spiritual exemplars.

Today one would historically and contextually situate and apply this level of socialist criteria to the most dedicated and humanly developed socialists, who embody the highest socialist ideals and principles. We focus on how these dedicated Gandhi-informed socialists live their personal lives, how they constitute and participate in their socialist groups and other social relations, and how they engage in their socialist engaged practices expressing their commitments, activist struggles, and constructive alternatives.

Second, Gandhi wants to interpret and apply his socialist vision to the practical level of the general society where most individuals are not at such a high level of ethical and spiritual development. This is the diverse level at which Gandhi offers most of his writings on the need for socialist transformation to a socialist society. Here Gandhi attempts to apply his commitment to a nonviolent, decentralized, democratic, sustainable socialism.

Today one would apply this level of socialism in relating to millions of human beings who are not prepared to dedicate their lives to a Gandhian socialist vision, but who are alienated from much of contemporary capitalism, and are sympathetic, or at least open, to different levels of socialist discourse and transformation when applied to the key issues in their lives. Such issues include adequate healthcare and adequate education for all, safe water and nutritious food for all, adequately paying and meaningful jobs for all, real physical, psychological, social, and economic security for all, and a sustainable environment for all.

Third, Gandhi finds that his contextualized socialist vision must also be interpreted and applied to social and economic levels dominated by capitalists, feudal landowners, and others opposed to socialism. Gandhi often writes about his absolute ideals, but he always identifies himself as a pragmatic idealist concerned with relating to and changing the real existing world. Gandhi may have been against capitalism and its private property relations, and he may have been for socialism and the goal of a classless society. How does his socialist vision relate to a present world of powerful capitalists, accumulated capital, exploited labor, capital-labor relations of domination, corporate-state-military monopoly capitalism, globalization, and so forth? In this regard, as we have seen, Gandhi the socialist often established complex, at time contradictory, and sometimes confusing relations with capital, capitalists, and capitalism.

Today Gandhian socialists living in societies dominated by capitalism must engage those realities and find complex and varied ways of relating to capitalists and capital. In some cases, the relations are so contradictory and antagonistic that the best that the Gandhian socialists can do is to expose the exploitative and oppressive relations of domination and then educate, organize, and mobilize, to resist, struggle, and lessen or overcome inequalities and domination. In other cases, Gandhian socialists may be able to establish more constructive relations with some capitalists and with existing capital in ways that at least partially satisfy food, healthcare, housing, education, employment, and other unmet needs, and may be viewed as gradual measures of reform that can open up socialist potential for greater transformation.

In this regard, we find severe limitations in Gandhian socialism, muddled thinking, and questionable compromises; but we also find important insights, valuable critiques, and contributions by a Gandhian socialist approach, that must be major features of any reformulated, more adequate, future socialism.

As Gandhi repeatedly tells us, he has absolute ideals such as the ideal of pure spiritual socialism or communism, but as a relative being, he only has limited relative truths. Therefore, in our experiments with truth, we are moving from one relative view of socialism to a more developed, relative view of socialism, with many limitations and failures along the way. This applies even to our first, highest level of ethical and spiritual development, since even Gandhi sometimes regards ashram events and satyagraha campaigns as failed experiments, and he typically blames himself for such miscalculations and failures.

There is no absolute Gandhi formula for socialism; no absolute or pure blueprint that can simply be superimposed on changing, complex, contextual realities. Gandhi does not offer some axiomatic theory of socialism in which we can start with his Truth, Nonviolence, and his other pure ideals as foundational axioms, and then rather simply, mechanistically, dogmatically, and nondialectically deduce what our historically situated socialism must be. Gandhi offers us valuable socialist principles, values, and commitments, but we can also learn from Gandhi's failed experiments and from the failures of later experiments in Gandhian socialism. Similarly, in a reformulated socialist theory, we can learn from the limitations and failures in modern, Western, non-Gandhian experiments in socialism, but we can also learn from valuable contributions of modern socialism in areas in which Gandhian socialism has been confused and inadequate, such as its lack of a critical historical and economic class analysis.

I will end by suggesting a very brief, bold conclusion: Gandhi's philosophical, ethical, and spiritual principles essentially and necessarily lead to some contemporary view of socialism, and they are fundamentally antithetical to capitalism, including its contextual formulations today. In other words, it is not only that Gandhi examined contemporary expressions of capitalism, analyzed how particular capitalist private property and other relations result in exploitation and suffering, and on that basis, identified himself as a socialist. In addition to this, and more fundamental to his ethical and spiritual approach, an understanding of satya, ahimsa, satyagraha, and other essential Gandhian values and principles and underlying ontology leads to a Gandhian socialist commitment.

Expressed briefly and inadequately, Gandhi has a holistic, ethical, and spiritual view of reality—often labelled Truth, God, and Self (usually as the universal ethical and spiritual Self or Soul) and identified with Nonviolence—in terms of the underlying, unifying, interconnectedness of all of life. It is not only that violence, ego, greed and attachment, oppression, exploitation, private property relations are immoral, since they lead to suffering and other negative consequences; they also violate the Truth or Reality, focus us on what separates and disconnects one from others, and trap us in ignorance and illusion. In earlier chapters, in presenting Gandhi's key formulations of means-ends relations and other topics, we analyzed how violent means do not lead only to immoral, untruthful, violent consequences. Violent means are also inconsistent with Gandhi's ontology, his theoretical and practical commitment to his view of the unifying, interconnected, meaningful, relational Truth and Reality. In this way, as presented throughout this chapter, Gandhi regards the central, defining characteristics of capitalism as inconsistent with his ontological approach to Truth and Reality. Therefore, Gandhian socialism, as grounded in principles of truth and nonviolence and exhibiting the characteristics we have delineated, is not only more moral and leads to more positive consequences, but also expresses limited, contextual ways of socially and economically realizing greater truth and reality through nonviolent egoless service, meeting the social needs and working for the welfare of all, and experiencing the ethical and spiritual unifying interrelatedness of Reality.

Notes

1. This chapter is a revision of "Gandhi and Socialism," *International Journal of Gandhian Studies* 1, no. 1 (2012): 109–37. This journal, edited by Sushil Mittal, published an excellent first issue, but did not publish any additional issues.
2. One can make the same observations about the diminished status of recent Western socialist leaders, and one can ask the same questions about the history, current state, and future of Western socialism.
3. Compared with many theoreticians and philosophers, I have attempted to include more of the historical narrative and contextual background and framework throughout this chapter and in earlier chapters. Nevertheless, a greater focus on historical narrative by historians and other Gandhi scholars would certainly enhance my formulations.
4. In this chapter, I will usually provide Gandhi citations to the original publications. Almost all of these quotations can be found in M.K. Gandhi, *The Collected Works of Mahatma Gandhi* (*CWMG*), 100 vols

(New Delhi, Publications Division, Ministry of Information and Broadcasting, Government of India, 1958–91). Most of the citations can also be found in either Raghavan Iyer, ed., *The Essential Writings of Mahatma Gandhi* (Delhi: Oxford University Press, 1991), as well as in Iyer's more extensive, edited, three-volume work, *The Moral and Political Thought of Mahatma Gandhi* (Delhi: Oxford University Press, 1986, 1986, 1987), or in R.K. Prabhu and U.R. Rao, eds, *The Mind of Mahatma Gandhi* (Ahmedabad: Navajivan Publishing House, 1967).

5. See Albert Einstein, "Why Socialism?" *Monthly Review* (May 1949).
6. Remarkably, the self-avowed socialist Bernie Sanders entered the 2016 presidential primaries very late, with little name recognition, hardly registering in the polls, little financial backing, and no established Democratic Party support. Hillary Clinton, by way of contrast, had previously run against Barack Obama and had been preparing for years to become the 2016 presidential candidate. When Sanders entered the campaign, and before the first primary vote, Clinton had already wrapped up the support and funding from her wealthy Wall Street and corporate allies, the endorsement of the hundreds of establishment super delegates, and the aggressive support of the mainstream Democratic Party establishment. Nevertheless, Bernie Sanders, with the appeal of his central attack on capitalist wealth and power, with growing class inequality, and with his support of anti-corporate socialist healthcare and other messages, kept winning the primaries. As Sanders repeatedly and correctly asserted, he polled far ahead of Clinton in the contest with Trump, and to this day (July 2017), he remains the most admired politician, and far more popular than the aggressively and violently corporate President Trump.
7. M.K Gandhi, *My Socialism*, compiled by R.K. Prabhu (Ahmedabad: Navajivan Publishing House, 1959).
8. *Harijan* (April 1940), p. 97.
9. *Harijan* (July 13, 1947), p. 232.
10. *Harijan* (August 4, 1946), p. 246. In *Harijan* (March 31, 1946), p. 246, Gandhi asserts: "I claim to be a foremost Communist although I make use of care and other facilities offered to me by the rich. They have no hold on me and I can shed them at a moment's notice, if the interests of the masses demand it."
11. *Harijan* (December 16, 1939), p. 376.
12. *Young India* (March 26, 1931), p. 49. The fact that one presents a critique of capitalism, expressing the desire to end or destroy capitalism, does not necessarily make one a socialist. There are many forms of nonsocialism, as seen in various forms of pre-capitalist and premodern

theocratic formulations; in anti-capitalist, individualistic, libertarian formulations, and in various postmodernist formulations that reject socialism as another hegemonic, grand narrative. However, Gandhi not only has many writings expressing his critique of capitalism, but some of these same passages, as well as numerous other writings, express Gandhi's identification as a socialist.

13. For example, even when it comes to a seemingly more limited topic central to his approach to modern capitalism and socialism, such as his views on "the machinery method" and "the machinery craze," Gandhi resists some dogmatic view and rigid application. In *Young India* (July 2, 1931, which appears in *CWMG*, 47: 89), he asserts: "Applications of the laws of economics must vary with varying conditions." See Chapter 6 in this book on Gandhi's approach to technology.
14. M.K. Gandhi, *An Autobiography: The Story of My Experiments with Truth* (Boston: Beacon Press, 1993). Gandhi's autobiography was first published in two volumes in 1927 and 1929.
15. *Harijan* (January 2, 1937), p. 375, and *Amrita Bazar Patrika* (August 3, 1934).
16. *Harijan* (February 20, 1937), p. 12. Gandhi goes on to state that he is engaged in solving the same problem faced by modern, Western, scientific socialists, but that his approach is always committed to nonviolence.
17. See, for example, Gandhi's formulations in *Harijan* (March 1, 1935); *Harijan* (April 20, 1940); *Harijan* (July 28, 1946); Pyarelal, *Towards New Horizons* [reprinted from *Mahatma Gandhi: The Last Phase* (Ahmedabad: Navajivan Publishing House, 1959)].
18. *Young India* (November 15, 1928), p. 381. After applauding the purest sacrifice and noblest renunciation behind the Bolshevik ideal, Gandhi asserts that Bolshevism freely sanctions the use of violent force, and this violates his firm conviction that "nothing enduring can be built on violence."
19. *Harijan* (October 25, 1952), p. 301. Gandhi's controversial formulations of trusteeship as a voluntary, nonviolent, socialist alternative are addressed in the section on his possible weaknesses and confusion.
20. *Young India* (August 20, 1925), p. 285. In terms of such formulations about the capitalist class looking out for the welfare of the laboring class "under them," it is relevant to mention Gandhi's previously quoted formulations of his socialism in which everyone is "equal," is "on the same level," with "none low, none high."
21. *Young India* (October 7, 1926), p. 348. I find it interesting that most of Gandhi's confusing writings on capitalism are from the 1920s, with some in the 1930s, and his clearest anti-capitalist positions are from the

1940s and especially the last few years of his life. One may note a similar development in the views of Martin Luther King, Jr. and Malcolm X late in their lives. A fuller understanding of this change in Gandhi's writings about capitalism would include a detailed historical narrative of the changing interwar contextual variables and political and social economy, and with Gandhi's constructive work and other practical, socialist experiments in nonviolent, truthful, sustainable living.

22. For example, see *Harijan* (June 1, 1947), p. 172; *Young India* (December 11, 1924), p. 406; "The Ashram Vows" (Speech at Y.M.C.A., Madras, February 16, 1916), in *CWMG*, 13: 225–35; "Letter to Madeleine Rolland," before March 22, 1935, in *CWMG*, 60: 326.

23. For examples of Gandhi's criticism of state socialism, see *Young India* (December 11, 1924) and *Young India* (November 15, 1928).

24. In writings, such as *Young India* (March 31, 1931) and *Harijan* (December 5, 1936), Gandhi argues against the inevitability of class conflict. In a fascinating formulation in *Harijan* (March 13, 1937), p. 40, Gandhi submits that communism, in the last analysis, "means a classless society—an ideal that is worth striving for." He then indicates that he parts company with communism when force is used to achieve this ideal. "The idea of inequality, of 'high and low', is an evil," but we cannot eradicate this evil by using violent means. In addition to Indian influences, there is also a long tradition in the West of religious and nonreligious utopian socialists and utopian communists who advocate the ideal of a classless society but oppose class struggle as violent and divisive. It is clear from *Hind Swaraj* and many other writings that Gandhi deeply appreciates some of the Western utopian and other thinkers and practitioners of "the other West," especially Tolstoy, Ruskin, and Thoreau, who critique and reject the dominant orientation of Western, post-Enlightenment, capitalist, "modern civilization."

25. Iyer, *The Essential Writings of Mahatma Gandhi*, p. 10. For a detailed analysis of Gandhi's very broad interpretation and remarkable reinterpretation of his key concept of yajna, see my Chapter 4, "How Can Gandhi Interpret His Favorite Bhagavad-Gita as a Gospel of Nonviolence?"

26. *Harijan* (July 20, 1947), p. 240.

27. *Harijan* (July 13, 1947), p. 232.

28. *Harijan* (July 13, 1947), p. 232.

29. *Harijan*, (July 20, 1947), p. 240. Similarly, one could show how Gandhi's Constructive Programme, intended to provide positive alternatives for implementing his social and economic values and programs, is a means for realizing his socialist vision for a new India.

See "Constructive Programme: Its Meaning and Place," *CWMG*, 75: 144–66 (dated December 13, 1941). In the historical narrative of Gandhi's priorities in the interwar period after he returns to India, one notes how he goes through active political periods in which he focuses on his major satyagraha campaigns, negotiations, and other political activities. It is important to note how he also goes through other periods, including 1922–8 and the mid to late 1930s, including his founding of his Sevagram ashram in 1936, when he tends to withdraw from active political life and focuses on self-purification, village and ashram life, and experiments with his Constructive Programme. In different ways, his engaged practices with satyagraha and his constructive work both develop his formulations and the revisions of his views of Gandhian socialism.

30. See, for example, *Young India* (November 26, 1931), p. 369 and *Young India* (January 14, 1932), pp. 17–18.
31. The key text in understanding how Gandhi changes his view and blames Hindus and other Indians for being dominated and exploited by the British under colonial rule is Tolstoy's "A Letter to a Hindoo," which Gandhi translates and which appears in *Mahatma Gandhi and Leo Tolstoy: Letters*, ed. B. Srinivasa Murthy (Long Beach, CA: Long Beach Publications, 1987).
32. "Constructive Programme," *CWMG*, 75: 158. In several previous chapters, we have analyzed Gandhi's egalitarian approach, and in the last part of Chapter 6, we presented a Gandhi-informed approach to the contemporary crisis of the growing inequality in India, the USA, and other parts of the world.
33. "The Ashram Vows," *CWMG*, 13: 230–1.
34. *Harijan* (June 3, 1939), p. 145.
35. *Harijan* (June 8, 1940), p. 159.
36. Gandhi, *My Socialism*, pp. 10, 12.
37. "The Practical Trusteeship Formula," was proposed by Gandhian coworkers Narhari Parikh and Kishorelal Mashruwala. M.L. Dantwala drafted the proposed document that was published in *Harijan* in 1952 and that we are quoting. A dedicated Gandhian, an influential Indian agricultural economist, and the founder if the Centre for Development Alternatives, M.L. Dantwala (1909–1998) authored Gandhi-informed publications including *Gandhism Reconsidered* (Bombay: Padma Publications, 1945).
38. *Harijan* (October 25, 1952), p. 301. As previously noted and as will be analyzed under weaknesses and confusion, some of these proposals by Gandhi on trusteeship, capitalism, and socialism are certainly

confusing and contradictory. What, for example, does Gandhi precisely intend by giving the capitalist owning class a chance to reform itself? For how long does it have such a voluntary choice? Does this trusteeship reform mean that wealthy capitalists, who possess the capital, can continue their capitalist economy, or that the trusteeship reform leads rather quickly to the socialist abolition of capitalism? Does it make any sense to speak of capitalism, with its capital and powerful ruling class capitalists, if private property is "permitted by society" (whatever that means), only to meet social necessity, and for the social good, and there will be a move toward an egalitarian society in which capitalists will not be allowed to be wealthy? As will be seen in the next section under the second weakness, what complicates this even further is Gandhi's other proposals to the effect that if the capitalists fail to act as trustees, we must deprive them of their possessions and that confiscation must be ordered when necessary.

39. Among key passages in which Gandhi formulates these views are the following: *Young India* (March 26, 1931), p. 49; *Harijan* (June 3, 1939), p. 145; *Harijan* (July 28, 1940), p. 219; *Harijan* (February 17, 1946), p. 10; *Harijan* (August 4, 1946), p. 246; *Harijan* (January 18, 1948), p. 517; M.K. Gandhi, *From Yeravda Mandir: Ashram Observances*, trans. V.G. Desai (Ahmedabad: Navajivan Publishing House, 1933 [1957]), pp. 35–6.

40. *Harijan* (February 16, 1947). From this passage, in which Gandhi maintains that the private accumulation of capital is not possible except through violence and what is gained by violence must be abandoned, it is difficult to reconcile this with his previous claims that he may be against capitalism but not against capital. Gandhi complicates the issue by concluding this quotation with the claim that the accumulation of capital by the State (which he elsewhere often maintains represents violence) in a nonviolent society, unlike private accumulation, is possible, desirable, and inevitable.

41. "The Ashram Vows," *CWMG*, 13: 230–1. As indicated in the earlier section "Gandhi's Writings on Socialism," Gandhi is here rejecting modern violent forms of socialism.

42. *The Modern Review*, Calcutta (October 1935): 412. Gandhi continues: "What I would personally prefer would be not a centralization of power in the hands of the State, but an extension of the sense of trusteeship, as, in my opinion, the violence of private ownership is less injurious than the violence of the State. However, if it is unavoidable, I would support a minimum of State-ownership." This is another case where Gandhi today would probably have revised such formulations, since

the private concentration of wealth and power in the hands of huge corporations dwarfs the size of the economies of most nation states, and state economic and military investments, subsidies, and tax policies have become a large integral part of the functioning of "private" corporate capitalism.

43. See Chapter 7, "Terrorism and Violence" and sections in Chapter 2 and other chapters in this book on how Gandhi allows some necessary violence. For an analysis of how Gandhi might respond to Hitler and to the November 26, 2008 Mumbai terrorists, see Douglas Allen, *Mahatma Gandhi* (London: Reaktion Books, 2011).

44. One could also apply this to Gandhi's complex, controversial, and still debated views about conflict in Kashmir at the time of Partition. More particularly, Gandhi gives a speech, "Kashmir Issue," on January 4, 1948, weeks before his assassination. Although he hopes to avoid war in Kashmir between India and Pakistan, he seems to provide a justification for necessary violence by India's military, if war is inevitable. In terms of the later Indo–Pakistani wars and conflicts, the dangerous nuclear confrontation, the human rights abuses and extreme violence and suffering of Kashmiris, one can reformulate a contemporary Gandhi-informed perspective. For example, this is what Gandhians Rajiv Vohra and Niru Vohra in their Swaraj Peeth Trust, inspired primarily by Gandhi's *Hind Swaraj*, have been doing in extremely violent areas of Jammu, Kashmir, and Bihar. These courageous Gandhians, recognizing how those in India, Pakistan, and Kashmir have been and continue to be entrapped in vicious cycles of extreme violence, are engaged in working with youth in the short-term and especially long-term nonviolent transformative project of Gandhi-informed dialogue, radicalization, exemplary leadership, conflict resolution, and peace-making.

45. Such contemporary crises as environmental and economic unsustainability, climate change, growing economic inequalities, alienation and dehumanization are analyzed in Chapter 6, "Is Gandhi's Approach to Technology Irrelevant in the Modern Age of Technology?" and in sections analyzing these contemporary crises in the chapter on terrorism and in other chapters in this book.

9

Rewriting Marginality
Minority Literature, Hermeneutical Insights, and Gandhian Challenges

An international conference Rewriting Marginality: Multidisciplinary Approaches took place during February 24–6, 2010. Organized by Hameed Khan, this remarkable conference was held at Dr Babasaheb Ambedkar Marathwada University in Aurangabad, Maharashtra, India.[1]

Personal Influences and Critical Questions

The international conference "Rewritings Marginality" had a major focus on American studies, especially American minority literature. I was born, educated, socialized, and am a professor and peace and justice activist in the USA. I am cognizant of the fact that even when I address topics on Buddhism, Hinduism, Gandhi, or Ambedkar, my approach has been shaped, positively and negatively, by my American experiences.[2]

In this regard, I am often most comfortable in identifying with an American dissident tradition, challenging the dominant socio-economic and cultural status quo, as reflected in the nineteenth-century literature of such writers as Whitman, Emerson, Thoreau, Frederick Douglass, Sojourner Truth, and Mark Twain. Interestingly, while he most emphasizes his critique and rejection of "modern (Western) civilization," Gandhi is deeply influenced by creative and innovative writers in the West. In terms of such influences in the West, Gandhi most identifies with a dissident tradition, "the Other West," "the Other America," that includes such writers as Tolstoy, Ruskin, and Thoreau.

This chapter will use the common adjective "American," but I usually prefer "US," since Canadians and Mexicans are also North Americans, there are numerous "Americans" in Central and South America, and the US appropriation of "American" at least partially reflects a history of dominant, hegemonic, economic, and political relations. In a rather informal and personal way of introduction, I share major influences of American minority literature on my own life in order to illustrate themes central to this chapter.[3]

Raised as a Jew and having experienced firsthand traumatic, youthful experiences of anti-Semitism, I was drawn to and influenced by the writings of Jewish-American authors. From my prepared list of 50 Jewish-American writers, I have selected the following authors, including a few who have been very influential writers outside the narrow disciplinary boundaries of literature: Isaac Asimov, Saul Bellow, Noam Chomsky, Bob Dylan, Allen Ginsberg, Joseph Heller, Tony Kushner, Lillian Hellman, Norman Mailer, Bernard Malamud, Arthur Miller, Lewis Mumford, Tillie Olsen, Grace Paley, Marge Piercy, Henry Roth, Phillip Roth, J.D. Salinger, Maurice Sendak, Neil Simon, Isaac Bashevis Singer, Gertrude Stein, Studs Terkel, and Elie Wiesel.

What, if anything, do these authors share in the ways they write about Jewish-American experience, Jewish-American identity, and Jewish-American marginality, or in their writings on marginality without any specific Jewish reference? Even if one restricts the comparison of Jewish-American literature and marginality to two writers, Ginsberg and Phillip Roth, who grew up a few miles from where I did, one can describe their sense of marginality. This would include their upbringing to be socially mobile to attain assimilated middle-class respectability, their sense of alienation and rejection of such meaningless 1950s socialization, and their creative literary responses. But their differences seem at least as dramatic as their similarities, and this raises critical questions about experienced marginality, identity, and creative responses.

Similar critical questions can be raised from a list of significant African-American writers influential in my personal life. Consider the following abbreviated listing: Maya Angelou, James Baldwin, Amiri Baraka (LeRoi Jones), Angela Davis, W.E.B. Du Bois, Ralph Ellison, Bell hooks, Zora Neale Hurston, Langston Hughes, Martin Luther King, Jr., Audre Lorde, Malcolm X, Toni Morrison, Ishmael Reed, Jean Toomer, and Alice Walker. What, if anything, does such a minority literature tell us about the multiple, multicultural, and multidimensional ways of writing about African-American experience and identity, constructing race and rewriting marginality?

Finally, similar critical questions can be raised from a list of significant feminist writers influential in my personal life. Starting with Simone de Beauvoir, my most significant feminist, formative influence, one may consider complex questions of gendered experience, identity, and marginality. Is there some shared or essential nature of being "woman" in the world, of constructing woman's identity, and of writing feminist literature? Not numerically a minority, like other minorities in the USA, how have women's literary and other voices been marginalized, and what is the relation of woman's experience, identity, and marginality to race, class, sexual preference, nationality, religion, and other contextualized variables.

Let me share an observation, drawn from my Jewish-American experience and literature, but equally true, even if expressed in radically distinctive and different ways, by all of the other literature we are considering. Being socialized as part of a marginalized minority can be an advantage, although not a guaranteed advantage, when it comes to literary and other cultural insights and creativity, creative nonviolent resistance alternatives and sustainable living. Being marginalized and often denied access to the dominant values and identities of the privileged and the mainstream status quo can result in existential suffering, tension, alienation, and conflicted identities. But this can also result in heightened sensitivity, critical thinking, rethinking and challenging dominant cultural norms, being open to deeper experiences and cultural innovations, and being more empathetic, and with greater capacity to identify with those who have been marginalized, oppressed, and exploited, that is, most of humankind.

Here we also see connections with the Gandhian perspective to be considered.

Of course, as we have also seen throughout history, writers, oppressed and socialized as part of minority groups, often attempt to reject their marginalized identities and identify with the dominant privileged perspectives of their racist, sexist, classist, violent societies. It is also true that writers, privileged, and socialized as part of dominating groups, sometimes reject their mainstream or dominant multidimensional and structural perspectives and privileges, and become active participants in rewriting marginality.

Philosophy and Literature

Regarding the themes of marginality and multidisciplinary approaches to literature, there has usually been a significant difference in how my discipline philosophy and literature have tended to approach these questions. Although one can find significant exceptions in philosophy and literature, philosophy, going back as far as Plato and Aristotle and even before, has more privileged abstract rational thinking. For most philosophy, the rational has been the real, and the more we are engaged in critical rational thinking, the closer we come to gaining access to truth and to understanding reality. In this regard, most traditional philosophy, East and West, in emphasizing the unifying objective nature of abstract rational truth, tends to devalue or dismiss the pre-reflective, the emotions, the imagination, and the nonrational as pre-philosophical, nonphilosophical, and antiphilosophical; as lacking clarity, order, and rigorous intersubjective criteria for objective verification. Literature, by way of contrast, has been more open to engaging the emotions and other dimensions of human experience not devalued as nonrational, the complex experiential world, ambiguity, enigma, and aspects of experience that resist being comprehended and explained by abstract reason.

There are notable exceptions to this clear-cut dichotomy. Most of my earlier scholarly work was in the phenomenology of religion, especially focusing on the works of Mircea Eliade, often described in the 1960s and 1970s as the world's leading theorist of religious experience, myth, and symbolism.[4] Eliade, whom I knew very well, writes frequently of his "dual vocation" as both a scholar of religion and as a literary figure. In his native Romania of the 1930s, after his return from three years in India, he first establishes his reputation as a leading writer of novels and novellas. Eliade frequently cites Henri Poincaré's perspectival formulation that "the scale creates the phenomenon." He always insists on his anti-reductionist methodological claim: the scholarly or "scientific" and the literary must be approached on their own, unique, sui generis, irreducible levels of experience and expression. In his anti-Enlightenment orientation, greatly shaped by the literature of Romanticism, Eliade often writes fiction of the imaginary "fantastic." Such literary creativity cannot be reduced to the perspectives of post-Enlightenment, secular, non-mythic, rational analysis, and explanation.

This could be classified as rewriting marginality, since Eliade portrays—usually with an emphasis on ambiguity, enigma, contradiction, and paradox and the unexpected disruptions and transcendence of normal dominant structural order—the reclaimed voices of oppressed and silenced Romanians, as well as Adivasis and other Indian peasants.[5] Eliade claims to decipher and then express in his literary works these hidden and silenced minority voices in the cosmic mythic religiosity, the rituals, and the ancient and traditional symbols of the peasants, with the rejection of the grey banality of meaningless, ordinary modern life. Yet, one finds in Eliade's phenomenology and hermeneutics that this sharp philosophical-literary dichotomy is not absolute, since his theories of religion, myth, and symbolism help inform and shape his literary creativity and rewriting marginality, and his literary vocation clearly influences his scholarly history and phenomenology of religion.

In the twentieth century, and especially in recent decades, this philosophy–literature dichotomy has often blurred, as when postmodernists and other philosophers describe philosophy as telling philosophical stories, constructing narratives, with no privileged access to universal objective truth or reality. This has been very tempting for proponents of multiculturalism and minority philosophy and literature, but there are serious limitations and weaknesses in some of these recent approaches. These approaches often present radical, insightful critiques of dominant, violent, disciplinary, economic, political, and cultural structures of authority and legitimacy, as they problematize, undermine, and subvert oppressive boundaries and structures. But, in my view, they sometimes deconstruct themselves into relations that are unintelligible except to the elite few, and leave us with fragmentation, disorder, and powerlessness, not to mention the temptation to become entrapped in one's rather narcissistic subjectivity.

The Perspectival Nature of Rewriting Marginality

A key point in existential and hermeneutical philosophical phenomenology is the upholding of the perspectival nature of our contextualized situatedness, of all of our approaches, and of all of our expressions, including rewritings of marginality. This claim about the perspectival nature of all experiential approaches and all knowledge is emphasized in some of the phenomenological works of Maurice Merleau-Ponty. One can find earlier variations of this philosophical orientation, as in the famous fable or tale of the blind men and the elephant that originates in India, has variations in Jainism, Buddhism, Hinduism, Sufism, and other literature, and illustrates that reality may be viewed differently, depending on your perspective. We can also point to one of the major philosophical doctrines in Jain philosophy, *anekantavada* (the many-sidedness of human existence) of all perspectival approaches, and of the nature of reality. This doctrine has a profound influence on Gandhi's ethical and philosophical theory and practice.

Such a philosophical approach, affirming that all approaches and all knowledge are perspectival, offers a radical critique and alternative to the modern, Western Cartesian approach and to other forms of traditional Asian and Western philosophical foundationism and essentialism that clearly reject the claims of other approaches as false or lacking reality. Such a phenomenological perspectival claim would seem to provide invaluable resources for and be very attractive to multidisciplinary approaches, multiculturalism, and others emphasizing inviolable differences and pluralism and diversity in their attempts at rewriting marginality. After all, such a perspective seems to decenter, subvert, undermine, and reject those traditional, dominant, hegemonic, universalizing perspectives that have subsumed, devalued, marginalized, silenced, and ignored the voices of minorities and the disempowered as backward, irrational, uncreative, illusory, and false.

Those dominant hegemonic approaches cannot reject marginalized voices as unworthy of great literary and philosophical attention. Such a perspectival approach to the rewriting of marginality may reject claims to abstract, universal, non-contextualized truth and reality, including traditional philosophical claims to objective, foundational essences of truth, rationality, goodness, beauty, and so on. But it leaves us with many unresolved issues with regard to relativism and essentialism. In this seemingly attractive perspectival anti-essentialism, are we left with minority literatures and rewritings of marginality characterized by unlimited, uncritical, facile relativism? Are we left with space for all voices to be heard, without the imposition of oppressive or any intersubjective criteria for assessing authenticity, creativity, depth of meaning, and truth? Am I simply telling my own philosophical or literary story, creating my subjective perspectival narrative of marginality, and you may like or dislike my formulations, but this has nothing to do with any claims to truth, authenticity, objectivity, or reality?

In this regard, most minority and other authors rewriting marginality would probably not be happy with the following, extreme, but common, perspectival relativism. I am offering, say, a Dalit rewriting of oppressive, caste-based marginality or a feminist rewriting of oppressive, patriarchal, or male-dominated marginality. I insist that in such a rewriting my Dalit voice or my feminist voice be heard and not judged, dismissed, or marginalized by other perspectives. From the perspectives of caste-based and male-dominated patriarchal narratives, we can appreciate why Dalits and women are portrayed as inferior, even if we find this offensive, dehumanizing, and unjust. However, in terms of the inviolability of differences and the limits of any perspectival philosophical or literary approach, I have no basis for asserting that my rewriting gets at a more profound or deeper truth than the dominant narratives of my oppressors. At most, I can make the relative claim that my rewriting gets at a more profound or deeper truth for me as an individual or for my particular social grouping.

As a matter of fact, dominant individuals and groups—while they may at times be made uncomfortable and even object to such minority literary rewritings—can usually adjust to and even "tolerate" such a perspectival relativism at universities and in society. This is because such a fragmented relativistic approach usually has no integral or necessary connection to engaged practices of resistance and transformation that threaten the corporate, economic, political, state, military, media, and other relations of control and domination.

Even this anti-essentialist perspectival relativism often does not remove all difficult claims to essentialism. In terms of minority and other marginalized literature, the rewritings may resist claims to absolute, abstract, universal, and essentialized truth and reality. However, the rewritings of marginality often express claims about unique or particular essentialized experiences and identities with respect to culture, race, gender, ethnicity, religion, and indigenous and tribal groups.

For example, here is a common pattern in Native American rewritings of marginality. Native Americans have experienced a devastating history of genocidal domination at the hands of modern, white invaders and oppressors. They have seen the destruction of their language, their tribal culture, and their religion, which has left them in their present desperate state of poverty, social crises, alienation, dehumanization, powerlessness, divisiveness, and inauthentic Indian existence. They must engage in a radical cultural renewal by reclaiming their authentic Indian experience, the basis of their authentic Indian identity, as transmitted through their ancient sacred myths and legends, re-enacted through their sacred rituals, and revealed by the Gods and sacred ancestors to their tribal spiritual leaders and other traditional sources of authority.

Such Native American minority literature, with its rewriting of marginality, is typically presented as a dramatic negation or oppositional relation to the dominant, white, modern values and orientation of the oppressive other. In some versions, following a frequent mythic pattern, there is the strong sense that by negating the modern, "fallen" recent history, one can reclaim some essentialized, pre-fallen, primordial, mythic, sacred state of being with access to the forgotten eternal truths and realities about the nature of human identity and its relation to the tribe, animals, the earth, and other dimensions of the sacred.

Without developing variations of such common patterns in minority literature, we may simply note a few relevant questions about such claims to relative essentialism in rewriting marginality. As will be seen in the next section, doesn't the fact that Native Americans in 2018 are socialized, usually negatively, within a dominant, modern, white, post-industrialized world shape and render impossible that Indians can reclaim and re-experience truths and realities in the same essentialized ways that tribal Indians did 400 years ago? In terms of the abovementioned points about the perspectival nature of all experience and all approaches and the consequent anti-essentialized relativism, why should any particular Indian not be free to submit that any tribal essentialism, any attempt to impose some traditional narrative as key to rewriting marginality, is just another example of hegemonic control and domination that is an obstacle to authentic experience and self-identity?

As will be seen in the concluding section, Gandhi's challenges and alternative formulations, including his rewriting of marginality, may help us to move beyond some of these troubling dead-ends that define much of contemporary anti-essentialist, anti-foundationalist, perspectival, contextualized philosophy, as well as other disciplinary approaches to themes of rewriting marginality. While emphasizing Gandhi's deep commitment to perspectival many-sidedness and how we are always moving at best from one relative truth to another greater relative truth, it will be important to recognize significant differences in Gandhi's philosophical approach and not identify him with fashionable forms of modern cultural relativism and recent postmodernist emphasis on relative particular differences that often dominate the rewriting of marginality.

Brief reference may be made to experiences of Indian Americans (Indo-Americans), since this illustrates the complexities and many, often contradictory, dimensions of minority experiences and self-identities. For a variety of reasons, Indian Americans, unlike most other minorities in the USA, especially racial minorities, enjoy a rather privileged existence. This is mainly because most Indians who came to the USA for advanced education and remained, have been from a very narrow, elite, highly educated and skilled sample of the population. With so many educated and talented engineers, scientists, doctors, and businesspeople, Indians usually obtained high-paying jobs and have among the highest per capita income of any group in the country. Consistent with their privileged class position, wealth, power, status, and lifestyle, they often express values divergent from those of oppressed minorities. Although they may have lived in the USA for 30 or 40 years and seem to have adopted dominant American values of the power elite far more than I have, they often express themselves privately in the language of conflicted and oppressed minorities. For example, seemingly wealthy and privileged Indo-Americans will sometimes say that they are in the USA, but their heart belongs to India. One may wonder: if so, why is your body not in India? In their conflicted self-identity, they will say that they are only "at home" as an Indian in India, when they have often experienced much less of India than I have. Even more perplexing, at least at first, is the fact that these modern, westernized, very successful engineers, scientists, doctors, and corporate and financial capitalists will sometimes fund and attend anti-modern, nationalistic, and chauvinistic conferences, such as those claiming that everything great, even in the modern world, can be found in the Vedas; or that by supporting the most reactionary, seemingly anti-modern and anti-Western groups and causes in India, one is showing that one is a true authentic Indian.[6] I offer these observations, without analysis or explanation, simply to show that multiculturalism, minority experiences and literature, and the rewriting of marginality can be very complex, multidimensional, and contradictory, especially when situated in different perspectival contexts and orientations.

Texts, Contexts, and the Interpretation of Meaning in the Rewriting of Marginality

Using work in philosophical hermeneutics, I have raised questions in previous writings about the relation of texts, contexts, and interpretation of meaning key to rewriting marginality. In my open-ended creative approach, every reading is a rereading, every interpretation a reinterpretation, and we are always concerned with how to relate contextual-textual horizons of meaning of authors with our contextual-textual horizons of meaning. In this regard, we are always contextually situated and must become aware of the contextualized givenness of our experiential world as part of the process of reconstituting marginality.

In presenting these hermeneutical formulations, our focus is on Gandhi and his most influential work, *Hind Swaraj*, because this brief book, really a dialogic manifesto and argument, is arguably the most influential Indian attempt at rewriting marginality.[7] The following hermeneutical observations with respect to Gandhi and *Hind Swaraj* are offered only briefly and inadequately. They can be applied to other illustrations of multiculturalism, minority literature, and the rewriting of marginality.

In analyzing complex hermeneutical questions of the dynamic relations between texts, contexts, and interpretations of meaning, I often have to respond to various questions with a clarifying question: which philosophy (or religious, social, political, or economic thought or vision) of Gandhi? Which Bhagavad-Gita? Which *Hind Swaraj*? Even, which Gandhi? Or, when referring to American minority literature, which George Washington? Which writing of the Constitution? Which Abraham Lincoln? Which writing of the Montgomery Bus Boycott? Which Rosa Parks and which Martin Luther King, Jr? Which writing of Wounded Knee? Which Black Elk? Which mythic account? Indeed, which America? How one responds to such questions is indicative of how one understands dominant power relations, minority literature, and the rewriting of marginality.

There is always a complex, often contradictory, dominant and hegemonic, secondary and oppositional, overt but also camouflaged and hidden, open-ended relational dynamic that holds between, say, Gandhi's (and our) contextual variables, his (and our) textual expressions, and his (and our) interpretations of meaning. To illustrate this hermeneutical project, we will briefly consider the example of how we are to read and interpret the meaning of *Hind Swaraj* and rewrite that account of marginality so that it speaks to us today.

First, to gain some understanding of what Gandhi intends in writing *Hind Swaraj*, we have to understand the complex relations of the contexts within which Gandhi lived, how he relates to other texts and contextual variables that influence him and led to his writing of *Hind Swaraj*, and how these contextual-textual relations inform Gandhi's interpretation of meaning expressed in *Hind Swaraj*. What was the horizon of meaning within which Gandhi lives and which gains expression in this work?

In situating *Hind Swaraj* contextually and interpreting Gandhi's intended meaning, our hermeneutical project is always approximate, is never certain, and is always open to multiple interpretations. We have Gandhi's text, how he expresses himself, but we always have to interpret the meaning of what is being expressed. Since there is a lot of diverse information, both in Gandhi's writings and the writings of others, and there are even so many contextual references and sometimes undeveloped or confusing contextual claims in the *Hind Swaraj* text, this has led to numerous, diverse interpretations of meaning with their rewritings of marginality.

In his 40 years in India, England, and South Africa before writing *Hind Swaraj*, there were numerous contextual influences on Gandhi's philosophy and practice. These include diverse philosophical, religious, social, political, economic, cultural, literary, legal, educational, and other "civilizational" influences. Gandhi is influenced both positively, by what he accepts, and negatively, by what he rejects, including, finally, dominant, oppressive, violent, "modern (Western) civilization." Yet, this is also complicated since most of Gandhi's explicit positive references in *Hind Swaraj* are to western authors, even if they are critics of the modern West, and only two of his 20 recommended readings in *Hind Swaraj* are by Indians.

Similarly, consistent with some Native American and other minority literature, Gandhi seems to praise in the loftiest, essentialized terms, the outstanding "ancient (Indian) civilization" as the oppositional embodiment of God, Truth, Morality, Love, and Nonviolence. Yet, in spite of his religious upbringing and some desperately sought guidance from the Jain Rajchandra, it is not clear that Gandhi, who was struggling with the question of what it meant for him to become an authentic Indian, has a deep understanding at this time of Indian philosophy, religion, history, literature, or culture, ancient or modern.

In terms of swaraj at the heart of *Hind Swaraj*, Gandhi relates to the context of nineteenth and twentieth-century Indian nationalist movements for independence from British colonial rule. He relates to the Moderates, who work for constitutional changes and reforms within the existing legal framework, and the Extremists, who endorse both legal and extra-legal or illegal means if necessary to gain independence. The latter include expatriate Indians, including those Gandhi had just met in England, and these include anarchists and those who advocate violence, terrorism, and assassination. Gandhi is familiar with how the Moderates and the Extremists struggling for independence from British colonial rule rewrite marginality in a wide variety of contradictory literature.

In short, in order to understand why Gandhi uses certain language, images, and symbols, presents certain arguments, rejects certain positions, and what he intends and means in writing *Hind Swaraj*, we have to understand how he is contextually influenced by Ruskin, Tolstoy, and other western sources; we have to understand how he is even influenced by certain modern political, constitutional, and social values, while rejecting the dominant post-Enlightenment, Industrial Revolution, materialistic, egoistic, unethical conceptions of development and progress of the modern West; and we have to understand how he is contextually influenced by his exposure to certain Indian ethical, political, economic, social, cultural, aesthetic, and spiritual sources and experiences, while rejecting, partially or totally, various traditional and modern Indian religious, political, social, and economic formulations.

For example, consistent with much of marginalized minority literature, Gandhi reacts in *Hind Swaraj* against the attitudes of modern civilization, with the colonial domination and humiliation of India, in his desire for swaraj. But he contextually rejects the dominant Indian approaches to political independence as false swaraj since they parrot the values of a violent and oppressive modern civilization of the West, and lack the deeper necessary ethical and spiritual meaning of swaraj as involving true self-rule grounded in morality, self-control, various virtues, and selfless service for meeting the needs of others.

In terms of our hermeneutical situation, not identical with Gandhi's contextual–textual horizon of meaning in 1909, how are we to read and interpret the meaning, significance, and relevance of *Hind Swaraj*? Should passages, say, dramatically and judgmentally portraying ancient Indian villages or modern Western hospitals be read as making historical, empirical, or factual claims, or should they be viewed at a deeper level as symbolic, metaphorical, mythic, or allegorical expressions in need of interpretation? How we answer such questions will shape how we accept, reject, reappropriate, and rewrite Gandhi's approach to marginality.

In our hermeneutical approach, every reading is always a rereading, every formulation is a reformulation, and every interpretation is a reinterpretation. The contextually situated text does not have some absolute, rigid, static, essentialized, true meaning. There is not one true, essentialized meaning of what it is to be an authentic Hispanic or Latino American, Jewish American, African American, Native American, American woman, or American worker. All contextually situated texts and rewritings of marginality are part of an ongoing, dynamic, open-ended process of new contextual developments, new textual readings, and new interpretations of meaning.

For example, there are significant contextual developments in Gandhi's life and world between November 1909 and his assassination in January 1948. Even in Gandhi's life, in his "experiments with truth" related to passages in *Hind Swaraj*, there are significant successes and significant failures, such as terminated satyagraha struggles, Hindu–Muslim communal violence, the Partition of India, and an independent Indian nation state that had little to do with Gandhi's conception of true swaraj. If we consider what has contextually developed from 1948 to the present, we live in a world that is often radically different from Gandhi's world.

Therefore, since our contextual situatedness always shapes how we read and interpret texts, how do our new contextual variables, including new hermeneutical developments, shape how we read *Hind Swaraj*, what it means to us, which passages seem significant and which voices are heard, which passages seem insignificant or irrelevant, and which voices are marginalized or silenced? Such central hermeneutical questions apply to how we read all minority literature, understand multiculturalism, and rewrite marginality.

In this hermeneutical project, we are always engaged in the complex task of how to relate two textual-contextual horizons of meaning: Gandhi's and our own. This is a dynamic process of contestation in which different people today will read and interpret *Hind Swaraj* in radically different ways: more literal and more symbolic interpretations, more sympathetic and more hostile interpretations, more conservative and more revolutionary interpretations, more narrowly religious and more ethically and humanistically nonreligious interpretations.

This does not mean that anything goes and that our hermeneutical approach to *Hind Swaraj* or to any other text of minority literature and rewriting marginality is completely arbitrary and subjective, as if we can read any meaning we like into the text. Using an example of rewriting marginality from American literature, there is a long history of "Negro spirituals" and other powerful cultural creations by American slaves. From the perspectives and rewritings of the slave masters and of the dominant white supremacist culture, these are expressions of the inferior blacks expressing their childlike "natural" bodily emotions, their passive and willing acceptance of their status as slaves, and even their gratitude for the masters' civilizing white man's burden. We now recognize that this hegemonic ideological rewriting from the perspective of the white masters usually distorts or silences the authentic voices of the oppressed and exploited slaves, whose expressions are often camouflaged, and express great fear and terror, alienation, anger, and the struggle and hope for freedom and liberation. The same analysis can be given of caste-privileged rewritings of the authentic subaltern voices in powerful Dalit literature.

There are misreadings and misinterpretations of meaning. The text—without one exclusively correct reading and without some non-contextualized absolute, essential meaning—is malleable and capable of multiple readings and interpretations, but it is not infinitely malleable. The text has a structure, intention, goals, arguments, means-ends analysis, relevant contextual variables, and so on. Any claim, for example, that Gandhi's *Hind Swaraj* expresses a modern, capitalist, industrial, technologically determined version of swaraj is based on a misreading and a misinterpretation. That is why our hermeneutical project must always include criteria of verification so that we can judge whether any particular reading and interpretation has great explanatory value in allowing us to assess the developing meaning, significance, and relevance of *Hind Swaraj* or of minority literature for our contemporary world.

It may at first seem both bold and pretentious, but consistent with our hermeneutical project and with Gandhi's philosophical approach and hermeneutical observations, to submit that our reading of *Hind Swaraj* today invites us to develop and improve Gandhi's textual formulation of 100 years ago. We are called upon to do with *Hind Swaraj* what Gandhi does with the Bhagavad-Gita, the Ramayana, and other texts. Through our rereading, rethinking, reformulating, and reinterpreting, contextually influenced by new information and new developments, our hermeneutical project is to raise critical questions, purify, expand, and improve *Hind Swaraj* so that it can become a more developed and more adequate text for the twenty-first century.[8] Does such a hermeneutical approach speak to a vision and practice of rewriting marginality that takes seriously the contextualism of class exploitation, sexism, racism, poverty, humanly-caused suffering, violence, war, imperialism, and the destruction of planet earth? Does such a hermeneutical approach to Gandhi after 9/11 view literature and philosophy as insightful, transformative, and empowering in helping us to realize our higher human potential?

Gandhian Challenges and Contributions to Rewriting Marginality

This section and the following two sections will raise a series of Gandhian challenges. How does Gandhi approach marginality? What voices does a Gandhian approach privilege? How does it incorporate multiculturalism, diversity, and differences within holistic, relational, unifying perspectives? By offering an interpretation of Gandhi's complex formulation of violence and nonviolence and his innovative ethical and ontological analysis of the relative-absolute distinction, I will suggest how rewriting marginality is central to the transformative process of reconstituting our relations to our self, our world, nature, truth, and reality.

Gandhi does have some interest in literature and in aesthetics. He often writes of how, from his youth and throughout his life, he is drawn to certain hymns and tales, especially those presenting exemplary moral individuals and lessons; he does have an interest in Gujarati literature; and in *Hind Swaraj* and other writings, he expresses his appreciation for the aesthetic theories of Tolstoy and Ruskin, with their radical critiques of modern, Western, industrial civilization and their anti-modern aesthetic alternatives. However, in my view, Gandhi is often quite repressed and limited in the range and depth of his aesthetic appreciation, and this is not what he most offers to multiculturalism, minority literature, and the rewriting of marginality.[9]

There are many, obvious, well-known features of Gandhi's philosophy and practice that are directly relevant to the themes of minority literature and rewriting marginality, and which can be presented without detailed analysis and development. Gandhi's famous Talisman relates directly to rewriting marginality. When we are in doubt as to what to do, including whether and how to relate to minority literature, multiculturalism, and marginality, Gandhi advises us to think about the most downtrodden, those with the least freedom, self-determinism, and real swaraj. Then we should ask ourselves what our action, including our literary production, will do to improve their lives. Then, according to Gandhi, all of our doubts will melt away.[10]

Oh, if only it were so easy. Think of Ellison, after the publication of his remarkable *Invisible Man* (New York: Random House, 1952), struggling for decades, unable to write his second novel. Or think of Baldwin, tormented and full of doubts about what it is for him to be an American, how to respond to racism, how to respond to vicious homophobic attacks by Mailer and by some Black writers with their super masculinist rewriting of their manhood. In his struggles for more authentic self-identity. Baldwin becomes an expatriate writer in Paris, where he is less marginalized and more at home. But because of civil rights and human rights developments, he later feels compelled to return to New York to resume his conflicted multidimensional minority existence with his new engaged practices and rewritings of marginality.[11] For most of us who struggle with writing and rewriting, it would be wonderful if we needed only to meditate on Gandhi's Talisman, and then our doubts would melt away, the creative juices would flow, blockages would become unblocked, our path illuminated, and profound literary productivity would soon follow.

Of course, it is not so easy, and it is not so easy for Gandhi himself, even with his commitment to identifying with rewriting marginality, as he often struggles in his life and in his writings. Think, for example, of the formative time of his two decades in South Africa. Although he deepens his identification with an overwhelming commitment to the minority Indian community, even finally rejecting the evils of Modern Western civilization, he keeps holding on to his identification as a loyal member of the British Empire, with his admiration for his idealized British Constitution and his idealized British legal system. Although his sympathies are with the Boers and with the Zulus, he identifies with, supports, and even participates in the British wars against the Boers and Zulus. In fact, although his approach to marginality should have led Gandhi to identify most with the plight of the most downtrodden, the indigenous Africans, Gandhi primarily focuses, often exclusively, on the plight of the relatively more privileged Indians.

In this regard, the remarkably empathetic and tolerant Gandhi, with his deep commitment to respecting the diverse paths of others, often seems incapable of appreciating and identifying with the cultural values and contextualized situatedness of Zulus and other Black Africans. In his attempt to rewrite marginality, by responding to the humiliation of Indians, he reminds them of the earlier superior ancient civilization of extraordinary ethical and spiritual teachings and literature. But Gandhi sometimes seems to regard native Africans in ways not totally dissimilar to how the British regard Indians: as rather primitive, irrational, uncivilized, backward human beings, lacking in the glories of modern civilization (or any civilization).

Although Gandhi supporters often defend him against all charges of racism, many of his writings, especially in South Africa, are blatantly racist. In recent years, the influential, progressive writer Arundhati Roy has made the best-known extreme attacks against Gandhi as a racist and as a casteist. Ashwin Desai and Goolam Vahed carefully document Gandhi's obsessional identification with the British Empire, his need to show Indian loyalty and service toward the Empire, including shocking ways in which he completely ignores or justifies extreme violence and suffering inflicted by the British on the Boers and especially on the Zulus, with the colonial, racist view of African native peoples as uncivilized savages.[12] In all fairness, and to Gandhi's credit, in his ongoing "experiments with truth," Gandhi is often conflicted and later very self-critical of many of his earlier positions and would have definitely rejected some of these earlier limited views about minorities, multiculturalism, and marginality.[13]

Returning to the basic Gandhian orientation with regard to minorities and marginality—privileging and serving the needs of the most downtrodden, exploited, oppressed, impoverished, unfree, and suffering among us—Gandhi offers the following exemplary model to writers, just as he does to other human beings: act through selfless service, morally and socially fulfilling your dharma, with character, self-control, and self-discipline. Act as a virtuous being, and this includes simplifying your needs, acting with fearlessness and courage, and embracing a non-egoistic attitude of nonattachment to success, failure, power, status, wealth, and other results of your actions. Such selfless identification with marginality and rewriting of marginality is not self-denying, but is the means by which the writer realizes one's deeper ethical and spiritual self. This is the basis for living a meaningful, nonviolent, significant, and truthful human existence.

What this means is that Gandhi's approach rejects the literary position that literature exists simply for the sake of literature, and it rejects the myth of objective neutrality. In our contextualized reading and writing of texts, our interpretations of meaning, and our rewritings of American marginality or of anything else, we are perspectivally situated in the relational many-sidedness of multicultural reality. While oversimplifying complex, often contradictory reality, there is great truth in the old American Labor Union song: "Which Side Are You On?" As the influential American historian and activist Howard Zinn entitles his memoir, which later turned into a documentary of his life: "You Can't Be Neutral on a Moving Train."

For Gandhi—while recognizing the many-sidedness of existence and the countless ways of rewriting history, culture, literature, socioeconomic and political relations, ethics, and philosophy—this means identifying with and privileging the voices, needs, and perspectives of those who have been most marginalized, silenced, exploited, oppressed, and dominated: African Americans, Native Americans, other minorities, women, gays, lesbians, bisexuals, and transgender people, those with physical and mental disabilities, helpless children and the elderly, and so on.

As an action-oriented person in his writings and practices, Gandhi would challenge some of minority literature and other multicultural writings. He certainly recognizes and describes in great detail how minorities, whether numerical or power minorities, are victimized by the state, economic, military, educational, and other structures and policies of those with dominant power. However, as influenced by Tolstoy's "Letter to a Hindoo," Gandhi is impatient with some of the focus on victimhood. Just as he advises Indians under the Raj, he would instruct marginalized peoples today that they are often their own worst enemies and are at least partially responsible, through their passive acquiescence or complicity and cooperation, for their own marginalization.[14]

Gandhi would focus on minority literature and rewriting marginality as transformative in changing the perspectival relations and understandings of those who have been marginalized. This focuses not only on the oppression, exploitation, injustice, racism, sexism, and so on, but also on opening up space for silenced and marginalized voices. This means opening up new literary spaces for the self-determining minority voices, by furthering the process of self-transformation, by socially and culturally transforming the conditions and potential for minority empowerment, and by offering new relations of cooperation, mutuality, noncooperation, resistance, and alternative constructive work.

In this selective perspectival privileging of the voices and needs of those who have been most marginalized, Gandhi never forgets the many-sidedness of human reality. In his ethical and ontological view of the unifying, interconnected nature of all reality, he emphasizes perspectival diversity and differences, but he continually expresses this as a fundamental unity with a respect for differences. He thus would empathize with, but be uncomfortable with many forms of essentialized separatism, with rigid disciplinary and cultural boundaries, and group and individual identities, which appear in much of multicultural, postmodern, and minority literature.

In this regard, Gandhi would have also emphasized, as he did throughout his life, the need to understand and engage other human beings, including those who uphold the dominant, oppressive and unjust worldview, perspectives, and relations of those with power. In Gandhi's approach, one attempts in the transformative process of rewriting marginality to depersonalize the evil, not defining the other human being as some essentialized "enemy," and working for reconciliation based on equal relations of mutual respect. In short, the oppressor is also given the opportunity to become a more developed ethical human being, free from the imprisonment of being entrapped in imposed violent, dehumanizing, and alienating structures of power.[15]

As the marginalized are empowered, all of us, even the former oppressors, are better off, since those who were marginalized and silenced can now contribute actively to solving our most pressing, shared contemporary crises and to creating diverse ways of living meaningful lives. The marginalized other, as no longer silenced and marginalized, is not only part of my authentic social relational world, including my own relational sense of self, but contributes to my own dialectical process of rewriting and reconstituting my individual social self as a more ethical and spiritually developed human being.

Gandhian Challenges to Approaches to Violence and Rewriting Marginality

What Gandhi most contributes to the themes of minority literature and rewriting marginality is not even this important, specific privileging of the marginalized oppressed and downtrodden. Numerous other writers also privilege the perspectives of the marginalized. What Gandhi most contributes is his radical challenge to us to rethink our approach to minority literature and rewriting marginality in terms of his key theoretical and practical values and principles. This especially consists of his approach to violence and nonviolence, and how this is grounded in the primacy of ethics and the ontology of truth and reality.

Gandhi was the most influential proponent of ahimsa in the twentieth century, and this section focuses on some of my work on Gandhi's remarkable approach to violence to illustrate how he may deepen and broaden our understanding of violence so that we approach minority literature, multiculturalism, and the rewriting of marginality in radically different ways. This section, with the new emphasis on minority literature and rewriting marginality will shorten and summarize much of the more detailed analysis in earlier chapters presented on the multidimensionality of violence and the violence of the status quo, the means-ends analysis of violence and nonviolence, and the preventive approach to violence. The concluding section will develop this by focusing on Gandhi's key distinction between the relative and the absolute, how this informs the approach to truth and nonviolence, and how this relates to an ethical and ontological view of the interconnectedness of all reality.[16]

Most of us who claim to be against violence and war and for nonviolence and peace use these terms in a very narrow sense, restricted to overt physical forces and conflicts. Minority literature often focuses on violent conquests, genocidal practices and exterminations, and overt, violent destruction of Native American culture with its sacredness of animals and nature. It focuses on the extreme suffering and violent exploitation of African slaves, and the lynching and beatings of African Americans seeking freedom and equality. It focuses on rape, domestic violence, and other oppressive expressions of misogyny in American history. A relevant Gandhian perspective must deal with such overt violence, but this is a relatively small part of the overall violence directed at minorities and the marginalized in contemporary USA and the world.

First, Gandhi deepens and broadens our perspective by continually pointing to the multidimensional nature of violence: overt but also hidden, concealed, and camouflaged dimensions of physical violence, inner psychological violence, linguistic violence, economic violence, social violence, political violence, cultural violence, religious violence, educational violence, and environmental violence. The history of writings on marginality, from the perspectives of the dominant power elite in the USA or any other society, with all of the silences, erasures, imposed definitions, racism, sexism, and classism, is in reality a history of imposed economic violence, linguistic violence, psychological violence, cultural violence, and so on.

For example, Gandhi places a tremendous emphasis on economic violence, which he usually equates with exploitation. In rewriting marginalization, minorities (and others) must deconstruct the dominant ideological justifications for economic exploitation, domination, and inequality. In some respects, Ambedkar is even stronger than Gandhi in emphasizing the violent economic basis of casteism, with its hierarchical relations of economic domination and exploitation, most violently of Dalits. In understanding the givenness of contextualized violence necessary for rewriting marginalization, Gandhi emphasizes the struggle to overcome unequal, asymmetrical relations of domination in which some people own and control the land, the technology or machinery, the wealth and capital, and they use such economic power to exploit and oppress impoverished disadvantaged minorities and the masses.

We are socialized into a modern world through language acquisition, family upbringing, educational training, religious and cultural institutions, and relations of rewards and punishments in which all of these dimensions of violence interact and mutually reinforce each other. Most privileged writings about minorities are very violent. Writings by minorities and other marginalized people not only express how they are violently mistreated, but also how they live and respond to themselves and to the marginalized others in very violent ways. Exploited and dominated minorities in the USA, as well as those marginalized throughout the world, are not exempt from this perspectival, many-sided process of violent socialization. They typically accept or adjust to their socialization as the inferior, marginalized other; and they often express their marginalized situation as the alienated, dehumanized, exploited, and oppressed other, with multidimensional violence, fantasies, alcoholic, drug-induced, and otherworldly forms of escapism, and other responses that are self-defeating and do nothing to transform their marginalized existence. Without understanding this multidimensionality of violence, we cannot grasp the underlying root causes and determining causal factors that must be addressed in the transformative rewriting of marginality.

Second, in accepting or just living in such a world, Gandhi emphasizes the structural violence of the status quo. This is business as usual, or simply, just the way things are. The fact that the dominant system seems to be functioning efficiently, even without examples of overt physical violence or disruption on the part of African Americans, Latino Americans, Native Americans, and other marginalized people, does not mean that it is based on nonviolent relations. The fact that minorities suffer and die, without acts of noncooperation, protest, and resistance, because they blame themselves, accept some religious justification for their suffering, or simply feel fearful, hopeless, and powerless, should not disguise the fact that this is a very violent situation. For Gandhi, the normal dominant economic and political systems, consumerist and technological systems, cultural and religious systems, with all of their marginalizations, are inherently violent.

During my 2015–16 sabbatical, in which I was based at Indian Institute of Technology Madras (IIT-Madras), there were many such illustrations of the structural violence of the power-defined and dominant status quo at IIT-Madras and throughout India. For example, shortly before I arrived, in an incident that received national attention, the Dalit students' Ambedkar Periyar Study Circle (APSC) at IIT-Madras was "derecognized" and banned by the dean. The fact that the APSC promoted dissenting, Dalit, Ambedkar and Periyar thought and initiated debates on the evils of Hindu caste-based discrimination was considered divisive and even charged as spreading hatred toward Prime Minister Modi and others with power. Even after the ban was lifted, this was a widespread caste-based attitude, and the APSC members and other marginalized students on campus often experienced alienation and lived under fear and insecurity.

By way of extreme status quo contrast, the IIT-Madras, with its reputation of enrolling privileged, Tamil, high-caste, Brahmin students, has many rightwing Hindu student groups, invites many aggressive and chauvinistic Hindutva speakers to campus, has daily Hindu and Hindutva rituals, and has many programs extolling the cultural, political, and spiritual glories of hierarchical, caste-based Hinduism. In terms of the structural violence of the status quo, it repeatedly struck me as remarkable and revealing that such ideological glorifications and practices that define Dalits as inferior and justify economic, cultural, and other violence imposed on untouchables (lower castes, tribals, women, and others) are promoted, and not deemed divisive, hateful, and violent by the powerful elite.[17]

In a Gandhian perspective, our understanding of the multidimensional violence, as integrated with the structural violence of the status quo, is necessary for analyzing our modern violent world of hierarchical domination and marginalization. Such a Gandhian rewriting of marginalization is necessary for getting at the root causes and basic relational determinants necessary for long-term preventive measures, significant transformation, and for effectively resisting such pervasive violence. Such a rewriting, privileging the needs and voices of minorities and other oppressed people, must not only critique and subvert the dominant violent structures of power, but it must at the same time propose nonviolent, transformative alternatives for rewriting and overcoming marginalization that are grounded in truth, nonviolence, and real self-empowerment and self-determinism. Such an expanded consciousness of a more complex, nuanced, overt and hidden, holistic, relational approach to violence radically changes how we understand and respond to our contemporary crises in the USA, India, and the world in which numerical and power minorities are so violently marginalized. Such a broadened and deepened approach to violence offers challenges for rewriting marginalization for transforming violent structures and relations into ones of truth, nonviolence, love, compassion, self-rule, and sustainable living. Gandhi repeatedly maintains that an understanding of the writings and marginalizations of violent modern civilization arises from modern versions of the doctrine that the ends justify the means. Such a modern approach is a foundationally and structurally unethical, means-ends system of violent values and relations that can only produce violent and untruthful versions of freedom, independence, peace, progress, and human development that perpetuate the ongoing state of multidimensional and structural violence. In this regard, Gandhi claims that minority literature, sometimes with courageous and self-sacrificing marginalized heroes, often expresses the necessity of violent means to achieve lofty ends. In his means-ends analysis, Gandhi maintains that these minority heroes often internalize and embrace the basic modern violent perspectival orientation and worldview of their modern oppressors. Gandhi's challenge in rewriting marginality emphasizes his analysis of integral, moral, means-ends relations in which we decondition the multidimensional violent causes and structures and interject compassionate, loving, truthful, nonviolent, sustainable, causal factors and structures to break the vicious endless karmic cycle of violence, exploitation, and oppression.

In transformative minority literature, concerned with overcoming marginality, we must emphasize both means and ends and their integral, mutually reinforcing relations. Gandhi places even more emphasis on the means because we often have much greater control over the means we use, whereas noble ends, such as ending all violent marginality, may be unattainable because they express ideals beyond our power of realization. Violent, impure means by minorities and other marginalized peoples will shape violent impure ends regardless of our moralistic, self-justifying slogans and ideology.

Violence, terror, exploitation, greed, hatred, war, poverty, racism, sexism, national and group chauvinism, and all dimensions and structures of marginality are not independent, eternal, absolute, or inevitable. They exist within a violent, phenomenal world of impermanent, interdependent relativity. Historical, psychological, economic, social, religious, and other forms of violence are caused and conditioned, and they themselves become causes, and condition other violent consequences that then become new violent causal factors that fuel our world of socialized and maintained marginality. Gandhi-informed perspectives challenge us to approach violence and rewrite marginality in new ways. These perspectives aim at transforming the causally connected, means-ends, interdependent whole, of which minorities and other marginalized are integral parts. They allow us to transform ourselves from approaches and views constituted through ignorance, violence, domination, and suffering to those based on more moral and spiritual, nonviolent, egalitarian, just, relational understanding and practice. This very process of means-ends causal transformation, by which one transforms relations with marginalized others in order to serve their real needs, unmet in present dominant violent relations and structures of marginality, is the very process by which one transforms one's own self toward greater freedom, real peace, real security, and self-realization.

Gandhian Challenges to Approaches to Truth and Rewriting Marginality

This brings us to Gandhi's usually overlooked analysis of dynamic relations between the absolute and the relative that is essential for providing a more nuanced, complex, and adequate approach to understanding all perspectival, contextualized situatedness and responses, including minority literature, multiculturalism, and the rewriting of marginality. The key absolute-relative distinction and analysis challenges contemporary antithetical responses to minorities, multiculturalism, violence, and nonviolence that emphasize either unlimited cultural, contextual relativism of minority and other values, or the alternative of some absolutism that imposes a supposedly universal model on diverse others. As we have analyzed in Chapter 2 and later chapters, a Gandhian perspective, by way of contrast, submits that such common, dichotomous formulations of absolute truth versus relative truth are inadequate. A more adequate dialectical analysis of the relative and the absolute has much to offer our rewriting and transformation of marginality.

As has repeatedly been shown, Gandhi himself sometimes conveys the impression that he is a simple, rigid, uncompromising absolutist with respect to truth, violence, nonviolence, war, peace, vows, principles and rules, and other ethical and spiritual concepts and values. Nevertheless, a more comprehensive examination of Gandhi's writings on marginalized minorities and other topics reveals a more subtle, nuanced, and flexible Gandhi who addresses the complexity of violence, struggles with linguistic, psychological, and other forms of violence, and recognizes the difficulty of resolving violent conflicts and contradictions in hierarchical human relations of domination and marginalization.

This recognition of complexity in real unjust situations of violent marginality, active resistance, and struggles to overcome marginalization must not minimize Gandhi's commitment to such absolutes as nonviolence, love, and truth. A Gandhian perspective should not be identified with certain, fashionable, modern approaches of unlimited relativism, complete subjectivism, or postmodernist interpretations that submit that what I am formulating in my minority literature of rewriting marginality is my construction of a Gandhi narrative without any claims to truth and reality. Gandhi, with all of his respect for diverse many-sided paths to truth and reality, would never agree that violent exploitative marginality is immoral from his nonviolent egalitarian perspective of serving the needs of those most dominated and oppressed and working for the self-determinism of the marginalized other, but it can be justified and be acceptable in terms of other anti-Gandhian perspectives.

As presented in earlier chapters, Gandhi frequently offers formulations of the absolute, especially his two major absolutes of satya (Truth, often equated with God and the spiritual Self) and ahimsa (Nonviolence, benevolent harmlessness, often equated with Love), and these are central to any Gandhian perspective on minority literature and rewriting marginality. Gandhi has an ontological view of Truth or Reality that reveals permanence underlying change, unity underlying diversity, and the most profound, ethical and spiritual realization of the indivisible oneness and interconnectedness of all of reality. Our rewriting of violent marginality must analyze how we are socialized and educated in ways that prevent us from realizing the reality or truth of the unity and interrelatedness of life.

As seen in the previous section, nonviolence and violence have very broad and deep meanings, as evident in their multidimensional forms and structures of the status quo. Our rewriting of marginality must analyze how we are socialized and educated in violent ways that prevent us from realizing and living consistent with the reality of nonviolence and love.

In Gandhi's challenging approach that is central to any relevant Gandhian perspective, satya and ahimsa must be brought into an integral, dialectical, mutually interacting and reinforcing relation. As previously seen in the means-ends analysis, we cannot use immoral, untruthful violent means to realize moral, truthful, nonviolent ends. However, beyond his ethical analysis, Gandhi is also making a major ontological claim that is often overlooked by others, including many that identified with minority literature. Nonviolence is a powerful unifying force that brings us together in caring, loving, cooperative relations; that allows us to realize and act consistent with the interconnectedness and unity of all of life. Violence, by way of contrast, maximizes ontological separateness and divisiveness, and is based on the fundamental belief that the marginalized other—whether individual, class, caste, gendered, racial, ethnic, religious, or national target of my hatred and violence—is essentially different from me or us.

For many understandable non-Gandhian reasons, much of the rewriting of marginality focuses on rather rigid cultural boundaries and minority identities, a world of extreme fragmentation, and the primacy of differences. In the broader and more inclusive Gandhian framework, in which minority and marginalized differences are affirmed, one maintains that all of human life and all of reality are interdependent and interconnected. What unites an upper-caste Hindu or a privileged white American with a Dalit or with an impoverished African American or with any other human being is, on the most meaningful level, more significant than what divides us. One upholds the primacy of a unity with a respect for differences. In the Gandhian perspective to minority literature and rewriting marginality, violence and hatred are not only unethical, but are also inconsistent with the absolute truth and reality, whereas nonviolence and love are the ethical, psychological, political, economic, and cultural means for realizing truth and reality.

With this foundation of absolute truth and nonviolence, it is tempting to formulate a Gandhian perspective to violence, oppressed minorities, and marginality in oversimplified and false ways, by ignoring or devaluing Gandhi's repeated emphasis on his essential methodological, epistemological, and ontological claim: all of us, whether marginalized or privileged and dominant, exist in this world as relative, finite, imperfect beings of limited, situated, embodied consciousness and existence. Ambiguity, contradiction, fallibility, and existential tension are defining aspects of our human mode of being in the world. Our knowledge is always conditioned, imperfect, and perspectival. As Gandhi repeatedly tells us, even he at most has limited "glimpses" of absolute truth and nonviolence. Our Gandhian challenging approach to rewriting marginality always expresses the attempt to move from one relative truth to a greater relative truth, closer to the absolute regulative ideals.

Here we can see the central place of empathy, care, mutuality, cooperation, and tolerance in a Gandhian open-ended perspectival approach to rewriting marginality. One of the most arrogant and dangerous moves is to make what is relative into an absolute. Even when we attempt phenomenologically to suspend our own value judgments, empathize with and listen to the minority voices, and express the self-determining voices of the marginalized others, our understandings and rewritings are always limited and imperfect. Recognizing the specificity, complexity, and necessary limitations of our contextualized situatedness allows us to grasp the relative partial truths of marginalization while rewriting marginality.

In doing this, our Gandhi-informed approach to rewriting marginality should be tolerant and open to other points of view. Others, as engaged in minority literature and multiculturalism, have different relative perspectives and different glimpses of truth that contribute to our understanding and transformation of marginality. As seen in our analysis of the interconnected unity of truth and reality, the other as the marginalized other is integrally related to my process of self-understanding, self-transformation, and more truthful, nonviolent, ethical, political, cultural, and spiritual self-realization.

In these last sections, this chapter has formulated how Gandhi broadens and deepens our understanding of violence and nonviolence, especially in their multidimensional and structural dimensions, and how he challenges us with his analysis of means-ends relations and relative-absolute relations. Gandhian perspectival insights and challenges are very relevant to how we approach minority literature, multiculturalism, and rewriting marginality. Such a Gandhian approach, when selectively reread, reinterpreted, reappropriated, and applied in new creative ways, has great relevance and significance for the major themes and issues relating to minority literature and the rewriting of marginality.

As expressed in earlier chapters on a wide variety of topics, I do not believe that Gandhi, as a remarkable human being but one with human weaknesses, has all of the solutions when it comes to minorities, rewriting marginality, or the nature and function of literature. Some of what he wrote about Dalits, indigenous peoples, women, and other marginalized people must be revised and reformulated to be significant for rewriting marginalization today. Some of what he wrote, reflecting the historical narrative and contextualization of Gandhi's personality and socialization, is backward, reactionary, provincial, and of no relevance today.

Nevertheless, just as minority literature and multiculturalism at their best can subvert the dominant sites and structures of hegemonic power, Gandhi's insights can serve as a catalyst, allowing us to rethink many of the assumptions, concepts, and perspectival ways that we approach dominant and subaltern relations of marginality. When integrated with complementary non-Gandhian approaches, we are afforded exciting possibilities for new, creative, meaningful rewritings of marginality.

As formulated at the beginning of Chapter 1, this concluding chapter on rewriting marginality illustrates the purpose and structure of this book. "Gandhi before 9/11" refers literally, but mainly symbolically, to the narrative of the historical and temporal contexts of the twentieth-century M.K. Gandhi, how he experiences economic, political, social, caste, gender, religious, and other marginality and how he responds and rewrites Gandhi-informed marginality. "Gandhi after 9/11" refers to our twenty-first century world that defines marginality by dominant non-Gandhian and anti-Gandhian perspectives with their values, relations, and structures of meaning. This final chapter suggests ways in which a Gandhi-informed approach can understand and respond to the contemporary crises of marginality as evidenced in growing inequality, racism and sexism, communal and religious persecution, nationalistic xenophobia, and other ways of stereotyping, dominating, dehumanizing, exploiting, and destroying the marginalized "others." It suggests ways that a Gandhi-informed rewriting of marginality can lead to transformative engaged practices that are more moral, nonviolent, sustainable, and truthful.

As seen in this book's subtitle, we must consider a Gandhi-informed, creative, nonviolent and sustainable response in the rewriting of marginality that is defined in the Gandhi after 9/11 world by so much immorality, untruth, multidimensional and structural violence, and unsustainability. It has been the central claim of *Gandhi after 9/11* that a Gandhi-informed approach, philosophy, and practice, when selectively appropriated and contextually reformulated, is invaluable for us today. It provides us with creatively nonviolent and sustainable responses to our contemporary crises of marginality, as well as the other economic, political, social, cultural, religious, technological, and environmental crises that define our twenty-first century world.

Notes

1. I was invited by Dr Hameed Khan to deliver the Keynote Address "Rewriting Marginality: Minority Literature, Hermeneutical Insights, and Gandhian Challenges" at this international conference. This chapter is a major revision of what was first presented as the keynote and was later published as "Rewriting Marginality: Minority Literature, Hermeneutical Insights, and Gandhian Challenges," in *Writing Today* 1, no. 1 (January 2012): 1–18.
2. As a meaningful personal note, especially since the international conference was held at the Dr Babasaheb Ambedkar University, there was a significant presence of Ambedkarite Dalits. This included a wide range of Ambedkarites. On the one hand, there were a small number of speakers who gave highly polemical, sloganeering, dogmatic, political speeches, uncritically glorifying Ambedkar and his philosophy, and attacking Gandhi as a proponent of hierarchical casteism of domination and as an enemy of all Dalits. On the other hand, the majority of Dalits, who had rarely read any Gandhi, had been socialized to be anti-Gandhi, often, in my view, for some good reasons. They were surprised by the more nuanced, contradictory, imperfect, contextualized Gandhi I presented, were eager to engage me in conversation, and often expressed sentiments to the effect that "well, that Gandhi is more acceptable to us as Dalits" than what we experience in contemporary, dominant, Hindu India. These experiences in Aurangabad are consistent with many dramatic meaningful interactions I had with Dalits at

the University of Hyderabad in 2010, at IIT-Madras in 2016, and in other parts of India.
3. In indicating that I am cognizant of how my American background to some extent shapes my understanding of Gandhi, Hinduism, or Buddhism, and in now sharing some of the personal influences on me of American minority literature, this does not mean that being from the USA necessarily provides one with any deep understanding of American literature, culture, politics, economics, Constitution, and so on. For example, the French diplomat and historian Alexis de Tocqueville is often cited in the USA as the most insightful historian of the experiment of American democracy. To provide an Indian illustration, my friends Professor Prafulla Kar of Baroda and Professor Hameed Khan of Aurangabad have specialized expertise in American culture and know far more than I do about American literature. In this regard, as relevant to Gandhi, Indians over the years have occasionally said to me that they do not want a Gandhi-informed lecture because "we are Indians, so we know Gandhi." Far more often, I have had Indians invite me to address their classes and other gatherings to speak on Gandhi, because they bemoan the fact that their students and other Indians know little about Gandhi, and, I suspect, they hope that I as an American who values Gandhi's legacy will shame some in the audience to learn something about this remarkable Indian.
4. As discussed in Chapter 4, my works focusing on the Eliade's history and phenomenology of religion and scholarly and literary creativity include Douglas Allen, *Structure and Creativity in Religion: Hermeneutics in Mircea Eliade's Phenomenology and New Directions* (The Hague, Paris, and New York: Mouton Publishers, 1978); Douglas Allen, *Myth and Religion in Mircea Eliade* (New York: Routledge, 2002), and more recently Douglas Allen, "Eliade's Phenomenological Approach to Religion and Myth," in *Mircea Eliade: Myth, Religion, and History*, ed. Nicolae Babuts (New Brunswick, New Jersey: Transaction Publishers, 2014), pp. 85–112.
5. In this book, little mention has been made of Adivasis (from the Hindi words for "of earliest times" and "inhabitants"). These "indigenous peoples," "the scheduled tribes," number more than 200 distinct groupings, and there are about 100 million Adivasis in India today. Some have been involved in national and state secessionist movements. From a Gandhi-informed perspective, in which we privilege the needs of the other, especially the most disadvantaged and least free suffering others, the largely rural Adivasis should be viewed as among the most impoverished and most exploited Indians. For a historical narrative of Adivasi

developments in the twentieth century, see David Hardiman, *Gandhi in His Time and Ours* (New York: Columbia University Press, 2003), pp. 136–53.

6. As was shown in Chapter 5 and especially in Chapter 6, such Indian perspectives and identities can be very complex and contradictory. We have seen how dominant "modern" Indians today often combine an ideology of aggressive Indian exceptionalism, incorporating premodern claims about the superiority of Vedic and other ancient Indian values, self-identity, and civilization, with their modern, Western modeled, neoliberal, capitalist, militaristic, globalizing, anti-Gandhi perspectives.

7. What follows in this chapter repeats and reformulates some of the analysis of *Hind Swaraj* presented in Chapter 5, "Personal Reflections on Reading *Hind Swaraj* and Indian Reactions" and especially the more detailed analysis of *Hind Swaraj* presented in Chapter 6 "Is Gandhi's Approach to Technology Irrelevant in the Modern Age of Technology?" In more general terms, what follows repeats some of my formulations of Gandhi's approach to violence and nonviolence, relative and absolute truth, means and ends, and other topics in earlier chapters. What this chapter adds to such formulations is the focus on minorities and rewriting marginality.

8. See Chapter 4 for an interpretation of how Gandhi attempts to reread, purify, reformulate, reinterpret, and apply the meaning of the Bhagavad-Gita so that it is significant for us today.

9. The most noteworthy disagreement with my position by an influential Gandhi scholar can be found in the writings of Anthony J. Parel, especially in his *Gandhi's Philosophy and the Quest for Harmony* (Cambridge: Cambridge University Press, 2006) and as developed in his *Pax Gandhiana: The Political Philosophy of Mahatma Gandhi* (New Delhi: Oxford University Press, 2016). Correctly emphasizing Gandhi's holistic approach grounded in the interrelatedness of all of life, Parel proposes a framework in which the key to Gandhi's philosophy can be found in his equally emphasized, mutually interacting balance of the classical Hindu four ends of life (the *purushartha*s): *artha* (wealth, aim of economic and political power), *kama* (aim of pleasure, sexual desire), dharma, and moksha. With his disciplinary training in political science, including earlier work on Machiavelli, Parel is very insightful in emphasizing the centrality of the end of artha, the political and economic, in Gandhi's philosophy; how Gandhi contributes to political philosophy; how many supporters and critics misinterpret Gandhi as a dogmatic utopian; and how Gandhi's political approach has great pragmatic significance.

In terms of my present reference to the literary and aesthetic in Gandhi, I disagree with Parel in that Gandhi, while he relates strongly to devotional literature and hymns, is the least developed by far in relating to the end of kama. Gandhi is often very narrow and repressed when it comes to the aesthetic appreciation, pleasure, sensuality, and sexuality of kama. In addition, in emphasizing a more pragmatic approach to artha that is more accessible to much of modern Western political philosophy and that correctly emphasizes the contextual relativism and significance of Gandhi's political thought and its applications, I would submit that Gandhi would strongly disagree with many of Parel's formulations, especially in that they are too flexible in allowing for contemporary violence and minimize some of Gandhi's focus on and interpretations of dharma and moksha and how they shaped his view of artha.

10. The facsimile of Gandhi famous "Talisman," entitled "A Note," can be found in D.G. Tendulkar, *Mahatma: The Life of Mahatma Gandhi*, Vol. 8 (New Delhi: Publications Division, Ministry of Information and Broadcasting, Government of India, 1990), p. 89, and is dated August 1947. The talisman is also published in Mahatma Gandhi, *The Collected Works of Mahatma Gandhi*, Vol. 89 (New Delhi: Publications Division, Ministry of Information and Broadcasting, Government of India, 1983), p. 125.

11. Among Baldwin's works focusing on the black experience and other forms of marginalization in America, we may cite his *Notes of a Native Son* (Boston: Beacon Press, 1955), *Nobody Knows My Name: More Notes of a Native Son* (New York: Dial Press, 1961), and *The Fire Next Time* (New York: Dial Press, 1963), in which Baldwin also intends to educate white Americans on what it means to be black in the USA. A powerful documentary film on Baldwin (1924–1987), featuring extensive footage with Baldwin and focusing on the creativity and complexity of his life and literature of marginalization, is entitled *I Am Not Your Negro* and was released in 2016.

12. See Arundhati Roy, "The Doctor and the Saint: Ambedkar, Gandhi and the Battle Against Caste," Introduction to B.R. Ambedkar, *Annihilation of Caste: The Annotated Critical Edition* (New Delhi: Navayana 2014); Ashwin Desai and Goolam Vahed, *The South African Gandhi: Stretcher-Bearer of Empire* (Stanford: Stanford University Press, 2015). The anti-caste publisher Navayana has published other recent works documenting Gandhi's racist writings. For some brief analysis of Gandhi's controversial views and positions taken in South Africa with regard to Boers and especially toward the marginalized Zulus and other indigenous Africans, see my Chapter 7, "Terrorism and Violence."

My own position is that Gandhi is a flawed human being, who often presents racist and casteist views, but he evolves and usually learns from his inadequate views. Most important, in my view, Gandhi's basic philosophy is anti-racist and anti-casteist, and we must selectively reformulate Gandhi's approach as contributing to the struggles against racism, oppression, exploitation, and injustice today.

13. Indian minority rewriting of marginality in South Africa, as expressed in some of Gandhi's racist and most controversial positions, continues throughout the twentieth century during the institutionalized white supremacy racism and as codified and legalized in the system of Apartheid (apartness) from 1948 until 1994. Under this white supremacist, political, economic, and legal system, South Africans were defined by four racial groupings: Whites, Indians (Asians), Coloureds ('mixed'), and the majority Blacks (Natives).

    Relatively privileged minority Indians experience racism and marginalization, but they often define the oppositional "other" as the least privileged and most downtrodden and marginalized Black Africans. Therefore, during their experiences of apartheid and the emergence of the Anti-Apartheid Freedom Movement, the majority of South African Indians were either complicit with apartheid or rewrote their marginality in ways that identified with the racist, violent, political, economic, and cultural orientation of the white masters.

    In fairness, there are many significant exceptions with notable Indians playing leadership roles in the struggles against apartheid. These Indians and other Asians do not identify with the ruling class, white supremacists. To provide a personal example, during my time in Durban, South Africa in 2000, I was deeply impressed with Ela Gandhi, the granddaughter of Mahatma Gandhi, who was a progressive force in the African National Congress and a Member of Parliament. As a peace and justice activist, she expresses many of the best values of Gandhi's legacy.

14. As we noted in Chapter 8, some of Gandhi's statements focusing on how Indians and other oppressed peoples should not blame the British and others oppressors for their oppression but should instead recognize that they are responsible for their lowly status as victims, can be misleading if abstracted, taken out of context, and not related to other variables. A reformulated Gandhian rewriting of marginality today must not be confused with the dominant-power ideological versions of "blaming the victim," as in the case of African Americans, Latinos, and others living in poverty, who are falsely stereotyped as lazy, irresponsible, immoral, get what they deserve, and have only themselves to blame for their situation.

15. This is clearly formulated by Martin Luther King, Jr., whose approach and philosophy are greatly shaped by Gandhi's formulations of the interconnected nature of truth and reality, nonviolence, and rewriting marginality. In his *Stride Toward Freedom: The Montgomery Story* (New York: Harper and Row, 1958) and later books, King submits that in the Civil Rights Movement struggle and eventual victory to overcome segregation and racism, the struggle is not between blacks and whites, it is between justice and injustice. In the eventual victory over racism and injustice, it is not only blacks and other minorities who are the winners. This will also be a victory for whites. They will be freed from their hatred, racism, violence, and dehumanizing relations that separate them from unifying truth and reality. They will thus be given the opportunity to live more ethical, truthful, humanly developed, meaningful lives.

16. For my earlier, more detailed formulations and analyses of Gandhi's approach to violence, nonviolence, and truth, see especially the following chapters in this book: Chapter 2, "Gandhian Philosophy: Theoretical Basis with Primacy of Practice," with the sections on "Gandhi's Theory and Practice of *Ahimsa*" and "Gandhi's Philosophy of Relative Truth"; Chapter 7, "Terrorism and Violence," with the sections on "Gandhi's Different Approach to Violence and Terrorism," "Economic Violence: An Illustration," "Gandhi's Means-Ends Analysis," "Gandhi's Preventative Approach to Terrorism and Short-Term Violence," and "Absolute Truth, Relative Truth, and Terrorism."

17. In using this illustration from my experiences at IIT-Madras to reveal the structural violence of the dominant status quo, it is important to note that there are numerous exceptions. Hundreds of faculty, administrators, and Tamil Brahmin students fully realize this double standard, this hypocrisy, and are deeply troubled by the marginalization, alienation, and suffering of Dalits and other marginalized members of the campus community.

Select Bibliography

Allen, Douglas. "Eliade's Phenomenological Approach to Religion and Myth." In *Mircea Eliade: Myth, Religion, and History*, edited by Nicolae Babuts. New Brunswick, NJ: Transaction Publishers, 2014, 85–112.

———. "Gandhi, Contemporary Political Thinking, and Self–Other Relations." In *Gandhi's Experiments with Truth*, edited by Richard L. Johnson. Lanham, MD: Lexington Books, 2006.

———. *Mahatma Gandhi*. London: Reaktion, 2011.

———. "Mahatma Gandhi after 9/11: Terrorism and Violence." In *Comparative Philosophy and Religion in Times of Terror*, edited by Douglas Allen. Lanham, MD: Lexington, 2006, 19–39.

———. "Mahatma Gandhi's Philosophy of Violence, Nonviolence, and Education." In *The Philosophy of Mahatma Gandhi for the Twenty-First Century*, edited by Douglas Allen, 33–62. Lanham, MD: Lexington Books, 2009. Also published in *The Philosophy of Mahatma Gandhi for the Twenty-First Century*. New Delhi: Oxford University Press, 2009.

———. *Myth and Religion in Mircea Eliade*. New York: Routledge, 2002.

———. "Social Constructions of Self: Some Asian, Marxist, and Feminist Critiques of Dominant Western View of Self." In *Culture and Self: Philosophical and Religious Perspectives, East and West*, edited by Douglas Allen. Boulder, CO: Westview Press/Harper Collins, 1997, 3–26.

———. *Structure and Creativity in Religion: Hermeneutics in Mircea Eliade's Phenomenology and New Directions*. The Hague, Paris, and New York: Mouton Publishers, 1978.

Allen, Douglas, ed. *The Philosophy of Mahatma Gandhi for the Twenty-First Century*. Lanham, MD: Lexington Books, 2009. Also published as *The Philosophy of Mahatma Gandhi for the Twenty-First Century*. New Delhi: Oxford University Press, 2009.
Ambedkar, B.R. *Annihilation of Caste: The Annotated Critical Edition*. New Delhi: Navayana, 2014.
Baldwin, James. *Nobody Knows My Name: More Notes of a Native Son*. New York: Dial Press, 1961.
———. *The Fire Next Time*. New York: Dial Press, 1963.
Bose, N.K. *Selections from Gandhi*. Ahmedabad: Navajivan, 1948.
Chadha, Yogesh. *Rediscovering Gandhi*. London: Century, 1997.
Dantwala, M.L. *Gandhism Reconsidered*. Bombay: Padma Publications, 1945.
Desai, Ashwin and Goolem Vahed. *The South African Gandhi: Stretcher-Bearer of Empire*. Stanford: Stanford University Press, 2015.
Descartes, René. *Meditations on First Philosophy*. Cambridge and New York: Cambridge University Press, 1986.
Dharampal. *Dharampal: Collected Writings*, 5 vols. Includes Dharampal, *The Beautiful Tree*, *Indian Science and Technology in the Eighteenth Century*, and *Civil Disobedience and Indian Tradition*. Mapusa, Goa: Other India Press, 2000.
Einstein, Albert. "Why Socialism?" *Monthly Review* (May 1949).
Eliade, Mircea. *Myth and Reality*. Translated by Willard R. Trask. New York: Harper and Row, 1963.
———. *Patterns in Comparative Religion*. Translated by Rosemary Sheed. New York: World Publishing Co., Meridian Books, 1963.
———. *The Myth of the Eternal Return*. Translated by Willard R. Trask. New York: Pantheon Books, 1954; also published as *Cosmos and History: The Myth of the Eternal Return*, 1959.
Feuerstein, Georg. *The Yoga-Sutra of Patanjali: A New Translation and Commentary*. Rochester, Vermont: Inner Traditions International, 1989.
Freud, Sigmund. *The Future of an Illusion*. Translated by W.D. Robson-Scott. New York: Liveright, 1961.
Gandhi, M.K. *A Bunch of Old Letters: Being Mostly Written to Jawaharlal Nehru and Some Written by Him*. Compiled by Nehru. New edition. New Delhi: Penguin Books, 2005.
———. *An Autobiography or The Story of My Experiments with Truth*. Translated by Desai, Mahadev. Ahmedabad: Navajivan, first published in 2 vols. in 1927 and 1929; 14th reprint. Also published as *An Autobiography: The Story of My Experiments with Truth*. Boston: Beacon, 1993.

Gandhi, M.K. *From Yeravda Mandir: Ashram Observances*. Translated by V.G. Desai. Ahmedabad: Navajivan Publishing House, 1957 [1933].

———. *Hind Swaraj and Other Writings*. Edited by Anthony J. Parel. Cambridge: Cambridge University Press, 1997.

———. *My Socialism*. Compiled by R.K. Prabhu. Ahmedabad: Navajivan Publishing House, 1959.

———. *The Bhagavad Gita According to Gandhi*. Edited by John Strohmeier. Berkeley, CA: North Atlantic Books, 2009.

———. *The Collected Works of Mahatma Gandhi*, 100 vols. New Delhi: Publications Division, Ministry of Information and Broadcasting, Government of India, 1958–1991.

———. *Truth Is God*. Ahmedabad: Navajivan Publishing House, 1955.

———. *Unto This Last: A Paraphrase*. Ahmedabad: Navajivan Publishing House, 1956.

Gaur, R.R., R. Sangal, and G.P. Bagaria. *A Foundation Course in Human Values and Professional Ethics*. New Delhi: Excel Books, 2010.

Gier, Nick. "Gandhi, Ahimsa, and the Self." *Gandhi Marg* 15, no. 1 (April–June 1993): 24–36.

Giroux, Henry A. *America's Addiction to Terrorism*. New York: Monthly Review Press, 2016.

Godse, Nathuram and Gopal Godse. *Why I Assassinated Mahatma Gandhi*. Delhi: Surya Bharti Prakashan, 1993.

Gopal, S. *Radhakrishnan: A Biography*. Delhi: Oxford University Press, 1989.

Gruzalski, Bart. *On Gandhi*. Belmont, CA: Wadsworth, 2001.

Haksar, Vinit. *Gandhi and Liberalism: Satyagraha and the Conquest of Evil*. New Delhi: Routledge, 2018.

———. "*Satyagraha* and the Right to Civil Disobedience." In *The Philosophy of Mahatma Gandhi for the Twenty-First Century*, edited by Douglas Allen. Lanham, MD: Lexington Books, 2009, 63–97.

Hardiman, David. *Gandhi in His Time and Ours: The Global Legacy of His Ideas*. New York: Columbia University Press, 2003.

Hoddy, Elizabeth. *The Banwasi Seva Ashram in Gandhi's Footsteps*. Govindpur, Sonbhadra, U.P.: Banwasi Seva Ashram and New Delhi: Gandhi Peace Foundation, 1999.

Hofmeyr, Isabel. *Gandhi's Printing Press: Experiments in Slow Reading*. Cambridge, MA: Harvard University Press, 2013.

Howard, Veena R. *Gandhi's Ascetic Activism: Renunciation and Social Action*. Albany, NY: State University of New York Press, 2013.

———. "Instrumental Rationality." *Stanford Encyclopedia of Philosophy*. 2013.

Iyer, Raghavan, ed. *The Essential Writings of Mahatma Gandhi*. Delhi: Oxford University Press, 1991.
Johnson, Richard L., ed. *Gandhi's Experiments with Truth*. Lanham, MD: Lexington Books, 2006.
King, Martin Luther Jr. "Beyond Vietnam: A Time to Break Silence," April 4, 1968, available at http://www.mlkonline.net/vietnam.html (accessed on May 15, 2018).
———. *Stride Toward Freedom: The Montgomery Story*. New York, NY: Harper and Row, 1958.
Kumar, Rahul. "On the Self-Other Relationship: Lessons from Gandhi for an Alternative Cosmopolitan Framework." *Gandhi Marg* 37, no. 2 (July–September 2015): 333–54.
Marcuse, Herbert. *Eros and Civilization: A Philosophical Inquiry into Freud*. Boston: Beacon Press, 1955.
———. *One-Dimensional Man: Studies in the Ideology of Advanced Industrial Society*. Boston: Beacon, 1964.
———. "Special Issue Refusing One-Dimensionality." *Radical Philosophy Review* 19, no. 1 (2016).
———. "Special Issue Refusing One-Dimensionality." *Radical Philosophy Review* 20, no. 1 (2017).
Murthy, B. Srinivasa, ed. *Mahatma Gandhi and Leo Tolstoy: Letters*. Long Beach, CA: Long Beach Publications, 1987.
Nehru, Jawaharlal. *A Bunch of Old Letters: Being Mostly Written to Jawaharlal Nehru and Some Written by Him*. Compiled by Nehru. New edition. New Delhi: Penguin Books, 2005.
———. *Nehru on Gandhi*. New York: The John Day Company, 1948.
———. *The Discovery of India*. New York: The John Day Company, 1946.
———. *Toward Freedom: The Autobiography of Jawaharlal Nehru*. Boston: Beacon Press, 1961.
Paranjape, Makarand R. *The Death and Afterlife of Mahatma Gandhi*. London and New York: Routledge, 2014.
Parekh, Bhikhu. *Debating India: Essays on Indian Political Discourse*. New Delhi: Oxford University Press, 2015.
———. *Gandhi: A Very Short Introduction*. New York: Oxford University Press, 2001.
Parel, Anthony J., ed. *Gandhi, Hind Swaraj and Other Writings*. Cambridge: Cambridge University Press, 1997.
———. *Gandhi's Philosophy and the Quest for Harmony*. Cambridge: Cambridge University Press, 2006.

Parel, Anthony J., ed. *Pax Gandhiana: The Political Philosophy of Mahatma Gandhi*. New Delhi: Oxford University Press, 2016.

Paxton, George. "Gandhi's Wars." *Gandhi Marg* 39, nos. 2–3 (July–December 2017): 135–55.

Pinker, Steven. *Enlightenment Now: The Case for Reason, Science, Humanism, and Progress*. New York: Viking, 2018.

———. *The Better Angels of Our Nature: Why Violence Has Declined*. New York: Viking, 2011.

Prabhu, R.K. and Ravindra Kelekar, eds. *Truth Called Them Differently*. Ahmedabad: Navajivan Publishing House, 1961.

Prabhu, R.K. and U.R. Rao, eds. *The Mind of Mahatma Gandhi*. Ahmedabad: Navajivan Publishing House, 1967.

Prabhupada, A.C. Bhaktivedanta Swami. *Bhagavad-Gita As It Is*. New York: Bhaktivedanta Book Trust, 1972.

Pyarelal. *Towards New Horizons*. Reprinted from *Mahatma Gandhi: The Last Phase*. Ahmedabad: Navajivan, 1959.

Radhakrishnan, Sarvepalli and Charles A. Moore, eds. *A Source Book in Indian Philosophy*. Princeton: Princeton University Press, 1957.

Radhakrishnan, Sarvepalli and J.H. Muirhead, eds. *Contemporary Indian Philosophy*. London: George Allen and Unwin, 1936.

Richards, Glyn. "Gandhi's Concept of Truth and the Advaita Tradition." *Religious Studies* 22, no. 1 (March 1986): 1–14.

Roy, Arundhati. "The Doctor and the Saint: Ambedkar, Gandhi and the Battle Against Caste." Introduction to Dr B.R. Ambedkar, *Annihilation of Caste: The Annotated Critical Edition*. New Delhi: Navayana, 2014.

Ruskin, John. *Unto This Last*. Edited by P.M. Yarker. London: Collins, 1970.

Sahasrabudhe, Sunil. *Gandhi's Challenge to Modern Science*. Goa: Other India Press, 2006.

Savarkar, Vinayak Damodar. *Hindutva: Who is a Hindu?* Bombay: S.S. Savarkar, 1969. Published in 1923 as *Essentials of Hindutva* and later retitled *Hindutva: Who Is a Hindu?*

Shirer, William L. *Gandhi: A Memoir*. New York: Simon and Schuster, 1979.

Shukla, Ved Mitra. "Significance of Advaita Philosophy in Mahatma's Gandhi's Life." *GITAM: Journal of Gandhian Studies* 4, no. 1 (January–June 2015): 214–24.

Tendulkar, D.G. *Mahatma: The Life of Mahatma Gandhi*, Vol. 8. New Delhi: Publications Division, Ministry of Information and Broadcasting, Government of India, 1990.

Terchek, Ronald J. *Gandhi: Struggling for Autonomy.* Lanham, MD: Rowman and Littlefield Publishers, 1998.

Terrorism, defined. *Antiterrorism.* Joint Publication 3-07.2. US Joint Chiefs of Staff. 24 November 2010.

———. 28 Code of Federal Regulations (CFR) Section 0.85 (l) (US Government Publication Office.

Tucker, Robert C., ed. *The Marx-Engels Reader.* New York: W.W. Norton, 1972.

Index

Absolute Truth 8, 27–8, 30, 33, 50–4, 166–9, 172–3, 245, 247–8, *see also* relative truth
Abu Ghraib prisoner scandal 147
Adi Shankaracharya 46, *see also* Shankara
Adivasis (tribals, original inhabitants) 4, 153, 224, 243, 249, 251–n5
Adorno, Theodor W. 116
Advaita Vedanta 19, 40–2, 44–9, 53–4, 70
Afghanistan: Obama administration policy and 161; terrorism and 140, 157; war on terrorism and 139, 172
African Americans 138, 153, 233, 238, 241–2, 247; physical violence on 242, *see also* violence
African National Congress 141
African slaves 241, *see also* African Americans
ahimsa 7, 9, 18, 21–7, 29, 31–3, 37n6, 63–6, 72–4, 77, 79–81, 194, 205, 246–7; as active nonviolent force 27; among *yamas* 64; commitment to 205; Gita and 26, 31, 65, 72–3, 77, 81; ideals of 51, 167; and I-me ego 26; and Jainism 72; *karma-yoga* and 50, 74, 79, 81; killing and 33, 205; love and 149; meaning of 66; moral philosophy of 27; non-attachment and 79; as nonviolence force 7, 27; philosophy of 32, 73, 151; practices of 25–7, 29, 146; for prevention 26; principles of 118; renunciation and 64; and *satya* 18, 29, *see also* Truth; in Shandilya Upanishad 64; Truth and Reality 29, 74, 80, 194; for unification 27; *in Yoga-Sutra* 64
Al Qaeda 138, 150, 156, 161, 168–9, 172, *see also* terrorism
al-Baghdadi, Abu Bakr 172

alienation 31–2, 35, 69, 99, 116–17, 221–2, 227, 239 (*see also* inequality; poverty); 16, 20, 24, 88, 116, 124, 186, 222, 234, 243; Descartes and 170; domination and 35; humanism and 109; marginality and 221; Marx and 31–2, 70; modern civilization and 117, 124, 209; of Native Americans 227
alternative technologies 127, 130
Ambedkar Periyar Study Circle (APSC) 242–3
Ambedkar, B.R. 11, 16, 92, 220, 241, 243, 250n2
Ambedkerites 4, *see also* Dalits; untouchables
anatta 48
ancient Indian civilization (Gandhi's Ancient Indian Civilization) 82n8, 101, 111, 113–4, 231, *see also* modern civilization
anicca 48
ankantavadi 45, 57n12, 225
anti-American terrorism 160, 162
anti-essentialism 226–7
anti-Gandhian(s) 9, 86, 89, 91, 93, 101, 153, 171, 246, 249; formulations of 90–2; Godse as 91; interpretations 189; Savarkar influence as 91; values 42, 129; victim-blaming formulations 196; vision of a modern India 12
anti-terrorism 163, 167, 169, *see also* war on terrorism
aparigraha 24, 151, 192–3
appropriate technology 15, 103, 122, 126, 132, *see also* alternative technology
Aristotle 21, 67, 223

Arjuna 62, 64–5, 67
Arnold, Edwin (Sir) 77
Arthashastra 49
ashram 9, 77, 109, 111–12, 153, 193, 198, 210; events of 212; experiments 112, 193; talks on Gita at 77; identity of self in 46, 66 (*see also* self); printing press at 111
Ashram Vows 153, 198
assassination 3, 6, 14, *see also* violence; of Gandhi 91, 158; of Martin Luther King 14; Sir William Curzon-Wyllie 103
Atman 45–6, 53, 57–8n9, 58n23, 62, 64, 66–7, 77; self as 46, 62, 64, 66, 77, *see also* soul; as higher soul 62; identity of self in 66; Krishna as 67; realization of Brahman 54, 74; *see also* Brahman-Atman

Bajaj, Jamnalal 204
Baldwin, James 222, 236
Bambatha Rebellion 145, *see also* Zulus
Beauvoir, Simone de 70, 222
Bhagavad-Gita 2, 26, 30–1, 45, 47–50, 60–81, 87, 112, 156, 183, 191; as gospel of nonviolence 30, 75–82, *see also* ashram, talks on Gita at; interpretation of 66–9; and nonviolence 65, 69–82
Bhagwat, Mohan 92
bhakti 47, 49, 61–2, 71, 74
Bhaktivedanta Swami Prabhupada, A.C. 73
bhakti-yoga 62, 73–4
Bharatiya Janata Party (BJP) 89–92, 100

Bihar earthquake 106–7; Gandhi on 106
Laden, Osama bin 138, 156–7, 172
body–mind–heart, harmonious development of 125
Boers 152, 236–7
Brahman 45–6, 53, 67, 76–7; Krishna as 67; sacrifice and 76
Brahman-Atman (Atman-Brahman) 45–6, 53, 54, 58n19, 62, 74, 77
Brahmins 152–3, *see also* caste: Hindus of upper
Branwasi Seva Ashram 109
British colonialism 103, 146, 188, 196
Buddha 40, 70, 160, 162, 171; formulation of *pratityasamutpada* 162, *see also* Doctrine of Dependent Origination
Buddhism 52, 196, 220, 225
Bush, George W. 141, 158, 172

Caliphate 172
capitalism 8, 94, 131, 148, 172, 181–2, 184–8, 190–2, 197–204, 206, 208–13; abolition of 188, 192, 200; attack on 188; capitalists and 188, 201; characteristics of 213; corporate 94, 131, 172, 182; as economic system 201; financial 3, 25, 94, 123, 125, 131; formulations of 190, 206; as irrational 208; Marx on 148; monopoly of 211; and private property 192, 202, 211; ruling class under 186; and socialism 185, 190, 192, 201; wealth accumulation in 148, 186, 202–3; and working class 186, *see also* labor

capitalists 3, 11, 32, 86, 102, 152–3, 185–8, 190–2, 200–5, 208–9, 211–12; dispossessing 203; and exploitation 203; financial institutions 182; labor-power and 186, 201; private owners as 186; as propertied class 201, *see also* land owners; and violence 203
Cartesian 118, 225
caste: Hindus of upper 87, 152, 247; lower 6, 111, 196, 243; oppression and 33, *see also* untouchability
casteism 4, 8–11, 16, 23, 27, 33, 51, 73, 80, 104, 111, 120, 237 *see also* untouchability
catalyst, Gandhi as 16, 35, 55, 140, 209, 249
chauvinism 89, 100–1, 244
Cheney, Dick 141
Christianity 114
civil disobedience 43, 104, 153, 195
civilization, *see also* modern civilization
civilizational: approach 116–17, 123; development 114, 117, 119, 121–2; transformation 119
class 8, 11, 23, 27, 33, 64, 120, 154–5, 181, 186, 205; exploitation 4, 33, 42, 186, 205, 235; lower 73, 186; struggle 129, 192–3, 203, 205, *see also* working class
classism 196, 241
climate change 15, 93, 107–8, 126–8, 209
Code of Federal Regulations (CFR) 141
Collected Works of Mahatma Gandhi, The 145, 157–8

communism 185, 187, 191, 206, 211, *see also* socialism
compassion 5, 7–8, 23, 29, 66, 79, 120, 122, 130, 244
conflicts 55, 79–80, 90, 203, 240; control of ego selves against 90; and disharmony with nature 79; and Gita 67; resolving 90, 166
Constructive Program (Gandhi's Constructive Programme, Constructive Work) 22, 38n12, 216–17n29
consumption 3, 25, 88, 93–4, 107, 126, 128; advertising and 25; and concept of development 88; ego-driven desires of 3, 107; increasing 128, 208; materialism and 117–18, 124; modern technological development and 93, 126; power and 94
contextualization 132, 249
cosmopolitanism 45–6, *see also under* dharma
courage (bravery): 8, 10, 102, 145–6, 158–9, 177n16, 196
cowardice 8, 152, 158–9, 177n17
crises: environmental 3, 16, 78, 250; of marginality 249–50, *see also* conflicts
critical thinking 123–4, 222
cultural violence 6, 69, 150, 241, *see also* violence
culture 4, 22, 88–9, 115–16, 128, 130, 170, 227, 231, 238; to backward natives 148; and human development 114; and modern 115–16; modern civilization 122; sustainable 132; swaraj approach to 116, 130
Curzon-Wyllie, Sir William 103, 158; assassination of 103

Dalits 6, 11, 16, 73, 120, 153–4, 226, 241–3, 247, 249; oppression of 16; as "untouchables" 4, *see also harijans*; untouchability
Dantwala, M.L. 217n37
decentralization 184, 193, 197
dehumanizing 31, 88–9, 99, 186, 226–7, 239, 249
democracy 11–12, 14, 102–3
democratic transformation 201
deontology 45, 167
Desai, Ashwin 237
Descartes, René 170, *see also* Cartesian
Dharampal 88, 97n6
dharma 46, 64, 115, 152, 197, 237; civilization 119; cosmopolitan 47; *karma* and 61; and righteous war 64
Dharmashastras 49
Dhingra, Madan Lal 103, 158
diversity 30, 48, 52, 71–2, 80, 91, 101, 123, 149, 184, 225, *see also* pluralism
Doctrine of Dependent Origination (*pratitya-samutpada*) 26, 48, 162, 178n18
domination 7, 10, 19, 24–5, 41, 87, 116–17, 128–9, 131, 140, 154–6, 191, 197, 200–3, 211, 226–8, 241, 245–6 (*see also* economic power; globalization; power); capital-labor relations of 211; exploitative and oppressive
downtrodden 42, 236–7, 240, *see also* marginalized; oppression
dukkha (suffering) 48, 162
duty 8, 10, 64–5, 95, 112

economic: exploitation 109, 156–7, 241; inequality 24, 109, 132; power 6–7, 24, 155, 241; system 170, 186, 192, 200, see also capitalism; *swaraj* 24; violence 6, 24, 150, 154–7, 163, 241
economics 5, 110, 151, 192, 196
education 4–5, 51, 164, 198, 210–11; systems of 148, 150, 170; violence and 6, 150, 207, 241
egalitarianism 5, 7, 10–11, 15, 25, 46, 103, 126, 131–3, 155, 197–8; and values 11, 13–14
ego-attachments 13, 112, 123, 196–7
ego-driven: desires 26, 107, 124–5, 130, 208; self 29–30, 63, 90, 107, 117–20, 130, 154, 164, 196–7, 208
ego-self 63, 117, 197
egotism 10, 34, 61, 65, 68, 232
ego-transcendence 50
Eliade, Mircea 83n18, 223–4
Ellison, Ralph 222, 236
Emergency, The 87, 96n3
empathy 165, 248
Engels, Friedrich 185–6
environmental: destruction 7, 10, 108–9, 132; values 5, 34; violence 2, 6, 23, 241, see also climate change
escapism, 7, 31, 242; imaginative 32
essentialism 28, 52, 78, 130, 225–7
ethics 5, 8, 21, 27, 88, 194, 204, 238, 240
ethnic 6, 27, 33, 68, 80, 120, 141–2, 149, 209, 227, 247, see also Adivasis; justifications for actions of 33; minorities 6, 141,
149; others 120; and terrorism 142; violence 120, 247
exploitation 5–8, 12–15, 42, 50, 87–9, 103–4, 128–9, 144, 155–7, 191, 195–6, 202–4, 211–13, 237–8, 241–2, 244, 246 (*see also* domination; oppression); blaming victims of 196; class 4, 33, 42, 186, 205, 235; economic 109, 152, 156–7, 241; and economic violence 155
"experiments with truth" 16, 20, 29, 53, 58, 77, 86, 107, 190, 210, 237
Extremists (in *Hind Swaraj*) 86, 103–4, 110, 231

freedom fighters 140–1
Freud, Sigmund 31, 39n15

Gandhi, M.K. 2, 40–1, 43, 231-2, 249; as Advaitin 47–54; assassination of 91, 158; as Bapu 3; civilization and 118–26; controversy and 40; as creative thinker 178n19, *see also* experiment with truth; as Father of the Nation 90; influence of 43, 62; as Mahatma (Great Soul) 3; means–ends analysis 159–63; philosophy, contextual influences on 231; and philosophy 10, 34; philosophy of relative truth 27–34; Roy and 237; and socialism 184, 186, 196, *see also* Gandhian Socialism; as socialist 187–8; Tagore and 106; talk-series on Gita 77; technology 118–33; and terrorism 157–9, 163–6

Gandhian socialism 181–4, 189–90, 193–213
Gandhians 4, 15, 33, 47, 86, 102, 130–1, 189–91, 248; against modern technology 15; and alternatives 122; Buddhism and 52; and development process 189; and Gandhian socialism 190; Godse and 91; and Nehru 102; and power 150; and technology 130–1
Gandhi-informed: approaches 8, 13–16, 99–100, 130, 151, 248–50; approach and globalization 15; approach and dominant assumptions 16; approach to technology 15, 99–100, 126; innovations 14, 93; perspectives 9, 127, 245; philosophy 10, 34; process of self-realization 118; socialism 184, 186, 196, *see also* Gandhian Socialism
Gautama, Siddhartha (Buddha) 40
gender 8, 11, 27, 68, 80, 120, 151, 205, 227, 249; oppression 33, 51; and patriarchal 111; and violence 23 120, 151, 206
genocide 138, 146, 205, *see also* Holocaust; Nazi; violence
Ginsberg, Allen 221
globalization 8, 15, 92, 94–5, 105, 123, 152, 182, 196, 211
God (Absolute, Truth, Self, Reality) 44, 46, 50–1, 53, 119–20, 194, 246
Godse, Nathuram 91, 158
Gokhale, Gopal Krishna 104

happiness 22, 65, 117, 120
harijans (untouchables) 152, *see also* castes; Dalits

hatredness 5–8, 14, 16, 23, 79–80, 88, 120, 153–4, 243–4, 247; and ego-attached experiences 30, 196–7; love against 5; as violent 149
Heidegger, Martin 31, 41, 116
himsa 37n6, *see also* terrorism; violence
Hind Swaraj 2–3, 26, 35, 86–95, 99–114, 117–19, 131, 158, 229–35
Hindu Mahasabha 91
Hindu nationalism, *see also* Hindutva
Hinduism 21, 63–4, 101, 196, 220, 225
Hindutva 3–4, 91–3, 97n9, 97n11, 100–2, 243
Hobbes, Thomas 22
Hoddy, Elizabeth 109
Holocaust 205–6, *see also* Nazi
Horkheimer, Max 116
human: flourishing 22–3, *see also* happiness; suffering 5
Hussein, Saddam 161

I–me ego 26, 78, 117, *see also* ego-attachments
immorality 5, 8, 10–12, 24, 26–7, 32, 34, 59, 62, 79, 111–12, 120–1, 213, 124, 246–7, 250; Gita and 112; of modern civilization 111; and modern life 124; and violence 250
imperialism 105, 196, 235
impoverished 42, 50, 92, 102, 122, 128, 152, 155–6, 191, 204, 237, 247; basic human needs and 155; economic growth and 128; economic violence and 155; inequality and 155, 241; in

268 Index

modern India 102; nonviolent transformation and 152; and self-determination of labor 195; spirituality and 42, 50; standard of living and 92; technology and 122; terrorism and 156
independence 3, 11, 152, 157–8, 182, 231–2, 244; movement for 181, *see also* noncooperation; *satyagraha*
Indian Americans/Indo-Americans 228–9
Indian civilization 57, 101, 111, *see also* modern civilization
Indian National Congress (INC) 91
Indian philosophy 21, 27, 40–1, 72, 87, 231
indigenous peoples, *see also* Adivasis
Industrial: civilization 235; revolution 115, 117, 232
industrialization 123, 182
inequality 5–7, 10–11, 13, 15, 24–5, 92, 94, 108–9, 128, 154–5, 197
injustice 5, 7, 13–14, 16, 28, 31–2, 42, 89, 108, 142, 153
"inner voice" 47, 51, 53, 57–8n19
innovations, Gandhi-informed technological 93, 95
insecurity 22, 140, 143–4, 155, 164, 173, 243
instrumental: rationality 88, 115–17; reason 115–16
interconnectedness 8, 13, 118, 120–1, 132, 187, 213, 240, 246–7
International Society for Krishna Consciousness (ISKCON) 73
intolerance 55, 80, 101, *see also* hatredness

Iraq 140, 157, 161, 169, 171–2; invasion of 139
Islamic State (IS) 23
Islamic State of Iraq and the Levant (ISIL) 23, 32
Iyer, Raghavan 193

Jainism 72, 196, 225
Jallianwala Bagh 145
Jews 120, 146, 153, 206, 221, *see also* Holocaust
jihadist 150
jnana 44, 46, 62, 66, 71
jnana-yoga 48, 62, 74
justice 2–3, 5, 14, 54, 79, 107, 120, 142, 208; struggle for 16; violence and 23

Kant, Immanuel 21, 167
karma 26, 44, 61, 76, 79, 160
karma-yoga 13, 49–50, 61–3, 70, 74, 77–9, 81, 151, 197, 203
karmic prakriti 54, 62, 76
karmic self-knowledge 64
Kashmir Issue 219n44
King Jr., Martin Luther 14, 43, 56n4, 216n21, 222, 230, 255n15; assassination of 14
Krishna 31, 62, 64–7, 74, 76, 83n12, 112; to Arjuna 62, 64; and perfection 31; on sacrifice 76
Krishnavarma, Shyamji 103

labor 24, 109, 187, 190–2, 195–6, 200–2, 204; as capital 191, 196–7, 201; exploited 195, 211; identification with 190; machine craze 108; wealth and 198
labor-power, and capitalists 186, 201
Lage Raho Munna Bhai 90

land owners 152, 205
language, violence and nonviolence 6, 23, 69, 150–1, 241–2
Lashkar-e-Taiba (LeT) 139, 150
Latino Americans 233, 242; physical violence on 242, *see also* violence
Lenin 185
LeT 150
lifestyle 128, 228
Lohia, Rammanohar 181
love 5, 7–8, 23, 29–30, 79, 109, 111, 120, 149, 166, 246–7
love-force (moral force, soul force) 5, 8, 13, 27, 80, 121; transformative 80

Madhyamika Buddhism 42
Mandela, Nelson 141
Manusmriti 49
Maoists 4
Marcuse, Herbert 116, 136n23
marginality 9, 221–3, 225–33, 235–8, 240–2, 244–50; American 238; approaches to truth and 245–50; approaches to violence and 240–5; crises of 249–50; history of writings on 241; of other 9; rewriting of 225–40, 245–7, 249–50; rewriting, African-American and 222; structures of 244–5; subaltern relations of 249; structures of 244–5; transformation of 245
marginality-rewriting of 223–42, 244–7, 249–50; Gandhi-informed 250; violence and 235–40
marginalization 11, 20, 45, 71, 73, 87, 138, 222–3, 225–7, 232–3, 236, 238–49; heroes of 244; others 247–9; people of 242, 249
Marx, Karl 16, 31, 70, 148, 185–6, 192, 199, 201, 203, 208; self-realization by 70; and socialism 185
Mashruwala, Kishorelal 217n37
materialistic/materialism 14, 68, 117–18, 193, 232
maya, karmic world of 54, 57n15
media 3, 5, 7, 13, 25, 94, 129, 227; ethics and 5; inequality and 7; power and 94; terrorism and 138; violence and 139, 143
Mehta, J.L. 41
Merleau-Ponty, Maurice 225
militaristic/militarism/military 3, 5, 8, 13–14, 90, 100, 129, 131, 138, 143, 150–1, 158
Mill, John Stuart 21, *see also* utilitarianism
mind–body–heart/spirit human being 106, 124
minorities 6, 87, 94, 143, 149, 197, 222, 225–9, 237–8, 241–5, 247; as disadvantaged 241; as exploited 242; Gandhian orientation with 237; literature of 220, 222, 226–7, 230–1, 233–6, 238–40, 244–9; as marginalized 246; as oppressed 247; as other 238; power and 238, 243; relativism of 245
missionary work 114
modern civilization (and Gandhi's Modern Civilization) 3, 9, 22–3, 25–6, 31–2, 35, 87–9, 95, 104–5, 113–15, 117–19, 121–4, 129–31, 159–60,

236–7; capitalism and 209; characteristics of 115; and colonialism 160, 232; desire of 123; and ego driven desires 26, 130; ethics and 88; Gandhi's claims on 111; Hind Swaraj and 117, 119; as materialistic 117; modern India and 104; and modern technology 87, 102, 104, 107, 113, 115, 121–3, 127, 130; resistance to 95; and standard of living 122, 129; untruthfulness of 111; values of 3, 89; violence and 23, 72; and Western civilization 104

modern socialists 207–9

Moderates (in *Hind Swaraj*) 86, 103–4, 110, 231

Modi, Narendra 90, 133

moral force 5

morality 9–10, 21, 27, 30, 34, 151, 157, 194, 207, 231–2; as Vedic value 4

multiculturalism 29, 224–5, 229–30, 233, 235–7, 240, 245, 248–9

Mumbai, 26/11 terrorists 32, 138–40, 143, 147, 149–50, 165–6, 168, 205, *see also* New York, terrorists in

Murti, T.R.V. 19, 41, 71, 87

mutual respect/mutuality 9, 239, 248

Nagarjuna 41–2, 52–3; Madhyamika philosophy and 52

Narayan, J.P. 181

National Democratic Alliance (NDA) 90, 91, 100

national other 80, 120

nationalism; 4, 170, 184; as imperialistic 8

Native Americans 138, 227–8, 231, 233, 238, 241–2; genocide of 138, 227; minority literature 227; physical violence on 242; *see also* violence

natural disasters 106–8, 147

Nazi: genocide 146, 205, *see also* Holocaust; occupation 153

Nehru, Jawaharlal 12, 90, 100, 102, 181–2; anti-Gandhian vision of 12; criticisms of 102; and democracy 12; descendants of 100, 102; and Gandhi's vision 102; and influence of Gandhi 181; vision of Modern India 102

neo-conservatives (neocons) 171

New York, terrorists in 14, 32, 138–40, 147, 149–51, 157–8, 165–6, 205, 236

Nietzsche, Friedrich 31

Nirguna Brahman 46, 53, 58n19, 58n23, *see also* Brahman, Brahman-Atman

*niyama*s (moral observances) 64

nonattachment 64, 78–9, 238, *see also* karma-yoga

noncooperation 129, 153, 239, 242, *see also* satyagraha

non-Gandhian 9, 16, 22, 42, 81, 86, 89, 93, 100–1, 129, 131, 182, 189, 212, *see also* anti-Gandhian; and anti-Gandhian perspectives 9, 249; approaches (*see also* Gandhi-informed approaches); experiments in socialism 212; Fabian socialism 182; Gandhian interpretations and 81; militarizing Hinduness

and 101; interpretations of 189; marginality and 249; minority identities and 247; perspectives 249; technology and 100; terrorism 165; violence and 22
nonpossession 24, 190, 192, 197
nonviolence 5–10, 21–3, 26–34, 51–3, 63–7, 77–8, 151–3, 164–70, 194–5, 204–5, 243–8, *see also* ahimsa; noncooperation; satyagraha; Absolute Truth of 27, 33, 169; Bhagavad-Gita as Gospel 30, 49, 65, 69–70, 72–3, 75, 77, 81, 112; cause of 168, 205; in classical Hindu texts 65; creative 14, 151, 153, 165; effectiveness of 157; Gandhi-informed analysis of 8; and Krishna 66; and pacifism 140; relative 13, 28; sustainable 153; transformative 152–3; truth and 195, 207, 212–13
nonviolent 4–5, 7, 32–5, 79–81, 86–7, 118–21, 129–33, 160, 163–4, 243–5, 250; active 13, 27; alternatives 25, 169, 207; force 27, 80, 121; resistance 34, *see also* noncooperation; satyagraha

oppression 8, 11–14, 16, 20, 31–2, 35, 55, 89, 103, 128–9, 133, 157–8, 191, 196, 222–4, 237–8, 242–3, 246–7; control over 200; democratic political rights for 11; and exploitation 246; by feudal landowners 191; for justice 120; as majority 129; minorities 229, 237–8, 247; in modern economic model 128; moral force and 5; neo-Vedanta and 55; nonviolence and 159; patriarchal 4; physical terrorism at 149; political rights of 11; relative truth and 51, 213; rewriting of marginalization 239–40, 243; and socialization 242; technology and 133; terrorism and 156, 158; as unfree other 50; violence against 120, 142, 155, 157, 205; women and 33 87
other, the 47, 86, 120, 140, 170–3, 195–9, 221–2

Palestinians 161, 171
Parekh, Bhikhu 106–7
Parikh, Narhari 217n37
Paris Agreement (the Paris Climate Accord), 2017 132–3
Partition, the 91, 146; Hindutva rhetoric on 91; violence and 157, 233
patriarchal 9, 64, 111, 196, 226
pauperism 109, *see also* poverty
peace 3, 5–8, 14, 22–3, 29–30, 43, 62, 69, 120, 142, 244–5, *see also* terrorism; violence, war and 5–6, 22, 30
peasants 25, 87, 92, 114, 123, 153, 155, 224
Periyar 242–3
Phoenix Settlement 111
Pinker, Steven 22–3, 37n9, 38n10
pluralism 8, 48, 101–2, 225
political: power 3, 10, 90, 92–3, 103, 117; realism 22; violence 6, 150, 241
poverty 5–6, 11–12, 154–6; alleviation of 102; as economic

violence 6; empowerment against 12; as humanly caused 24; and inequality 10; and involuntary suffering 123–4, 152; and moral living as political 5; structural violence and 24; and suffering 156; universal law, greed and 198; and victim blaming 196; and violence 155; and wealth accumulation 11, 14, *see also* economic violence

power 24–5, 90, 94–5, 117, 122–3, 132–3, 147, 154–5, 193–4, 197–8, 238–9; anti-Gandhi modern 94; centralization of wealth and 186; control of distribution and 155; corporate capitalist 95; decentralized 207; dominant power 100, 119, 143, 158, 230, 238, 241; economic 6–7, 24–5, 155–6, 182, 241; globalized 15; hierarchical 147, 154; hierarchical 147, 205; labor 116, 186, 201, *see also* working class; military 147; political 3, 10, 90, 92–3, 103, 117; rightwing orientation 90; rightwing orientation, *see also* Hindutva; socialist model of 207, 193; state 95, 131, 193; structural relations of 90; structures of 148, 239, 243; technological 129; truth as 194; wealth concentration and 24–5, 92, 94, 102, 132, 155, 186, 191, 201

Practical Trusteeship Formula 198, 217n37

private property 152, 197, 199, 201, 203, 212; abolishing 192; in capitalism 192, 202, 211, 213, *see also* capitalists

purusha 62

racism 6–8, 14, 29, 80, 120, 142, 151, 157, 162, 196, 222–3, 227–8, 235–7, 239, 241, 244, 247, 249 (*see also* caste; class); Mailer and 236; triplets of 14; victims of 42, *see also* Holocaust

Radhakrishnan, Sarvepalli 19, 41

Rahul, Kumar 45–8; on Gandhi as Cosmopolitan Advaitin 45–7

Rajchandra, Jain 231

Ramanuja 41, 65, 87

Ramayana 48, 69, 234

Rashtriya Swayamsevak Sangh (RSS) 91–2, 100

rationality 115–16, 207–8, 226

reconciliation 165, 169, 239

reformulations, selective and creative of Gandhi 15–16, 28–30, 33–5, 49, 99–100, 206, 232–5

relative nonviolence 13, 28

relative truth 8–9, 13, 27–33, 50–4, 63, 80–1, 166–7, 228, 245, 248; philosophy of 27–34

religious: divisive 8; fundamentalisms 8; systems 7, 242; terrorisms 8, 150; violence 6, 150, 241

renunciation 13, 32, 50, 61, 64, 66, 77, 112; Gita and 61; *karmic* world of 49–50, 61; philosophy of 27–34; welfare and 63

resistance 131, 159, 161, 227, 239, 242, 246; action-oriented nonviolent 34; to dominant values 95; King Jr. and 43;

modern culture and 116; nonviolent 69, 129, 222 (*see also* noncooperation; satyagraha); Palestinian 161; satyagraha movements as 111; Sunni terroristic 161; technology against 129; and terrorism 170; truthful force of 13; and violence 13, 32, 154, 170
Richards, Glyn 44, 46
Roth, Phillip 221
Roy, Arundhati 237
Roy, M.N. 181
Ruskin, John 76, 221, 232, 235

sacrifice 63, 75–6, 118–19, 203, *see also* yajna
Saguna Brahman 46, 58n19, 58n23
Sanders, Bernie 185, 214n6
sannyasa 66
sarvodaya 11–12, 151, 154, 193
satya, see also truth (*satya*)
satyagraha (truth-force, love-force, soul-force) 13, 22, 44, 51, 95, 104, 125, 146, 151–3, 195, 212, *see also* experiment with truth; campaign 13, 22, 44, 51, 95, 104, 125, 146, 151–3, 165, 195; as failed experiment 212; proactive force of 104; termination of 233; writings on 165
satyagrahis 9, 51, 146, 159, 210
Savarkar, Vinayak Damodar 90–1, 97n9, 100–3, 158; anti-Gandhian influenced by 91; and "Hindutva" 91
science 4–5, 22, 88, 110, 114, 123, 127, 144, 207
security 22–3, 138, 143, 155, 161–2

Self (soul) 6–7, 23, 27, 45–6, 48, 50–4, 62–7, 69–70, 117–21, 170–1; as *Atman* 46; as autonomous 117; and Buddha 171; Descrates and 170; ego-defined 196; ego-driven 117–19; to egoless consciousness 171; higher 62, 117; I–me–ego 78; individual 117–19, 170; social 117, 240; transformation of 163; unspiritual 26, 118; worldly 117
self/ego-sacrifice 122
self-alienation 70, 170, *see also* alienation
self-control 62, 125, 130, 232, 238
self-determination 125, 195, 208, 236, 243, 246
self-development 15, 86, 121
self-discipline 63, 118, 125, 238
self-empowerment 123, 243
selfishness 29, 154, 164, 171
self-justifications 141
self-knowledge 74, 125
selfless action/service 5, 30, 63, 72, 76, 120, 122, 130, 197, 208, 232, 237
self-other relations 26, 34, 45, 47, 54, 70, 90, 99, 119, 170
self-purification 38–9n14, 45–7, 151, *see also* self-sacrifice (*yajna*)
self-realization 44–5, 50, 62–3, 70, 74, 76, 80, 86, 118–19, 121, 163
self-renunciation 63
self-rule 12, 118, 125, 131, 196, 232, 244
self-sacrifice (*yajna*) 63, 103, 118, 125, 130, 151–3, 159, 165
self-suffering 146, 151–3, 159, 165

self-transformation 121, 239, 248
Sevagram ashram 109, 216–17n29, *see also* ashram; Branwasi Seva ashram
sexism 7–8, 16, 152, 157, 196, 235, 239, 241, 244, 249
sexist 8, 196, 223
Shandilya Upanishad 64
Shankara 19, 41–2, 44, 46, 48, 53, 56n11, 56n12, 58n19, 65, 71
Shia militias 161
Shiv Sena 91
Shukla, Ved Mitra 43–5, 47–8; on Gandhi as Advaitin 43–5
Shyamji, Krishnavarma 158
"Simple Living and High Thinking" 123–6
Singh, Bhagat 175–6n11
slaves/slavery 110, 138, 141, 186, 200, 234, 241
social: democracy 12; domination 117; violence 6, 23, 150, 241, *see also* violence
socialism 8, 51, 181–95, 197, 199–202, 204–12; Gandhi and 188–93, *see also* Gandhian Socialism; alternative 209; forms of 184–5, 193, 206; formulations of 182, 184–5; identification with 188, 193; interpretation of 210; meaning of 185; nonviolent 193; as rational 208 *see also* capitalism; as spiritual communism 210, *see also* spiritual communism; writings on 183
socialists 181, 183–5, 187–8, 190, 193–4, 198, 202, 206–12; Gandhi as 184; and Gandhian socialism 181, 206–9, 211

socialization 77, 164, 170, 221, 242, 249
socio-economic democracy 12
solipsism 119, 170
Soul 5, 7–8, 27, 44, 46, 48, 50, 61–2, 188, 208, 212, *see also* Atman; Self
soul-force 5, 18, 13, 27, 80, 121, 195
South Africa 112, 141, 231, 236–7
spiritual: communism 210; forces 121; self-realization 248
spirituality 8, 10, 40, 54, 72, 151, 194, 196, 204, 207
starvation 25, 108, 152, 198, 202, *see also* impoverish; pauperism; poverty
sthitha-prajna 47, 82n5
struggles, Gandhi-informed grassroots 95
subjectivism 71, 166, 189, 246
suffering 4–8, 31, 47–8, 63, 72–3, 75–6, 124–5, 151–6, 158–60, 162–3, 203–4; absorb 203; inflict 203; voluntary 8, 152–3
Sufism 225
Sunni terroristic resistance 161
sustainability 1–2, 8, 10, 14, 181, 209
sustainable: living 118, 126, 151, 170, 183, 189, 197, 222, 244; self-development 122
swadeshi 12, 22, 24, 51, 95
swaraj 12, 15, 22, 24, 30, 34, 46, 51, 95–6, 103–4, 159, 195–6, 99–105, 229–36; civilization 118, 125, 131; culture 94, 125, 130; meaning of 176n12; as our "birth right" 104; philosophy

131; technology 109, 118–19, 121–3, 126–31
Syadvadi 45–6

Tagore, Rabindranath 106, 134n10, 134n12
Talisman 236
Tata, J.R.D. 204
technology 3, 15, 88–90, 92–4, 99–101, 103–5, 107–10, 112–18, 121–3, 125–7, 129–33; approach to 126–33; appropriate 126, *see also* alternative technology; control of 123; modern 3, 8, 10, 89–90, 92, 104–5, 113–14, 116–17, 121, 127, 130–1; swaraj approach to 116, 125
terrorism 1, 8, 10, 22–3, 27, 29, 32, 81, 104, 138–51, 154–73; Absolute Truth, relative truth, and 166–70; anti-American 162; approach to violence and 149–51; Code of Federal Regulations (CFR) on 141; and intentionality 144–8; Islamic 162; multinational corporate 32; on Palestinians 161; and USA 161, *see also* Afghanistan
terrorists 8, 103, 139–42, 144, 156–9, 163–8, 205; individual 144, 150; killings 140; in Mumbai 32; in New York 32; 9/11 or 26/11 32, 139, 149–50; European 156; expatriate 159; freedom fighters as 141; Muslim 161; Pakistani 8; Saudi 156
Thoreau, Henry David 216n24, 221

Tilak, Bal Gangadhar 104
tolerance 8, 9, 29, 51, 153, 167, 248
Tolstoy, Leo 72, 221, 232, 235, 238
transformative: action 13–14; marginality 245, 248; nonviolence 7, 152–3, 204–5; practices 7, 77, 204
tribals, *see also* Adivasis
Tripathi, R.K. 41
true socialism 184, 195, 197, 199, 208
Trump, Donald 132, 158, 162, 168, 172
trusteeship 8, 87, 181, 188, 190, 192, 197–9, 203–5; doctrine of 192; formulations of 203; vision of 204
truth (*satya*) 7–10, 26–30, 44–54, 67–8, 77–81, 170–2, 189–91, 194–5, 212–13, 226, 243–8, *see also under* ahimsa; Absolute 8, 27–8, 30, 33, 50–4, 166–9, 172–3, 245, 247–8; force 5, 7, 13, 27, 80, 195; as God 194; Krishna as 67; nonviolence in 29, 195; paths to 29; and Reality 9, 27, 29–30, 48–9, 52–4, 67–8, 74, 79–80, 213, 226–7, 246–8; relative 8–9, 13, 27–33, 50–4, 63, 80–1, 166–7, 228, 245, 248
truth-force 13, 80, 195

unfree 50, 63, 76, 119, 123, 125, 199, 237
untouchability 4, 6, 35, 45, 51, 73, 106, 132, 152, 106, 154, 173, 205, 243, 250, *see also* casteism
Lakhavi, Zaki ur-Rehman 139

utilitarianism 159, 167
untruth/untruthfulness 8, 11,
  26–8, 30, 32–4, 48–50, 62,
  78–9, 89, 104, 111–12, 120–1,
  194–5
unity 7–8, 13, 44, 48–50, 52, 56,
  106, 120–1, 187, 192, 246–7;
  of all of life 247; desire union
  or 49; in diversity 246; with
  the higher self 62, 101; over
  diversity 48; realizing our 121,
  197; rejection of 120; respect
  for differences 10, 27, 50, 121,
  247; self-realization of 80; truth
  of 246
Upanishads 21, 26, 48–9, 62–3

Vahed, Goolam 237
vairagya 44
Vaishnava bhakti 62
values 3–5, 11–14, 25, 34–5, 69,
  89–90, 92–3, 99–100, 102–4,
  129–31, 170–1; oppressive
  12; revolution of 14; system of
  violent 244; transformative 14
varna 45, 74, 85n23, *see also* caste
varnashrama 45
Vedanta 20, 40–1, 49–50, 183
Vedantin 41, 43, 47, 49–50, 53–4
Vedas 48–9, 63, 76, 229
victim-blaming formulations 196
victims 42, 142, 154, 159, 165,
  196, 206
violence 4–13, 22–34, 72–3,
  77–9, 87–9, 103–4, 120–1,
  139–73, 192–200, 202–9,
  239–48; communal 23, 152,
  154; contemporary 23, 81,
  153; cultural 6, 69, 150,
  241; economic 6, 24, 150,
  154–7, 163, 241; economic

inequality as 24; educational
  6, 150, 207, 241; external
  149; genocidal 153; Hindu-
  Muslim communal 233; inner
  6; institutional 203; internal
  149; and justification of war
  146; killing as 6, 23, 32–3, 64,
  104, 107, 112, 149, 165, 205;
  legitimate 104; linguistic 6, 23,
  150, 241; multidimensional
  156, 242–3; as negative force
  142; physical 6, 23, 149–50,
  241–2; psychological 23, 150,
  154, 241; revolutionary 184;
  and rewriting marginality
  240–5; short-term 163, 165;
  structural 6–7, 23–5, 35, 80,
  153, 203–5, 207, 242–4,
  250; and suffering 151–4;
  terrorizing 142, 172
violent force 22, 32–3, 141
voluntary trusteeship 205
Vyasa 75

wage-laborers 114, 153, 186, 201,
  see also labor; labor power;
  workers; working class
war 5–10, 13–14, 16, 22–3,
  28–33, 88–9, 111–12,
  144–6, 151–2, 161, 244–5; in
  Afghanistan 139; brutality of 6;
  contextualism of 235; on Iraq
  161, 169; justifications for 32,
  112, 146, 169; for peace 120;
  on terrorism 139, 147, 160–1,
  168, 171–2
wealth 14, 22, 89, 117, 132,
  152, 156–7, 185–6, 197–201,
  203–5, 228–9; concentration
  of 11, 25, 92, 94, 102, 105,
  108, 123, 155; concentration

Index 277

of economic 24–5, 117; control of 103; ego-attachment to 123; obsessions with 90, 198; possessions 107, 155
wealthy 132, 152, 156–7, 185, 188, 198, 200–1, 203–5, 229, *see also* capitalists
Western socialism 191, 202
women 6, 70–1, 73, 196, 226, 238, 243, 249
workers/working class 51, 87, 152, 154–5, 186, 196, 201, *see also* labor; capitalists and 200

xenophobia 249, *see also* Holocaust; Nazi; violence

yajna (self-sacrifice) 63–4, 75–7, 103, 118, 125, 130, 151–3, 159, 165, 193
yamas 64
yoga 62, 64, 66
Yoga-Sutra 62–4
yogi 42, 62, 66, 75, *see also sannyasa*

Zinn, Howard 238
Zulus, 145, 152, 177n16, 236–7

About the Author

Douglas Allen is professor and former chairperson of the department of philosophy at the University of Maine, USA. He served as president of the Society for Asian and Comparative Philosophy and is the series editor of Studies in Comparative Philosophy and Religion.
Author and editor of 15 books and 150 articles and scholarly journal articles, he has been awarded Fulbright and Smithsonian grants to India. His books on Gandhi include *Comparative Philosophy and Religion in Times of Terror* (2006); *The Philosophy of Mahatma Gandhi for the Twenty-First Century* (2008); and *Mahatma Gandhi* (2011).
He is recognized as one of the world's leading scholars in phenomenology of religion and the philosophy of Mahatma Gandhi. He had the honor of addressing the General Assembly on the United Nations International Day of Non-violence, October 2, 2017.